BROKEN ARROW

BROKEN ARROW

How the U.S. Navy Lost a Nuclear Bomb

JIM WINCHESTER

CASEMATE

Philadelphia & Oxford

Published in the United States of America and Great Britain in 2019 by
CASEMATE PUBLISHERS
1950 Lawrence Road, Havertown, PA 19083, USA
and
The Old Music Hall, 106–108 Cowley Road, Oxford OX4 1JE, UK

Copyright 2019 © Jim Winchester

Hardcover Edition: ISBN 978-1-61200-691-8
Digital Edition: ISBN 978-1-61200-692-5

A CIP record for this book is available from the British Library

Printed and bound in the United States of America

For a complete list of Casemate titles, please contact:

CASEMATE PUBLISHERS (US)
Telephone (610) 853-9131
Fax (610) 853-9146
Email: casemate@casematepublishers.com
www.casematepublishers.com

CASEMATE PUBLISHERS (UK)
Telephone (01865) 241249
Email: casemate-uk@casematepublishers.co.uk
www.casematepublishers.co.uk

Contents

Introduction

On a morning approaching Christmas long ago and far away, the author half-heard from another room a morning radio news item that went something like this: "A declassified report says that a Skyhawk jet fell off an aircraft carrier carrying a nuclear bomb...." This report was baffling to a schoolboy in New Zealand where the tiny air force had Skyhawks, but never aircraft carriers or nuclear weapons (as far as he knew). His mother thought it was probably an American one and he put the story to the back of his mind.

In fact, the event had taken place 21 years previously aboard the USS *Ticonderoga*, a U.S. Navy carrier involved in the Vietnam War. The news story broke when a reporter received a list of "Broken Arrow" accidents after a Freedom of Information Act request.

A Broken Arrow is the loss or destruction of a nuclear weapon. The Pentagon acknowledges that 32 occurred between 1950 and 1980, but by keeping this 1965 event secret until 1981 and then issuing misleading information, it lost control of the story when the full details emerged in 1989, leading to a major diplomatic incident.

Accidents were routine on aircraft carriers, from the cut finger to the broken back, from the fiery ramp strike to the soft catapult shot. In the 1960s a carrier almost never returned with all the planes or men it sailed with, even in peacetime, but only one carrier on one cruise managed to lose a thermonuclear weapon. This book centers on one unusual accident, or looked at another way, a relatively common one with big consequences.

Some assume that many people must have lost their jobs or at least their promotion prospects over the accident. No one did. Keeping the accident secret meant not having to account for it. By the time it was publicized, everyone involved had retired or forgotten about it

The U.S. government has never been honest about this story, continuing to redact relevant documents to this day. Until I neared completion of this book the one thing I agreed with was that pilot Douglas M. Webster did not meet the Pentagon's criteria for inscription on the Vietnam Memorial Wall. Then I discovered evidence that they had already broken their own rules and added the name of a casualty in a very similar case, which differed only in the nuclear aspect, to the Wall.

Former A-6 Intruder pilot Ken Davis said: "I recollect when a B61 [nuclear bomb] got dinged (not lost, mind you, just a dented nosecone) during a shipboard loading exercise—and entire forests were decimated as a result." They undoubtedly were in the *Ticonderoga* case too, but most of the documentation was probably quietly shredded or burnt years ago. Despite multiple copies being distributed, the actual Broken Arrow message of December 5, 1965 has not yet turned up in any archive, nor has any evidence of a later search for the bomb.

An attack pilot who had several nuclear weapons-related roles, culminating as head of the Navy's European command's nuclear plans and policy section told me he was taught all about the USAF's nuclear accidents, but said, "No, I was told, the Navy never experienced a Broken Arrow."

This may be the biggest Cold War story you've never heard.

Acknowledgements

The author would like to thank: Masayo Duus, for allowing me to quote from *Toppu gan no shi* (*Death of a Top Gun*, Kodansha, 1997), and Ichiro Yamaoda for his translation; *Ticonderoga* and Air Wing Five veterans, in particular Randy Wilson who helped start me on this journey, and Delbert Mitchell, who helped me finish it.

The USS *Ticonderoga* Association (www.bigt.net), in particular Ed Trotter and George Passantonio, John Lunsford and Lloyd Frank; *Ticonderoga* and VA-56 veterans Bill Blythe, Walter Mallett, Robert Strother, John Deasey, Ron Babcock, Frank Barrett, George Floyd, Ray Green, Carl Kernan, Dave Lesley, Denny Macke, John Madigan Jr., Bob Martin, Gene McCallister, Jerry Slagle and Chuck Wilber; VA-56 pilots and families Austin Chapman, Jim Delesie; Jack Holland, Van Hough, Dennis Palmer; John, Sam and Bill Paisley, Michael Rawl and Jay Shower.

The A-4 Skyhawk Association (www.a4skyhawk.info), particularly Bob Hickerson; Doug Siegfried, the Tailhook Association (www.tailhook.net); Library and Archive, The San Diego Air and Space Museum; Flor Thomas, Naval History and Heritage Command; Sandra Lewandowski, Roberto Marquez, Liz Poe, NNSA; Tim Frank, Arlington National Cemetery; John Wilson, the National Archives; Ken Davis and Robert Glass, the Coffelt Group; Dr. Mary Curry and Dr. Robert S. Norris, the National Security Archive; Don Davis, American Friends Service Committee Archives; Local History & Genealogy Center, Warren-Trumbull County Public Library; Michelle Drobnik, Ohio State University Archive; Brian Godsen, www.packardtimeline.com; Alex Wellerstein, and Jim Yuschenkoff, USS *Intrepid* Museum.

Gary Verver, the late Hugh Magee, Bob Krall, Mike Eberhardt, Scott and Eileen Irwin, Sean and Ava McDermott, Dennis and Laura Pratt, Joe Kaposi, Brian Loudenslager, J. J. McBride, Ken Davis, Nick Stroud 'The Aviation Historian', Ian Bott, the late Robert F. Dorr, Robert Hewson, Tim Senior and Jennifer Campbell.

The Lieutenant (Junior Grade) Douglas M. Webster Memorial Fund is used to help young people of Warren, Ohio develop their personal ethics and physical abilities through participation in YMCA and High School athletic activities. To donate, make checks payable to the Community Foundation of the Mahoning Valley, indicate the Douglas M. Webster Memorial Fund in the memo line, and mail to: Douglas M. Webster Memorial Fund, Community Foundation of the Mahoning Valley, 201 East Commerce Street, Suite 150, Youngstown, OH 44503. www.cfmv.org.

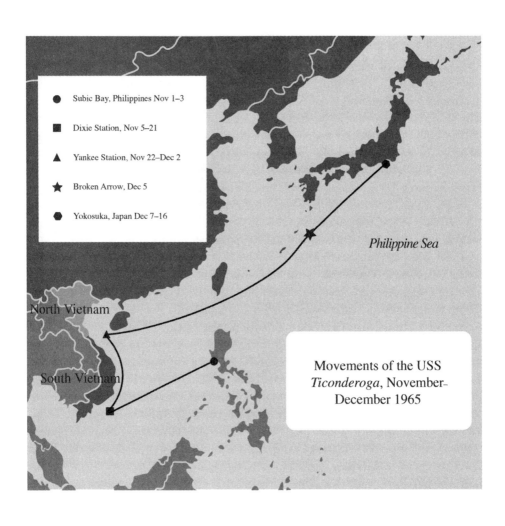

- Subic Bay, Philippines Nov 1–3

- Dixie Station, Nov 5–21

- Yankee Station, Nov 22–Dec 2

- Broken Arrow, Dec 5

- Yokosuka, Japan Dec 7–16

Philippine Sea

North Vietnam

South Vietnam

Movements of the USS *Ticonderoga*, November–December 1965

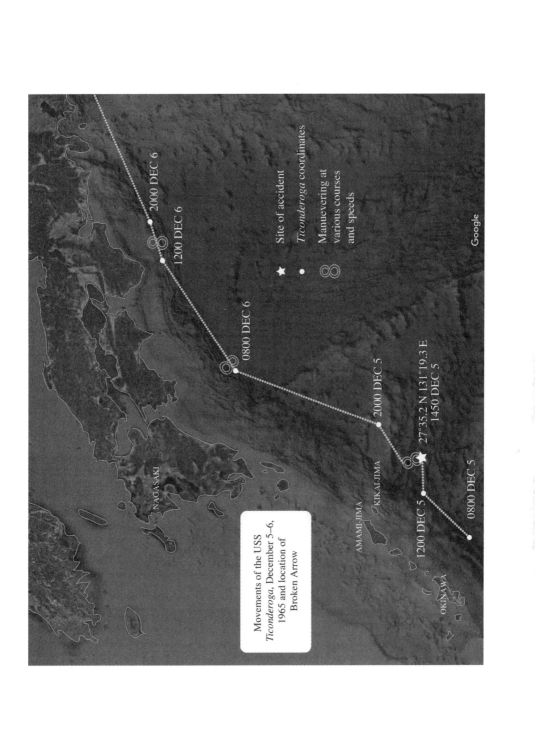

Movements of the USS *Ticonderoga*, December 5–6, 1965 and location of Broken Arrow

NAGASAKI

AMAMI-JIMA
KIKAI-JIMA

OKINAWA

2000 DEC 6
1200 DEC 6

0800 DEC 6

2000 DEC 5

27°35.2 N 131°19.3 E
1450 DEC 5

1200 DEC 5

0800 DEC 5

Site of accident
Ticonderoga coordinates
Manuevering at various courses and speeds

Google

CHAPTER I

Eve of Destruction

Sunday, December 5, 1965
En route Special Operations Area in the South China Sea to Yokosuka, Japan

Halfway through its second Vietnam tour, the 42,000-ton aircraft carrier USS *Ticonderoga* ploughed on through a blue-green sea towards Japan, leaving behind the war. After ten days on the line on Yankee Station, the carrier operating area off North Vietnam, and sixteen days on Dixie Station, its southern counterpart, the crew of just under 3,000 sailors and airmen were looking forward to a few days' rest and recreation in Yokosuka, south of Tokyo.

Steaming northeast at 20 knots, emitting a plume of yellow smoke generated by four of the eight boilers, *Ticonderoga*, nicknamed "*Tico*" or the "Big T" by its crews, was surrounded by a screen of four destroyers. They included the *Turner Joy*, which like *Tico* had been involved in the Tonkin Gulf Incident the previous August, the catalyst for the full involvement of the United States in the Vietnam War.

American involvement in Vietnam had escalated from that date. In 1964, there were only around 23,000 American "advisors" in Vietnam. On March 8, 1965, U.S. Marines landed unopposed in Da Nang and by the end of the year there were 200,000 American troops in country.

In February, President Lyndon B. Johnson had ordered strikes against the North dubbed Operation *Flaming Dart*, which had little military effect. At the beginning of March, Operation *Rolling Thunder* began. This was a campaign of gradually escalating strikes aimed at demonstrating U.S. resolve and pressurizing Hanoi to stop supporting the insurgency in the South. On December 2, 1965, *Ticonderoga* completed its part in the latest phase, *Rolling Thunder 42*. Despite some signs the North's economy was weakening, Hanoi was "…demonstrating no willingness to terminate support for the military struggle in South Vietnam," read the gloomy assessment of Pacific Command's secret monthly report.

Overnight the carrier had begun paralleling the Ryukyu island chain, passing about 80 miles from Okinawa at midnight. With no night flying scheduled, most of the crew slept. Those standing the middle watch were looking forward to some extra bunk time on Sunday morning when reveille was not normally called at sea. Super typhoon Faye had expended itself near the Kurile Islands ten days before, but some remnant of its power still stirred the Pacific and the seas grew heavy enough for water to come over the carrier's bow and wash onto its wooden flight deck.

Aboard *Tico* were five squadrons of fighters and light-attack aircraft and no fewer than six smaller detachments of heavy bombers, reconnaissance, jamming and early warning aircraft, transports and helicopters. All in all, nearly 75 aircraft formed Carrier Air Wing Five (CVW-5), flown, maintained, loaded and administrated by nearly a thousand aircrew and airmen.

The main striking elements of Air Wing Five were the two squadrons of Douglas A-4 Skyhawk jet fighter-bombers. Attack Squadron VA-144 "Roadrunners" flew the A-4C "Charlie," which entered service in 1960, and the VA-56 "Champions" flew the improved A-4E "Echo," delivered to the Navy from 1963. VA-56 was one of the first squadrons to receive the new model, outwardly similar to its predecessor, but with a more powerful, more efficient and not least, more reliable Pratt & Whitney J52 turbojet engine. The A-4E could also carry more weapons, on five underwing pylons, than the A-4C could with three pylons, one or two of which were invariably devoted to external fuel tanks.

First flown in 1954, the original Skyhawk was designed around the dimensions of early nuclear weapons such as the Mark 7 (Mk 7), with up to 61-kiloton yield, nearly three times the destructive power of the "Fat Man" bomb dropped on Nagasaki in 1945. This 15-foot weapon with its long tail fins required a lot of ground clearance, which in turn meant the Skyhawk had a stalky undercarriage and was not unknown to fall onto a wingtip or tip onto its tail if mishandled on a rolling carrier deck. By 1965 tactical atomic or "special" weapons had become smaller, lighter and more powerful, improving the Skyhawk's striking power, but somewhat negating the need for its long legs.

The Champions had 14 A-4Es and a complement of 185 men, 24 of whom were officers, and 19 of those pilots. Some of the men and machines had flown the first official bombing missions over North Vietnam in August 1964 when Air Wing Five had retaliated for North Vietnam's purported attacks on the destroyers *Maddox* and *Turner Joy*.

One of the Champs' junior Skyhawk pilots was a little shorter than most of his squadron mates but he was athletically built. He was a high school gymnastics champion from small-city Ohio with a broad grin, thick dark eyebrows and prominent ears that were emphasized by his short military haircut.

Twenty-four-year-old Douglas Morey Webster had been commissioned as a lieutenant (junior grade) in the United States Navy a year ago to the day. He was on his first combat tour and in the last three weeks had flown 17 missions including strikes on heavily defended targets such as the Hai Duong road and rail bridge.

By early December, *Tico*'s crew had worked for 28 days straight and were approaching exhaustion. Pilots flew two or three missions a day. Airmen and sailors worked 16-hour days or longer in tropical heat. Apart from a few special spaces, there was no air conditioning aboard the veteran carrier.

Even routine operations can be dangerous on a carrier loaded with jets, fuel and munitions. This very day an engine room fire aboard *Kitty Hawk* on Yankee Station would kill two sailors and injure 29 more. Every day *Tico*'s log dutifully recorded injuries ranging from the trivial to the severe.

For the flight deck crews, known to other sailors as "the gang on the roof," the hazards were legion. Intakes could suck a man into an engine and exhausts could blow him overboard or into the path of another aircraft. Propellers could chop him to pieces. A jet landing short—the dreaded ramp strike—could throw flaming debris down the deck, sweeping men with it. A snapped arresting cable could slice a man in half. The deck was almost always slick with pools of oil, fuel and hydraulic fluid. A rough non-skid surface gave grip, but wore away under constant pounding from aircraft and vehicle tires, jet blast and rotor wash.

When the ship turned into the wind for flight operations, the wide open deck was buffeted by a constant pants-flapping gale of 30 knots or more, which, when added to jet blast and prop wash, could turn dropped items like nuts, washers and pieces of locking wire into high-velocity projectiles, dangerous to man and machine alike. The shrieking of jets, the drone and vibration of piston engines and the eye-stinging exhaust fumes combined with high ambient temperatures taxed men on the flight deck even further. All this for an extra 55 dollars a month hazardous duty pay.

The pilots and aircrew were less exposed, but even strapped in a closed cockpit high above the deck were subject to the same risks from crashing aircraft and ordnance explosions, plus the ones associated with catapult launches and arrested landings. Fires on the carriers *Forrestal*, *Oriskany* and *Enterprise* would kill nearly 240 men during the next three years. On an average cruise without major accidents it was not uncommon for a dozen men to not return home from a carrier deployment in the 1960s.

Even bed wasn't totally safe. One *Tico* sailor tore his scrotum on a stanchion while climbing from his bunk. Another fell out of his, fracturing his lower back.

The only event of note that morning had been a slight change of course to avoid a Greek freighter, Manila-bound from Portland. The rough overnight seas had brought some water into the hangar bay through the open aperture of No.2 Elevator but by afternoon it was a bright early winter day with the sun shining through broken cirrus and 68-degree temperatures. The wind was only 10 knots and visibility was 25 miles. Some crew noticed a slight swell developing around lunchtime, but nothing that could rock the ship or affect the planned loading evolution. The most notable occurrence on the deck log so far had been a sailor who had cut his nose on a swab wringer.

A still from Department of Energy film *Always/Never* shows W Division sailors preparing a B43 thermonuclear bomb for movement from SASS to the flight deck. (*Always/Never*)

Crewcut

On December 5, there was no scheduled flying, no launches, no landings, no engines turning. Many off-duty crew were taking a chance to relax on the flight deck. In two days, the carrier would be in Japan for ten welcome days of shore leave.

Not everybody was sunning themselves. Working away four decks below, in a compartment called SASS (Special Aircraft Service Stores) behind a door marked:

> RESTRICTED SECURITY AREA
> KEEP OUT
> AUTHORIZED PERSONNEL ONLY
> IT IS UNLAWFUL TO ENTER THIS AREA WITHOUT WRITTEN PERMISSION
> OF THE COMMANDING OFFICER.
>
> Sec-21, Internal Security Act of 1950

Tico's Weapons Division was assembling nuclear weapons.

At 1300, preceded by the drill call bugle, an exercise was called over the ship's loudspeaker system, on 1 Main Circuit (or 1MC), broadcast to all. "Now all members of the Crewcut detail, man your stations."

For most of the crew it was a no-notice event, but the W Division had been preparing for the weapons loading drill codenamed "Crewcut" for a week. The assembled weapons were rolled on their handcarts across the linoleum floor one at a time into the small elevator that connected SASS with the hangar deck.

At 1335, exercise preparations were interrupted by a bugle call, a pause and one alarm blast:

> Fire on the 02 Level, port side, center, compartment 13E!

The ship's bell joined in with a rapid ringing, a pause, a single ring:

> Fire on the 02 Level, port side, center, compartment 13E!

It only took five minutes to deal with the fire and Crewcut preparations continued. All participating crew were at their exercise stations by 1358 and the loading drill began.

In the hangar bay aircraft electronics technician Randy Wilson watched the Skyhawk with only passing interest. Although a member of VA-56, he had only reported aboard *Tico* after the ship sailed from San Diego and had just finished his mandatory ninety days of messcooking before being allowed to work on the squadron's aircraft. Only qualified crew who had passed a stringent course could wear a loading badge and take part in special weapons exercises.

Despite not having a role in the Crewcut drill, Wilson planned to hitch a lift on the elevator up to the flight deck. He was in the squadron maintenance shop when an electrician working on an A-4 on the flight deck called down on the sound-powered phone for someone to bring him up a part. The shop petty officer gave Wilson the part and told him to take it to Erickson on the flight deck. Coming out of the shop at the rear of the hangar deck, he looked across and saw that the elevator was down, and ran over to catch a ride up to the flight deck, along with the A-4 they were preparing to push onto it.

Other sailors carried on their regular activities. Charles Hall was standing in a chow line that was forming near a hatchway by the nose of the lead A-4 as sailors gathered to go down one deck for lunch. Ed Ofstad was working in the chartroom where he was in charge of the ship's fathometer. With time off, Radarman Gene McAllister climbed several sets of ladders to "Vulture's Row" on the carrier's island and was using the 8mm film camera he had bought in Hawaii to film flight deck operations, part of a chronicle of his sea duty he was making for his parents in Missouri.

Jim Little of W Division was roaming the line of aircraft, watching the airmen of the squadrons attach the weapons, looking for any discrepancy in procedures. Jim was a gunner's mate technician, a less descriptive rating than the already obsolete one of nuclear weaponsman.

The W Division men maintained their secrecy and black humor (often expressed in the form of unofficial cloth patches featuring mushroom clouds) in the face of a job that most civilians could barely comprehend: storing, maintaining, assembling

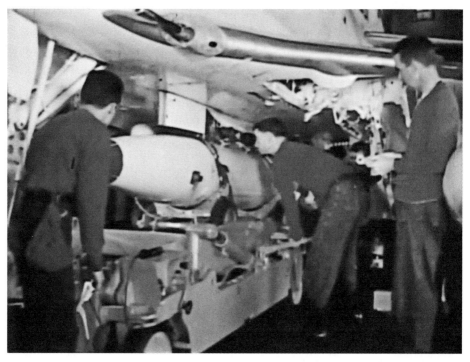

Under supervision of a technical monitor, the B43 is raised to connect with the A-4's centerline pylon. (*Always/Never*)

and transporting the weapons that would kill hundreds of thousands, if not millions, if ever used.

Tico had three aircraft elevators. No.2 Elevator, abeam of the bridge on the port side had once jutted out over the sea like an afterthought, but since the carrier's late-1950s modernization now formed the end of the angled flight deck when raised. When lowered to hangar deck level it was directly exposed to the wind and spray from the sea.

W Division's John Peters handed over the weapon to a six-man crew from GM (Guided Missile) Division, the ship's missile-loading specialists. A pair of armed Marines came with it. Chief Tom Chambers' men gasped when a gray tarpaulin was pulled off to reveal that the sleek white bomb was a war reserve weapon, "Y1" stenciled in black on its side.

Randy Wilson headed to No.2 Elevator, crossing Hangar Bay 3 where the ship's boats were kept, then into bay 2 skirting the line of aircraft and their busy crews, who were making the final connections of some weapon to the pylon under the centerline of the first aircraft destined for the flight deck.

Each of the Skyhawks in the drill was connected to a low-slung yellow tractor called a "mule," except the one at the head of the line. This was an A-4E with the

The pilot and technical monitor check the preflight settings on the B43. (*Always/Never*)

number 472 painted in black on the nose, marking it as the 13th aircraft of the fourth squadron of Air Wing Five, whose code letters "NF" sloped up the tail fin against the candy-striped rudder.

The Skyhawk had been turned to face tail-on to the elevator opening. Awaiting it on the flight deck was a mule and driver who would tow it forward to one of the catapults where it would sit for one minute. Instead of being shot off the bow on a mission that might be the first action of World War III, the cockpit occupant would wait while the deck crew went through their own procedures to simulate a launch before his jet was towed forward to No.1 Elevator and lowered back to the hangar for unloading again.

Without a tractor connected, the aircraft had to be pushed by hand onto the elevator. With no fuel aboard, the Skyhawk would have weighed just under 6½ tons, but loaded as it was today with two full external fuel tanks, a 2,000-pound weapon and a pilot in flight gear, today it weighed slightly over 12.

Shifting this mass across the hangar deck was no big deal with enough hands available. With its nose raised in the air at the end of the long landing gear strut, the high leading edge of the wings and the drop tanks gave reasonably good hand holds for a dozen or so men to overcome the tons of inertia and get an A-4 rolling backwards. Stopping it could sometimes be a little harder.

This scene of an A-4 movement onto an *Intrepid* elevator gives an idea of the manpower involved. Note the tiller bar man and safety supervisor. (USS *Intrepid* Cruisebook)

In addition to the plane pushers, supervisors and towbar handler were two wing watchers, making sure the wingtips cleared obstacles, and three chockmen following the moving aircraft with battered metal chocks, two short blocks connected by a three-foot long metal bar, adjustable to fit different wheel sizes. Chocks were always employed for moves because aircraft brakes could lose effectiveness over time if not used. Champ 472 hadn't flown since *Tico* left Vietnam four days ago.

These particular chock men were trainees. A shortage of qualified personnel aboard *Tico* in late 1965 meant that some petty officers were doing the work of commissioned officers, and lower-ranked men were doing 18-hour days, grabbing catnaps where they could.

Although an ostensibly basic task, chocking a moving aircraft was a delicate operation. When the supervisor's whistle blew, the chocks had to be thrown around the wheels at exactly the same time on each side so that the jet didn't spin around. On a closely packed carrier deck, a moment's delay in stopping an aircraft could cause collisions that could take a fighter out of service or trap and crush a man's arm. Each chock man had to keep a close eye on the other to time his throw exactly to match his counterpart's.

Each Skyhawk needed a qualified man aboard to operate the brakes, which were applied by pressing down on the top parts of the rudder pedals with the toes. Plane Captain Bob Redding had ridden the brakes as 472 was brought from its parking place, but now a pilot appeared from a hatchway, dressed in olive-green fatigues, a parachute harness and a survival vest, carrying his helmet in a green bag, a knee board hanging loosely from his left leg. On the deck surface by the pilot's brown flying boots were a number of puddles of seawater mixed with the rainbow swirls of kerosene that had dripped from a nearby refueling hose.

The pilot and a chief busied themselves beneath the aircraft, checking the bomb's connections and settings, then the pilot signed for it and was handed an Atomic Energy Commission receipt acknowledging he was temporary custodian (for maneuvers) of one B43 Y1 freefall weapon.

The word came down from the flight deck that they were ready topside to begin receiving jets. Peter House, the hangar deck petty officer, walked over to the pilot and asked if he wouldn't mind getting aboard as it was time to break down the aircraft, releasing it from its chains prior to moving.

Bob Redding climbed down from the Skyhawk and went off to chow, handing it over to Airman Richard Edmister, a head taller than most of his colleagues and with flaming red hair. Edmister was holding the ladder when Doug Webster appeared beside him. Webster scaled the ladder and settled in the cockpit. The plane captain followed to help Webster strap in to the aircraft with the four quick-release fittings that connected him at the waist and the shoulders to the ejection seat. Edmister connected Webster's right shoulder fitting, but Webster said he would do the rest himself.

Edmister pulled the safety pin from the seat, making it live, primed to catapult the pilot free of the aircraft in an emergency and lower him safely by parachute. The seat had a zero-zero capability, meaning it would just about save a pilot stopped still on a runway or deck, but it wasn't made live until the aircraft was ready to go onto the elevator, lest it was activated and shot the pilot into the hangar ceiling.

Passing Webster his hard helmet, glossy white with the red boomerang symbol of his squadron on each side, Edminster watched him begin to string his microphone lead to the socket and climbed back down the ladder, which an airman in blue shirt and dungarees quickly took away.

In all, Webster sat in the cockpit for five to ten minutes before the elevator was lowered and the next stage of the movement began. He finished buckling in and completed the required cockpit checks with his helmet on his thigh or resting on the control stick.

Petty officer Howard was taking a bomb cart up to the flight deck on the elevator and watched the plane pushers heave against the wing to get the Skyhawk moving. To plane director C. L. Lindsey, who was supervising the move, the blueshirt plane pushers looked like "hundreds of bees" around the Skyhawk.

As well as the blueshirts and two brownshirted chock and chain men shouldering tiedown chains, there were a couple of yellowshirted supervisors keenly observing their work. Whistles hung around their necks to blow warnings as everyone except the pilot was facing away from them and unable to see hand signals.

The only known complete photo of the lost A-4E, seen landing on *Tico* with a load of bombs and rocket pods. Trapping aboard with unexpended ordnance was unusual and put a strain on the landing gear. (John Deasey)

As the A-4E had no powered steering and its nosewheel simply turned like a castor in the direction the plane was moving, one sailor held a tiller bar connected to the nosewheel hub and steered in reverse as the blueshirts provided the brute force needed to push it onto the outer end of the elevator.

The elevator didn't quite fit flush with the hangar deck floor, being about two inches higher when lowered. A shallow wooden ramp along its length marked with red and yellow warning stripes joined the metal surface of the hangar to the wooden elevator. To get the Skyhawk onto the elevator, this minor obstacle needed to be overcome. The sailors pushed the heavy jet, loaded with fuel, a bomb and a pilot backwards towards the elevator. On the first attempt the mainwheels failed to climb the small incline and it rolled back at them a short distance. Sometimes it took three or four tries to get an A-4 on the elevator, but there were more than enough hands on the job.

Free Fall

Randy Wilson heard a loudspeaker blare: "Stand by for a turn to starboard." As any sailor will tell you, a boat is a vessel that leans inwards as it turns and a ship is one that leans outwards, towards the outside of the turn. The ship shook as it began the turn, enough that everyone would have felt it, and the deck tilted to port, towards the water.

The blueshirts had begun their second try at pushing the Skyhawk onto the elevator. It picked up speed, got over the ramp and kept going.

Doug Webster's focus appeared to be on something other than the director's signals, as he was looking down or looking back into the hangar. Several things then happened in a very short time. Lindsey blew his whistle as the nosewheel reached the yellow line on the elevator. Webster raised himself slightly and looked over the cockpit side. The whistle blew again and the yellowshirt crossed his arms with closed fists in front of him in an X shape, signaling to *hold the brakes*. The blueshirts who had been pushing started to grab what they could and pull instead. The jet was accelerating backwards towards the edge.

Left wing watcher petty officer D. R. Hall made a third whistle blow and the chockmen went into action, casting their metal chocks at the main wheels. Webster looked up.

Gene Ott had thrown his chock at the sound of the second whistle, but the left wheel rolled over it. He grabbed and threw it again, but missed. The right wheel had been stopped by C. D. Sherman's chock, although maybe at the expense of the tire, which was torn.

Webster had his hands on the windscreen frame and to some seemed to be applying all his force to the foot brakes. To others he looked like he was trying to stand up, but the straps were holding him back. He had a desperate look on his face and appeared to be trying to say something but couldn't get the words out.

With one wheel stopped and the other still rolling, the Skyhawk twisted. The left wheel hit the low guardrail on the elevator edge. The nose reared up. Someone shouted, "Get the hell out!" The open canopy swung down on Webster's hands as the aircraft tipped backwards.

The tiller bar lifted off the elevator, pivoted and struck Gene Ott in the hip, knocking him to the deck and almost over the edge. As he looked up, all he could see was the white belly of the aircraft. The plane pushers stumbled and fell face first onto the elevator.

The last line of protection was a literal safety net. This protruded a couple of feet around the edge of the elevator but was designed to catch men, not a 12-ton bomber. The Skyhawk, now standing almost vertical, dropped over the edge into the net, left wheel first. The net failed. For a moment the jet seemed suspended in the air. Then it completed its arc and fell onto its back into the Philippine Sea with a huge white splash.

The blueshirts got to their feet and rushed to the edge. They watched the Skyhawk start sinking into the blue-green sea, disappearing from view as the ship ploughed on. The last view of 472 anyone ever had was its white belly, with a single B-43 one-megaton nuclear weapon gripped on the centerline.

Petty officer Martinez on the left wing called "Plane overboard!" into the radio handset he was carrying. It was vital that a rescue effort was launched as soon as possible and that the chain of command be notified so that they could start doing whatever it was that they did when an atomic bomb fell into the ocean. It hadn't happened before.

Edmond Chevalier, the ship's weapons officer, also ran—to an intercom telephone by the hangar door. Selecting the 1MC circuit, he shouted, "Man overboard, port side! Launch the whaleboat!" The man overboard bugle was played.

The "Angel," the carrier's Seasprite rescue helicopter, was readied and was airborne within two minutes, searching the sea behind the carrier.

Jim Little also ran to a hangar bay phone, grabbed a pad of forms and prepared a message with the bare details of the accident to be sent up the chain of command.

Silhouetted against the opening of No.2 Elevator, a rainbow of filthy shirts and jerseys, red, yellow, green, blue, brown and white, looked out towards where a million-dollar attack jet had just been and now in its absence was only empty sea, a destroyer and, beyond the horizon, the Ryukyu Islands of Japan.

A khaki-clad chief with a clipboard ran up to VA-56 ordnanceman Paul Pizzarella, standing at the aft end of the elevator. "Was there a bomb on that plane?" he asked. The reply was to the point, "There was a fucking pilot on that plane."

CHAPTER 2

Looking for the Sky to Save Me

Fifty-odd miles to the southeast of Cleveland in Ohio's Mahoning Valley lies the small city of Warren. At the heart of the "Rust Belt" of former industrial cities, it was once at the cutting edge of technological developments, becoming in 1911 the first town in America to get electric street lighting, courtesy of the Packard Electric Company, which was founded by Warren natives James and William Packard in 1890. By the end of the decade the Packard brothers started producing automobiles, but moved that business to Detroit in 1903, leaving the Warren plant to make the wiring and electrical components.

Other than the Packards, notable Warren residents include the creator of Charlie Chan, the director of *Home Alone,* the drummer from Nirvana, and the first man to walk on the moon.

Neil Armstrong, who lived an itinerant early life, resided briefly in Warren and on July 26, 1936, the six-year-old future naval aviator and moonwalker took his first flight with his father, a ride in a Warren Airways Ford Tri-motor from a small airfield on Parkman Road. A replica lunar module now stands on the site.

Five years to the day after Armstrong's first flight, Douglas Morey Webster was born in Warren to parents Morey and Margaret. Thirty-year-old Morey was a full-time clerk at the Warren YMCA and was only earning around 1,500 dollars a year. When their only son was born the Websters were renting rooms in a house on Porter Street, not far from the city's central Courthouse Square, for 40 dollars a month. Doug's cousins, the McKees, lived just down the street.

Morey Rayman Webster was named after his maternal grandfather Warren Morey (who carried freight across the Great Plains for the U.S. Army), and grew up in Warren with five sisters. Morey's mother Lucy Irene Morey was from Cortland in Trumbull County, and his father Harvey Elijah Webster was from Michigan and worked in construction. Harvey was probably working on a project when his only son was born in Evansville, Indiana, in September 1911. Morey was about five-foot-seven and wiry. His son would inherit his stature as well as his high forehead and distinctive arched eyebrows.

Two years Morey's junior and of Norwegian descent on her mother's side, Margaret Moe Logsdon was from the prairie town of Calmar, Iowa. Nearby Decorah had one of the largest Norwegian communities in America and the surrounding countryside was farmed by families of Scandinavian stock. With five daughters and one son, John and Anna Marie Moe Logsdon were doing their best to increase Calmar's population (849 in 1910), but it has only just held its own a century later. Margaret went to rural schools in Allamakee and Winneshiek counties and graduated from Decorah High School with four years' secondary education. In 1930 she was still in Iowa but five years later the census records her in Chicago. The Great Depression hit the plains states hard, with approximately three-and-a-half million people moving elsewhere in the decade to 1940. In Chicago Margaret met Morey, where he was doing a degree in engineering. Times were hard and Morey may not have completed his studies because in the 1940 census he declared two years of college as the limit of his education.

Morey and Margaret were married in Chicago the day before Morey's 26th birthday. By 1940 the couple were living in Warren, and a year later, their only son was born.

In Warren, Margaret Webster got a job at the local branch of the American Cancer Society and stayed there the rest of her working life. The director of education for the charity was Donna Ailes, the glamorous wife of Morey's colleague Bob. Their sons would become best friends.

The war brought with it huge expansion in employment in Warren, particularly at the plants of Packard Electric, and changed the fortunes of the Webster family. In 1942 Morey began work at the Packard Electric plant on Dana Street, where pre-war they produced wiring for General Motors cars, having become a GM subsidiary a decade earlier, but by now had moved exclusively into manufacturing for the war effort. In the same year Packard Electric developed the first PVC-coated wiring, which had superior durability and electrical resistance, and pioneered the use of molded plastics in automotive electrical systems. In the next three years the plant's wiring harnesses were installed on the engines of thousands of tanks, torpedo boats and B-29 bombers.

Morey himself worked in Labor Relations (essentially the personnel department) and may have been excused military service because of the plant's war work and the high blood pressure he suffered all his life. Soon after Morey joined Packard the Websters moved to their own house on Edgewood St Northeast, a long street of one- and two-storey wooden houses with porches a few blocks from Warren G. Harding High School. Douglas Webster had clear blue eyes and dark brown hair tinged with red. When he was a boy he loved drawing airplanes, mainly fighters, usually with himself as the pilot. A family photo shows Doug aged about three sitting in a pedal plane, a 1941 Murray Pursuit. With oversized goggles and a cloth cap sitting backwards on his head in the finest Wright Brothers fashion, little Doug looks truly happy.

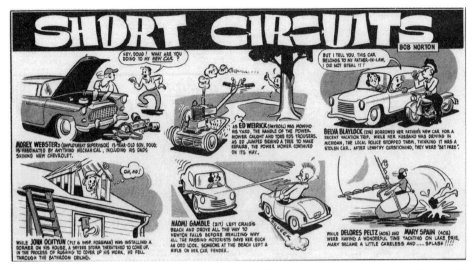

Teenage Doug's exploits as an amateur auto mechanic featured in this cartoon from the June 1955 *Cablegram*. (*Cablegram*)

He was full of energy. A few Christmases later Doug got a bicycle and was desperate to ride it, but he was sick and couldn't go outside. His parents eventually relented to his pleas to ride it inside and he went around and around the tiny house, from the kitchen to the hall to the living room and back.

As he grew, Doug took part in many activities and excelled at whatever he tried his hand. He joined the Boy Scouts in elementary school and his father also participated with Warren's #2 Troop at the First Methodist Church Hall. In middle school Doug was selected as a state representative and later was on the committee of the Boy Scouts of America.

Doug loved to read and passed a high-school level reading and writing test in fourth grade. He would read any mechanical, scientific or aerospace magazines he could get his hands on and tried to put his knowledge to practical use. One day in 1955 Morey came home to find the hood open on his brand-new Chevy and his son beavering away underneath it with engine parts scattered on the driveway.

"What are you doing to my new car?" exclaimed Morey.

"Well, Dad, I just wanted to check the correlation of the valves to the tappets," was 13-year-old Doug's earnest answer.

The post-war consumer boom kept Packard Electric busy and by 1953 there were 6,000 employees in the plant. A new facility opened to make small electric motors used in cars, washing machines, vacuums, and refrigerators. Morey took an active part in the plant's social life. The company's weekly newspaper the *Cablegram* documented some of the highlights over the years: Sports Committee 1947, Variety Review 1948, Picnic Committee 1949, Kiddies' Xmas party committee 1950–51,

Packard Electric's dive squad trained at the Warren Municipal Pool. Morey Webster (on ladder) and Bob Ailes (behind ladder) were enthusiastic volunteers. (*Cablegram*)

Chairman Welfare Committee 1951, supervising finish-line operations at the first Trumbull Soap Box Derby 1958 and winning a prize at the Packard Golf League 1958. His vacations and pastimes also featured in the gossipy regular column of happenings in the Labor Relations department. An unsuccessful 1956 duck hunt in Canada warranted a panel in the "Short Circuits" cartoon—warm weather kept the ducks in the lake's center and Morey spent a week without getting near one, the cartoonist drawing him firing his gun at distant birds but falling short.

In late July 1954, Morey's older sister Ruth Flowers drowned in Rice Lake, Ontario, where she and her husband ran a guesthouse. She was bought home to Warren for burial. The first *Cablegram* of August led with a story about Packard Electric's establishment of an amateur dive team that would be offered free to county fire departments "In case of drownings where the body needs to be recovered." Among the 14 trained divers was Morey, then 43, balding and thin as a twig, and Bob Ailes, who was just balding.

When heavy floods came to Warren in February 1959, Morey and some colleagues helped ferry affected people through the icy waters to shelter at the Packard Music Hall and National Guard Armory in company-supplied station wagons.

In 1957, when Doug was 16, Morey and Margaret divorced. The reasons for the split are now lost, but it caused almost as big a gulf with Doug and Morey as it did with Margaret. Morey moved in with a relative called Dutch Schmidt and Doug went to live with his mother.

In 1959 Morey's name appeared on the *Cablegram*'s list of star donors to the United Way, as did, across the page, Jean S. Rawl. The next year the two were adjacent as Jean S. and Morey R. Webster. Nine years younger than Morey, the former Jean Simpson had been nearby Youngstown's first drum majorette and served in the Navy Women's Reserve (the WAVES) during the war. At Packard she worked in Salaried Personnel as secretary to the director of employee relations Kenneth M. Thompson and had a teenage son, Michael, from her first marriage. He was six years younger than Doug. "When my mother was divorced there weren't a lot of divorced people in Warren, Ohio," Mike Rawl told the author. "It was a time when divorce was fairly rare and so you kind of had that scarlet letter hanging on you. So it was tough, it was financially difficult, but I'll give her credit, she went to work and I went to school early, a year-and-a-half early, I wish I hadn't but it gave her the ability to work. I started kindergarten when I wasn't quite five, so my whole career through high school and junior high school I was a year or more younger than the other kids in the class."

Morey and Jean married at the First Methodist Church at the end of July 1960 and honeymooned in the Pocono Mountains. "When he and my mother were married we were living in a little house in Warren in Francis Avenue, and I thought to myself, *'Yeah, maybe we'll wind up in a decent-sized house'*—and he moved in with us."

Having grown up in the depression, Morey knew the value of a nickel and watched his money very carefully. Nonetheless, he seemed to have some left for his pastimes and vacations. He and Jean went yachting around Lake Erie in late 1962 and on a trip to Ireland in the spring of 1964, where they visited some of Jean's many Irish relatives and had an exciting time in London. There seemed to be a new car every few years. The 1955 Chevy Doug had partly dismantled was replaced by a 1958 Bel-Air two-door hardtop, which was offered for sale in the *Cablegram* in October 1961. By March 1964, Morey was driving a new Buick station wagon.

As someone with influence over hiring and firing, lots of people wanted to be Morey's friend. Mike Rawl says: "It was always important to him to present an image of incorruptibility and high values and standards and kind of a gruffness almost. He wasn't gonna do any favors for anybody. If you got a job it was on your merits. At our house almost every week or two somebody would come by with a ham or a bottle of booze or something trying to influence him to hire their nephew, and he would grudgingly accept them but he wouldn't make any promises."

Mike found it hard to measure up to his stepbrother. He suffered in comparison with the extraordinary kid that Doug was. If Mike came home with a trophy or some other achievement, Morey would dismiss it with sarcastic comments or just "pfft." Mike felt there was a kind of shared sadness between Doug and Morey that they didn't have the relationship they could have done if it wasn't for the divorce.

Over time, as Doug became more independent, Morey became more generous towards his stepson. He encouraged Mike to get summer work at Packard. He didn't give out the job any more than he did for the relatives of the gift-givers, but he told Mike how to apply and he bought an old car for Mike to drive to work.

After his divorce, Morey took up a new pastime—flying. He went solo in April 1958 and started logging the 40 hours needed to make lone cross-country flights, gaining his private pilot's license that November. He bought a small plane then traded it up for a Piper Tri-Pacer. His workmates wanted him to organize the next picnic at Skeets Airport and give rides. They also noted that he would gaze out the window hoping for flying weather while the other men discussed their golf progress.

Mike Rawl describes Morey as an anxious man with high blood pressure, always having to watch his diet and stay thin. He didn't smoke, but there were few drugs to control the condition in those days. His health meant he couldn't keep his pilot's medical certificate (his last—third class—medical certificate was dated September 1963) and had to sell his airplane. Instead he bought a houseboat and he and Jean took vacations on the Allegheny River. Mike lived on it one summer while he was working at Packard. Mike says: "I've never seen many photos of Doug, I've never seen any of his childhood. Morey didn't have any around the house. It was just *strange*. The more you look back on it the stranger it was, that they could have co-existed in this little town within minutes of each other but for all those years not a hint of relationship between them, until Doug went to college and became a little more independent. I'm sure Doug was protective of his mother and was worried that to form a relationship with his father would be a betrayal of his mother and he was angry with his father over whatever caused them to split up. Morey did *something*, I don't want to guess what it was."

One day at the YMCA, Mike helped a teacher he knew unload canoes from a trip. Jimmy Lewis asked if he'd like to help guide a trip and Mike wound up doing it for several years, taking kids on the Allegheny River and up in Canada. Although Mike hadn't known it when he agreed to help, Doug had done the same trips with Jimmy a few years earlier. Jimmy gave Mike Doug's old paddle with his name carved roughly into the wood. The handle of the paddle broke but Mike kept it and it came in useful when he went to college and the fraternity he joined required that its members have a paddle. The frat brothers all signed it and Mike still treasures it. Nearly fifty years later Mike called Jimmy to talk about high school days and although the former teacher and later principal of the Junior High, now in his eighties, had trouble remembering Mike, he hadn't forgotten Doug.

"Well, you remember Doug, don't you, Doug Webster?" asked Mike.

"Doug! Of course I remember Doug, everybody remembers Doug Webster. Oh my God, Doug was just fabulous, he was the best guy I ever had. He was absolutely outstanding."

"How is Doug? I haven't seen him in so long," Jimmy asked.

"Don't you remember, Doug was killed," Mike said.

"Oh … that's right," Jimmy said sadly.

Bob Ailes' son Roger was one of Doug's best friends, living a few blocks away on Belmont Street. His father also worked at Packard Electric, beginning as a mill iron operator in the maintenance department and working up to foreman. Bob Ailes was an enthusiastic Mason, becoming the chaplain of the local lodge and rising through the various arcane ranks of the order. Morey also joined and once took his stepson along to a meeting, but Mike wasn't impressed by the guys in their funny hats. Bob's sons didn't join the order either, to his great disappointment.

Doug and Roger were more interested in airplanes. The 1950s was an exciting time for American boys fascinated by flight. The space race was getting underway and magazines were full of the latest aeronautical developments. Doug's room was full of model airplanes and books on flying and pilots. Nearby Youngstown Air Force Base opened with an air show in 1952, flying F-84s and later supersonic F-102 fighters to defend the Mahoning Valley's industries in the event Russian bombers attacked from the north.

Margaret later said she didn't know Doug planned to join the military, but knew he would have something to do with airplanes. Roger Ailes once told how he and Doug went downtown to join the Marines but their recruiting center was closed and the Air Force wouldn't have Roger because of poor eyesight. He didn't say if the Navy office was open and spotted something in Doug, but when his friend graduated and headed to Ohio State in Columbus, he joined the Navy Reserve Officer Training Corps (NROTC) and began his journey to becoming a naval aviator. Roger went to Ohio University in Athens, unsure of what to study but determined to fly fighter planes. He stuck with the Air Force ROTC for a couple of years, but again his eyesight and other health issues thwarted his ambitions.

Like Doug, Roger was also experiencing a family breakup. Just before he was due to come home on vacation from university he got a call saying he would have to make arrangements to stay at Doug's house. The reason was that his parents were getting divorced. This was the first he'd heard of it. Donna married a fundraiser from the cancer society and moved out to California. Bob moved in with his mother.

When Roger got back to Warren his parents' house was sold and his childhood belongings gone. Roger spent the winter break living with Doug and Margaret. In the New Year he left Warren for good and after graduation he went into the growing industry of television.

School Days

Doug went to Warren G. Harding High School on Elm Road. Milton Mollenkopf had been principal at the school for 30 years, but it was facing change as he neared retirement. The baby boom generation saw a massive expansion of the school and by the time Mike Rawl graduated a few years after Doug there were eight hundred in his year alone and the school was split in two. One of the highlights of Doug's time at WGH was the visit of Vice President Richard Nixon in October 1956.

While Harding was a big player in athletics and basketball, it was a powerhouse in football. Future NFL hall of famer and two-time Super Bowl champion Paul Warfield was a year behind Doug in school. Some regarded him as the most famous person to ever come out of Warren.

Doug loved sports and had taken up swimming in elementary school, but, like his father, he was skinny and was sometimes teased for it. His mother worried that people thought she wasn't feeding him properly. Somebody suggested that he take up weightlifting, which he did in middle school, before finding his true calling in gymnastics at Harding. As home became less attractive he spent a lot of time in the gym.

Because Margaret was at work when Doug finished school, he spent his afternoons at the YMCA where his father had once worked and did a lot of swimming with Roger. His dedication led to being honored as the Warren YMCA's first "all-American fitness boy" and his photo hung in the entrance for many years. Somewhere in his youth, perhaps at the pool or on a canoeing trip, he once saved a drowning man, he wrote in an essay about his life for a high school assignment.

Doug showed great aptitude for gymnastics, and the head of athletics at WGH, John Thompson, a former gymnast himself, almost built the school's athletic program around him, according to Mike Rawl. Doug developed his arms and shoulders until he was almost triangular ("sort of an exclamation point") like coach Thompson. Morey and Mike went to see Doug compete at the University of Pittsburgh, where he won. "His specialty was the rings and he was phenomenal on those," says Rawl. "You can imagine the kind of strength that it took to do the 'iron cross' on the rings. Hold your legs straight out in front of you and your arms like this and then you go straight into a standing position with your feet up and then you come down and flip around. It was just fabulous." "When Doug had his back to you it was all muscles," Margaret remembered years later. "He used to walk out to the garage on his hands."

It was not just athletics. Doug was in the honor society and on the student council and the drama society, playing the part of the old man Mr. Seiko in *Teahouse of the August Moon,* a play about cultural misunderstandings between American servicemen and Okinawans.

Doug didn't suffer fools gladly and held others to the same standards he expected from himself. Sometimes he would come over to Morey and Jean's house to do his homework. One evening Mike was heading out to a dance and unwisely started to shine his shoes while wearing a long-sleeved shirt and got shoeshine on the shirt and Doug was right down his throat with "Jesus, you stupid son of a bitch!" and "How could you do something like that?" His hot temper would get him in trouble at college.

Otherwise Doug's life was that of a typical 1950s Midwest teenager. Malts at Islay's Dairy, movies at the Robins and Daniel Theaters (both owned by Daniel Robins, whose brother David married the sister of movie mogul Jack Warner), tinkering with cars, scout camps, daydreaming about being a jet pilot. At least once Doug dated Carole Rigsby, daughter of Packard Electric's general manager Carl C. Rigsby, taking her to the amusement park.

University

On graduation from Harding in 1959, Doug headed to Ohio State University in Columbus, 170 miles away, but close enough to take a bus to visit his mother at weekends. Although he considered journalism, his chosen major was economics, specializing in industrial relations management, his father's specialty at Packard.

OSU was one of the Big Ten schools of the northeast and Midwest, known for emphasizing both athletics and academics. Most of the students came from Ohio's suburbs and rural communities and although sometimes dismissed as "cow college," OSU was changing. By 1963 it had its own nuclear reactor, and social change was accelerating. In 1960, 98 percent of the 25,000 or so OSU students were white, but by October 1963 the university saw its first civil rights sit-in.

The university president had the ability to veto any visiting speaker he deemed subversive, such as former student Philip Luce, then a left-wing radical, later a right-wing radical. The Speaker's Rule was repealed after protests in 1965. The biggest controversy in Doug's years was probably over the faculty's decision to keep the Buckeyes out of the 1961–62 Rose Bowl, which saw vandalism of houses of those who had voted against going, even though it upheld a previous decision that Big Ten schools would not participate. Effigies of faculty members were hung around campus.

By the end of the decade, Buckeye students' concerns had become less parochial. At OSU in the spring of 1970, riots that some regarded as more violent than that year's infamous Kent State protests broke out, with students calling for equal rights, equal representation and an end to the Vietnam War. The university was closed for nearly two weeks.

When Doug arrived, students under 21 were expected to lodge in halls of residence. Doug's room was in Smith Hall, a brand-new dorm. The men's dorms had paid maids, otherwise the beds would never have been made. Women were required to wear dresses (not slacks) to the dining commons even in winter.

Students were ineligible for the military draft, however, when Doug arrived at Ohio State, Reserve Officer Training Corps was compulsory for male students. Students demonstrated against this—"End the hidden student draft" read one banner—and in June 1961 it was made voluntary. Nonetheless over 80 percent of freshmen (and a few freshwomen) signed up for it and Doug enthusiastically joined the Navy program. For one thing, it paid for his tuition, fees and books and a stipend of 50 dollars a month, and would also hopefully lead to a career as a naval aviator. As well

Doug (third row up, second from right) was (briefly) Phi Gamma Delta fraternity brother with golfer
Jack Nicklaus (second row up, fourth from right). (*Makio* yearbook)

as teaching military discipline, it gave Doug the chance to learn to fly, to travel and
experience life on Navy ships.

Doug also joined a fraternity in his freshman year, the Omicron Deuteron chapter
of Phi Gamma Delta, known as "FIJI." Fraternities were seen as vital to having a
social life in those days, although were also bastions of conformity that didn't suit
everyone. The frat photo in the 1960 *Makio* yearbook shows 70 young white men
in suits and ties. Doug is one of only a few wearing a light-colored suit. One of
his frat brothers was pharmacy student Jack Nicklaus (Class of 1961, although he
never graduated), who was called "Blob-O" by his frat mates for being a little out
of shape, even though he was already a U.S. amateur golf champion. Nicklaus was
made chairman of the frat's "Hell Week" initiation ritual in 1959 and spent a lot
of his free time "quaffing Blatz beer at the Rathskeller." Each spring the fraternity
held a Fiji Island party on a farm outside of Columbus, where brothers dressed up
as South Sea islanders and fell over after too many mixed drinks.

Nicklaus chose FIJI because of the "big guys and good athletes" who made
up its brothers. Its concentration on sport may have attracted Doug too, but he
apparently disliked its emphasis on socializing and ran afoul of its disciplinary system.
Frat discipline was administered by a board of regents who appointed a judicial
commission with its own "chief justice" who dealt with infractions of dorm rules.

Doug encountered this system with serious consequences, says Mike Rawl. "He
was trying to study and this guy was playing music loudly and Doug went over
and knocked on the door and asked him to turn it down and he went back and sat
down and the guy just kept on playing the music and Doug went across the hall

At Ohio State University, Doug was an accomplished gymnast, specializing in the rings. He was ranked 17th in the discipline in the United States in 1962. (The Ohio State University Archives)

and said if you don't turn it down … and the guy said 'do what you want to do' and Doug came back and socked the guy in the mouth and then got tossed out of the fraternity."

When this happened Doug lost his state scholarship, making the ROTC program even more important. He moved out to an apartment off campus.

The Navy ROTC gave Doug the chance to see some of the world. On one summer vacation he went on a midshipman's cruise, joining an aircraft carrier operating out of Naples as part of the Sixth Fleet. This may have been the *Independence*, one of the new supercarriers built from the outset to carry jet bombers and nuclear weapons, and much bigger than the *Ticonderoga*. He also spent time on a destroyer and flew in a Navy attack jet. He used the Navy's extensive air transport network to visit cities all over Europe.

In Doug's college years Vietnam was only a distant troublespot and no doubt far from his mind when he committed to a Navy career. The ROTC gave him the opportunity to learn to fly and by the time he graduated he had a private pilot's license, issued on June 6, 1963.

Mike Rawl remembers coming across Doug in downtown Warren one day. "He'd come home from Ohio State, and he was just standing in front of a store with one foot up against the wall and one foot down and he was reading *Catcher in the Rye* and he'd grown a beard. And I walked up to him and I said, 'I didn't know you were back in town' and he didn't have much to say to me, he was just reading his book."

It was at OSU under coach Joe Hewlett that Doug really developed his gymnastics talents and frequently scored over 90 points out of 100 in his specialty, the still

MARCIA LEA BRAZINA
2702 LIBERTY ST.
EASTON, PA.

ENGLISH

spring
when the world is puddle-wonderful

e. e. cummings

and not to be young is a mere
disguise

Marcia Brazina was a graduate student from the east when she met Doug at Ohio State. Soon they were going steady. (*Koiné* yearbook)

rings. The only sophomore on the rings in the 1961 squad, he was "the surprise of the afternoon" in one of his early meets, beating Michigan veterans. He competed in another meet against a Canadian Olympian, coming 11th, but showing great promise. By early 1962 he was ranked 17th in the nation in the rings discipline despite a pulled muscle that cost him at least one meet.

In a Big Ten Meet in March 1963, Doug came fifth but was only half a point from first place and was Ohio's only medal winner. In the regular season he won eight out of ten rings contests that year. In his senior year he became the Buckeyes co-captain with Dick Affeldt and was the Western Conference still rings champion.

We can only speculate how far Doug might have taken gymnastics had his Navy commitment not taken him in another direction. Very shortly after his death, Ohio State established a memorial award in Doug's honor, given to the gym team's most valuable player. Its first award was made in April 1966—while *Ticonderoga* was still in Vietnam waters—to Dick Petrilla, a ringman from Warren. The next year the OSU's *Lantern* newspaper's report of the "coveted" award described Doug as "an NROTC graduate who died in Vietnam landing on an aircraft carrier." The official myth had already taken hold.

One day a new graduate student arrived from the east to begin a master's degree at OSU. Mike Rawl remembered the story as she told it: "I was moving into the apartment right next to Doug's at Ohio State and it was on the second floor and I pulled my U-Haul truck up down below on the street and I just started unloading the truck and I looked up and I saw this guy up there and he was sitting in the sun in his shorts and had a beer and he was reading you know and looking down at me and I just unloaded the truck and took trip after trip after trip carrying this stuff up the steps and when I finally got it done and I put the door of the truck down he leaned over and he said 'Can I give you a hand with anything?'" And that was Marcia Brazina's introduction to Doug Webster. Soon they were going steady.

Marcia was tiny, like Margaret, under five-foot tall, a brunette of Russian Jewish heritage with a winning smile. The daughter of Dr. Reuben and Evelyn Brazina from Easton, Pennsylvania, she already had an undergraduate degree in English language and literature from Connecticut College for Women in New London and had come to OSU to study for a Masters in English. She had been a reporter for the college paper the *ConnCensus* and the literary editor of her college yearbook *Koiné*. Her father had been an army dentist in the Pacific and Japan and had returned to civilian practice in Nazareth after the war.

Navy Blue

On August 23, 1963, at Columbus, Ohio, Doug signed papers to join the Navy proper. The following month he graduated with a BSc in business administration. The athletics department had nurtured his competitive spirit and improved his already extraordinary physical condition. NROTC had given him a grounding in naval tradition and discipline and a taste of carrier aviation. He had a pilot's license. He was as prepared as he could be for a career as a naval aviator.

Doug had achieved his goal of being selected for training as a naval aviator and packed his bags for Officer Candidate School at Pensacola, Florida. While Doug trained, Marcia returned to Pennsylvania to teach in the Muhlenberg College English department.

Pensacola calls itself the Cradle of Naval Aviation, being where the first naval air station was established in 1914. The town had a naval history dating back to 1826 when construction of a navy yard began, 13 years before Florida became a state.

Then, as now, the base has golf courses and brick homes in colonial Georgian style with white porticos where some of the senior officers live with their families. Amidst the manicured lawns and tropical plants are rows of student barracks. Palmetto trees line the roadways and the long beaches have white sands, which the locals claim are the whitest in the world. In summer, a Gulf breeze moderates the humidity, but in winter it can drop below freezing at night. The environment must have been a pleasant surprise for Midwesterners like Doug, but he wouldn't have time to enjoy the sunshine. Trainees who brought along golf clubs were soon disabused of the notion that they would get any link time and shipped them back home.

For Doug and his fellow candidates, pre-flight training began with ten days of "shock treatment" indoctrination, beginning with a Reveille bugle at 0515 and Taps at 2130. "Indoc" started on a Wednesday and it was only on the second Sunday that candidates got any afternoon or evening liberty, and only then if they were performing satisfactorily and had no demerits. Weekend liberty only came after the third week.

Gymnasiums were located in the old seaplane hangars but Doug seems to have put his passion for gymnastics aside. He would have had no trouble meeting the Navy's fitness standards or passing their swim qualifications.

Students were either Aviation Officer Cadets with degrees, like Doug, or Naval Aviation Cadets (NavCads) who had some college credits but weren't graduates. There were also a few officers switching branches, who took an abbreviated course. The Navy had 17,000 commissioned pilots in 1964 and trained nearly 3,000 men to become officer pilots or aviation observers every year. This required numerous training bases in the Southern states and hundreds of training aircraft. Student naval aviators (SNAs) moved between them at each stage of their training.

Pre-flight school was in Building 633, another imposing porticoed brick structure with a huge brass bell in a frame outside. Inside were the classrooms where Doug would spend around 450 class hours over about 22 weeks.

The academic department taught naval orientation, leadership, aviation science, the principles of flight and aero engines, and study skills. A math or engineering degree wouldn't hurt, but the instructors prided themselves on being able to pass a candidate with only eighth-grade math. The military department taught drill, discipline, courtesy, and bearing, things with which Doug was familiar from ROTC.

The physical Training and Survival Department covered physical fitness, swimming and survival techniques. In the air station's pools, Doug learned survival-swimming techniques, which differed from sport swimming. For some reason the Navy prefers a frog kick to a scissor kick and breaststroke to overarm. Much of what a confident swimmer like Doug knew would have to be unlearned.

Named after the archetypal hapless student aviator of flight safety cartoons, the "Dilbert dunker" was a cockpit section of an SNJ trainer plane, mounted on a ramp pointed towards the bottom of a swimming pool. The student climbed a ladder on the rig and was strapped into the pilot's seat by a sailor. When ready, he gave a thumbs-up and another sailor pulled a lever on the wall. The cockpit was released, rode the rails into the water and promptly turned turtle. The student was told to brace himself for impact and to remain calm, orient himself, unstrap his harness and swim clear, even as water rushed painfully into his sinuses.

In the last days of basic training the candidates were taken to the huge Eglin Air Force Base reservation for survival training. A three-day field survival course (called a "problem") saw them out in the woods with only a map, compass and knife. Food had to be gathered or caught and that included opossum, raccoon and rattlesnake.

Doug seems to have had little trouble passing basic training, and in a short ceremony a couple of days after returning from Eglin, Doug was commissioned as an ensign in the United States Navy. It seems Margaret was there to share the occasion. A photo shows her in a short-sleeved black dress gazing proudly up at her son in his dress whites, gloves in hand and hat at a jaunty angle. The bare arms, the sunglasses she holds and the green foliage suggest Florida rather than Ohio.

Doug already knew how to fly but now he had to learn again the Navy way, with checklists and standardized procedures. Primary flight training began with a dozen flights in the two-seat T-34 Mentor with one instructor, then a check ride with a different instructor. In the cockpit Doug was "Mister Webster." If progress was satisfactory, he would go solo on his 13th flight.

Towards the end of the eight-week course the student got to choose the path of their Navy career, between jets and propeller aircraft, and in mid-January Doug sent his mother a letter from Fort Worth, Texas.

Jan 18 1964

Dear Mom,

After having bad weather for a week, the skies are finally clear and we are having a gorgeous day. I just finished my initial flight training eight days ago. Yes, I passed. Actually I was the fourth out of 24 students who took the jet pilot training course. I chose the jet pilot program over the prop because I want to become a commercial airline pilot when I get out of the Navy. I am moving again, though! The Navy is shipping me to the Naval Air Station in Meridian, MS in a few days.

Doug didn't find getting good grades easy. He worked so hard that by the end of this phase he felt he was only one step away from a mental hospital.

That same week a brand new Skyhawk rolled out of the Douglas factory at Long Beach, California. Bureau Number 151022 was the first of the second-to-last batch of A-4Es built. It was flown to Lemoore and handed over to the Navy the next day, to VA-56 Champions.

Meridian

At Meridian, Doug learnt to fly jets with one of the base's two training squadrons, which between them flew around 120 T-2A Buckeye jet trainers. It has been said that the hottest thing about the Buckeye was its red-and-white paint job, but it was a jet. Like Doug, it came from Ohio, being built in the North American Aviation plant near Columbus, across town from OSU.

After two weeks of training with Navy and Marine instructors in the back seat, it was time to go solo. It was a nervous day for any student aviator, made more so when the T-2 of one of Doug's fellow students caught fire and he had to eject. Stan Smiley was also on his first jet solo and parachuted into woods south of the base. Smiley recovered from this setback and went on to fly Skyhawks, but was shot down and killed over Laos in 1969.

There seem to have been some technical issues with Meridian's Buckeyes. On Doug's last dual hop the day before, he had hydraulic problems on his T-2 and his instructor had to use an emergency brake on landing.

Over 20 weeks at Meridian, Doug endured many hours of lectures on such subjects as aerodynamics, principles of flight, aviation psychology and so on. He made honor roll and was third in his class.

Doug doesn't seem to have had his own car and usually walked around the sprawling base. One day he set off from the barracks for simulator training in the base operations area, a walk of nearly three miles along a road through the woods. As he trudged along Fuller Road it began to rain hard and he was getting soaked. A black Volkswagen Beetle pulled up and Steve Richardson, a tall fellow student from Washington State who was on the previous course, opened the door and offered him a lift to the simulator building. Doug would serve with Steve on *Ticonderoga* and never forgot his kindness.

Doug did 50 hours of basic jet familiarization and instrument flying in the T-2A, moving on to three more months on the twin-engine T-2B, concentrating on formation flight training.

This was the summer of the "Mississippi Burning" murders in nearby Neshoba County. President Johnson ordered all hands at Meridian to participate in the search for the missing three civil rights workers. One student ensign apparently said he came to fly, not to search. Reportedly he was flown to Washington that afternoon and was out of the Navy by sundown.

Around this time Doug had moved on to Chase Field at Beeville, Texas. Here he flew training versions of the Grumman Cougar, an early swept-wing fighter. The Cougar was a true naval fighter with folding wings and cannon and in it he learned air combat maneuvers, strafing, bombing and low-level navigation. The intense training was causing him doubts about his suitability as a jet pilot, but not as much as one of his fellow students, who suffered from terrible nausea and threw up before every flight. He dropped out of flying training on the doctor's recommendation. Doug continued his solo flying and began night flying, which he found nerve wracking. He enjoyed aerobatics, particularly doing rolls.

The final stage was carrier landing training, beginning with field carrier landing practice, making dozens of landings on an airfield marked as a carrier deck, using a mirror landing system, then actual carrier qualification on the carrier *Lexington* in the Gulf of Mexico where Doug made the requisite two touch-and-go and six arrested landings.

Finally, after a year-and-a-half of training, Doug stood proudly in front of the flag as a captain pinned the wings of gold on the breast of his bridge coat. At the same time he received the silver bars of a lieutenant (junior grade) and got his orders to report to Naval Air Station Lemoore, California for Skyhawk conversion training and then to Attack Squadron Fifty-Six. It was December 5, 1964.

Douglas M. Webster receives his aviator's wings of gold on December 5, 1964, a year to the day before his death in the Philippine Sea. (U.S. Navy)

Lemoore

In the New Year Doug and Marcia moved to Naval Air Station Lemoore, which would be Doug's permanent base. Almost as soon as he arrived he was sent on escape and evasion (E&E) training. Since the conflict in Vietnam had escalated, E&E training had become much more intense and realistic. Aviators were dumped in the desert and had to make their way to a checkpoint without being "captured" by instructors. No matter how long they avoided capture, all trainees wound up in a mock prison camp where they were kept hungry, shouted at and forced to undergo various punishments and humiliations.

In late March, Doug began to fly the A-4 with VA-125, the West Coast training squadron. The two-seat TA-4 was not yet in service, so Doug's first Skyhawk flight was also his first solo flight in the nimble fighter-bomber. Instructor pilots would fly alongside students rather than with them. Hugh Magee flew as Doug's instructor on a number of VA-125 syllabus flights and remembered him as a "fine lad and an excellent stick."

In early May, he was sent to Fallon, Nevada to undertake nuclear weapons training. During this time he was not allowed to write or call anyone off the base, not even Margaret on Mother's Day.

Chapel of Love

On June 3, Doug and Marcia got married in the base chapel at NAS Lemoore. Margaret couldn't make it to the wedding due to work commitments and Morey wasn't there either, but not long afterwards he was able to come out and spend a week with the newlyweds. After years of being apart, there seemed to be some sort of rapprochement between father and son. Mike Rawl thought Morey was the happiest he had ever seen him when he got back to Warren, having begun to forge this new relationship with Doug.

Margaret did get out to Lemoore at the beginning of August and stayed with Doug and Marcia for four days in their house in Hanford. When he could find time around his training, Doug played tourist guide, showing his mother the gold rush towns of central California.

Now that he was flying the A-4, Doug had to renew his carrier qualifications with 15 day and eight night landings on *Kitty Hawk*. His performance was good, landing on the first attempt all but once, making him first of his group, which included two of his future squadron mates, to qualify and return to Lemoore. Even then he wrote to his mother that night landings were scary.

Completing A-4 carrier qualifications was the final hurdle before Doug could join a fleet squadron, one whose mission was "To conduct offensive surface to air attack operations with conventional and nuclear weapons."

CHAPTER 3

We are the Champions

Located in California's central valley between Fresno and Bakersfield, Lemoore was flat and isolated, which made it a good place for a Master Jet Base. It had some quirks when it opened in 1961. The concrete ramp was still fresh and the hangars were gently sinking into it, making the doors hard to open. The garden sprinkler system for the base housing was centrally controlled and would come on at random intervals, adding extra fun to backyard barbecues. To those used to Miramar on the outskirts of San Diego, Lemoore was a god-forsaken spot.

Lemoore was home to the Navy's West Coast light-attack squadrons. Three belonged to Air Wing Five and would sail together on *Ticonderoga*. Doug's assigned squadron was Attack Squadron Fifty-Six (VA-56), known as the Champions after their radio call sign.

The aviators of the Champions were from all over America, men in their twenties and thirties, all white and college-educated. Some were Naval Academy graduates or frat brothers, some were from military families, some had been successful football players. Many had nicknames, but these weren't used as individual radio callsigns in the way that would become the fashion in later years.

The skipper or "Champ One" was William Nealon, from a military family in Boston. He had joined the Navy at 18 and served on the carrier USS *Tarawa* when it helped evacuate American civilians during the Chinese Civil War. He had been nuclear warfare plans officer for NATO staffs in Naples and the executive officer at Naval Air Station Oceana before being assigned command of VA-56 in early 1965. Unusually, he hadn't served the traditional position of squadron executive officer (XO).

Nealon's XO was Carl Ray ("C. R." or "C. Ray") Smith from Florence, South Carolina. Smith was a 1949 Naval Academy graduate and had flown combat in Korea. His wife Virginia was an admiral's daughter and they had three sons and two daughters.

Render Crayton's unusual first name was his grandmother's surname. He was from South Carolina, but was a Georgia Tech textile engineering graduate who called

Champs pilots at Yuma in early 1965, VA-56 having won the "E" for efficiency award for West Coast light-attack squadrons. Back L-R: Callahan, Fox, Halverson, Crayton, Shower, Paisley, Gehman. Front L-R: Palmer, Pfeiffer, Simmons, Nealon, Belcher, Delesie, Schmidt. (U.S. Navy)

Atlanta his home town. Somewhere he got the nickname "Royal Mind." At 32 he was balding and maybe the tallest in the squadron by a small margin. In 1965 he married Patsy. Before joining VA-56 he did a tour as an advanced flight instructor at Corpus Christi, one of his students being future Senator John McCain. Now the operations officer, he had been the maintenance officer and was well known for carrying a marker in his flight suit pocket that he used to circle spots of corrosion on A-4s. Also raised in Georgia, the current maintenance officer John Paisley was married to Sam and had four children. He'd had a few years out of the Navy obtaining an aeronautical engineering degree and a short spell flying for Braniff Airlines.

John Olene "Jack" Holland was the safety officer. Sometimes he got called "Jacqueline" as a play on his name. He had flown A-1 Skyraiders from *Lexington* on a previous tour. An amateur moviemaker, he would sometimes fly with an 8mm camera mounted in the cockpit of his Skyhawk. Albert Jay Shower, known as Jay or "Jaybird," was the son of a wartime Eighth Air Force Bomb Group commander and a Naval Academy graduate. His first flight, aged ten, was in the co-pilot's seat of a B-29. His wife Bonnie would have their second child just before the squadron left for Vietnam. Texan Lou Herzog, aged 33, had previously flown with another A-4 squadron and later took over as the Champ's safety officer. He and his wife Patricia had three daughters.

The Junior Officers

Edwin "Ed" Pfeiffer was a soft-spoken, sandy-haired 26-year-old bachelor from Palo Heights, Illinois with a broad grin. He was the president of his fraternity at Ripon College in Wisconsin, where he had studied math and physics. Admin officer stocky Job Belcher Jr. was from the Navy town of Norfolk, Virginia, aged 31 and married to Joan. His fellow pilots called him "Joby" or fondly, "Smally Hog." To the line crews he was, perhaps inevitably, "Burp." Jim Delesie, 25, from Flint, Michigan, was an Annapolis science graduate. His wife Margaret had a son, Jim Jr. at Lemoore in 1965. He was the squadron's airframes and powerplants officer. Jim Halverson, 29, tall and slim with a big smile and somewhat large ears, was married to Patti Jo. Somewhere he picked up "Cool Breeze" as a nickname, but was sometimes called "Halverpuff." Bob Simmons from Pennsboro, West Virginia, was 28. He sometimes sported a mustache before it became the fashionable thing for naval aviators. Dale Palmer had just transitioned to flying the A-4, having come from a utility squadron in Okinawa where he had ejected from an FJ-3 Fury. His family called him "The Japanese Tourist" because he loved taking photos and home movies so much.

Tall with black hair and blue eyes, electrical engineering graduate and ham radio enthusiast Tom Gehman from Woodbridge, New Jersey, was nearing the end of his time with the squadron. Tom Callahan from Rochester, New York, was also to leave the squadron before the end of the year.

As well as the pilots, there were several non-flying officers in the squadron. Former enlisted man "Jumping Jack" Kaufman was the ordnance officer, responsible for the squadron's weapons crews. Mike Morgan was the air intelligence officer and Carl Dila served as the flight surgeon.

More pilots were to join the Champs after they deployed. Bill Cain would arrive before Christmas. Van Hough had orders to the Champs, but was still training with VA-125, where he was awarded the Top Gun award for best student in his class. Hough, Tony Merrill and former enlisted man Jim Maslowski would report to the squadron in early 1966.

Three other lieutenant junior grades (LTJGs) arrived at the squadron with Doug Webster. Annapolis graduate Austin Chapman was from Tryon, in the Blue Ridge Mountains of North Carolina. A high school football star, he was tall with thinning red hair and was nicknamed "Big Red." Pragmatic Edwin "Fast Eddie" Phelps III was from Lawrence, Kansas. His wife Sara had just had a baby daughter. His hobby was going up in the mountains and mining gold. Pale with flaming red hair, Bob Sturgeon from Atlanta had graduated Georgia Tech with a degree in aerospace engineering.

With his fairly modest Midwest background, preference for individual as opposed to team sports and being the first in his immediate family to serve in the military, Doug Webster was a little different to his squadron mates.

Austin Chapman says: "We had finished the training and instead of getting orders to a squadron already in Vietnam, they sent us to one that was nearly ready to go. They were trying to get everybody up to between 20 and 22 pilots for 14 aircraft. By the time we got there I think they were down to 18."

They were nearly down two more in July. While flying a practice bomb run near Turlock, California, Job Belcher ejected from an A-4E because of a mechanical problem, suffering only a minor abrasion from his parachute harness. The aircraft was on the books of VA-125 and may have been borrowed to make up a shortfall. Eleven days later, Virgil Jackson Jr. ejected safely from his VA-56 A-4E before it crashed and burned five miles north of Woodlake, near Sequoia Park. The aircraft crashed in the front yard of Leonard Hanson's Sentinel Butte home, destroying his house and slightly singeing the neighbor's dog. "Virg" Jackson left the Champs after this mishap, but went on to fly in Vietnam and later command his own squadron.

Broad-shouldered John Paisley wasn't initially the biggest fan of the Skyhawk. "When I had orders from the training command to VA-56 I had mixed emotions. When I first climbed into the airplane I was absolutely *appalled*. My shoulders touched the sides, the canopy was right *here* with the helmet. You turn your head the wrong way and you are going to hit the canopy and the only two places you could put your arms outstretched were down by your knees or up over the glare shield. But about the time you get to weapons training and you're flying the thing about three times a day and about thirty minutes a mission, you become accustomed to it, and I was very, very happy to fly that airplane in combat. For one thing it was rather small and hard to hit, and for the most part their [the enemy] weaponry was World War Two, much like ours. We were hard to hit, we were not blazing fast, but fast enough, and it jinked very well, so I just felt fortunate. I think it probably saved my life. I know a lot of [Skyhawks] got popped, on the other hand I think we were more fortunate than the larger aircraft."

In early August 1965, the overhaul of a Champs Skyhawk, a veteran of the Tonkin Gulf incident, was completed at Alameda. Before it was accepted, rework facility pilot Bob Krall had to test fly it four times, which was unusual. "The first flight was a refly (meaning the bird didn't perform well enough to accept the aircraft after overhaul). The following two flights checked on the 'fix' of the discrepancy that necessitated a refly in the first place. The fourth flight was a 'sell,' meaning that the aircraft met all requirements to accept the aircraft for transfer," says Krall. He signed Bureau Number 151022 over to a ferry pilot who flew it back to Lemoore where the Champs maintainers painted on its new side number, 472.

Boomerangs to Champions

When it was established at Miramar, California in June 1956, Attack Squadron Fifty-Six was known as the Boomerangs, its insignia representing a safe return from a deadly strike. VA-56 was the first jet light-attack squadron with a dedicated all-weather nuclear attack mission. Illustrating the rapid changes in naval aviation, in less than three years of existence the squadron had deployed only once but flown several types of aircraft: the Grumman Panther and Cougar and the North American Fury, followed by early model Skyhawks.

It was at the 1959 Naval Air Weapons Meet, held over ten days in December at the Marine Corps field at Yuma, Arizona, that the squadron truly established its reputation. VA-56 competed with 16 Navy and Marine squadrons, each representing their respective fleets and fighter or attack community. With only a couple of months' notice and little time to prepare, the Boomerangs were chosen to represent the West Coast light-attack squadrons, while their East Coast counterparts had been practicing for their whole training cycle. A new official list of radio callsigns had been issued shortly before the meet, but only a few squadron officers knew that VA-56 was now the "Champions." Skipper Larry Walker announced the new name as they arrived in the pattern at Yuma.

More than a decade before the famous Topgun air combat school opened at Miramar, the Yuma weapons meet was dubbed Operation *Top Gun*, and the progress of the contest, which tested skills such as bombing, rocketry and weapons loading was followed in the newspapers as if it was a sports tournament, with a spectacular firepower demonstration from the final awards ceremony being televised. Unfortunately the climax of the broadcast, a simulated nuclear weapon attack by a Skyhawk, was a bit of a dud when the mushroom cloud pyrotechnic failed to go off. "It must have been wet," said the TV commentator dryly.

When the scores were tallied, VA-56 won the jet light-attack category with 8,489 points, only 25 more than VA-12 from Oceana. The Fourth Naval Air Weapons Meet turned out to be the last and so the victors kept the trophy and the Champions name stuck.

Workups

In March 1965, Commander William G. Nealon took over the squadron from Wesley McDonald, who went off to command Air Wing Fifteen, and later became a rear admiral. Less than a month later the Champs lost their executive officer when Robert Tigner crashed north of Twentynine Palms, California on a practice bombing mission.

Bill Nealon was not universally popular, particularly with the junior officers. Austin Chapman thought he was an aloof person and very rigid in his command

VA-56 transitioned to the A-4E in July 1963. The Champs executive officer Robert Tigner was killed in the crash of this aircraft in April 1965. Note the "baby carriage" radiation shield behind the pilot. (via Gary Verver)

structure. "It was not a difficult relationship at all, just a more formal one. He just didn't get down and grovel with the young JOs very much." Nealon was critical of Jay Shower's formation keeping and wanted him to stay at a 90-degree bearing to his wing during maneuvers. Shower was skeptical that this could be done. "Sir, with all due respect, could you demonstrate this to me the next time we have an Alpha Strike out of Fallon." The CO replied, "Darn right. I'll put you in my position. We'll do this 20-degree orbit turn and I'll show you how we do it." Shower thought this was a physical impossibility and was proved right in front of the whole squadron as he did as instructed but when he leveled off, Nealon's jet shot away in another direction with about a hundred miles per hour overtake and took a long time to get back in formation. "And he was mad at *me* for having him do it, but he screwed up because he did it in front of all the squadron members," said Shower. "We were at the bar one night and one of the other guys had a go-around with him and he came up to Bill Nealon at the bar and he said, 'Skipper!' as he pushed his finger at the CO's chest. 'Skipper, you're doing it wrong....' It wasn't the incident I had, it was an incident he had. And I'm glad it was him punching the skipper and it wasn't me."

When off duty at Yuma, the Champs found various ways to amuse themselves. Eddie Phelps fancied himself as a bit of a prospector and one weekend he took Jay

Champs skipper Nealon signaling he's ready to take external air to start up his A-4. (John Paisley via Bill Paisley)

Shower on an expedition to search for gold. They drove over the first range of hills and into a dry creek bed. They met a prospector who showed them how to pan for gold and sold them a shaker tray and showed them how to filter sand through it, bouncing out the lighter stuff and eventually leaving pure gold. They wound up with a five-gallon can of enriched sand, which they hauled back to Lemoore. The next weekend Shower had duty as squadron duty officer and spent the entire weekend from Friday evening, all through Saturday and Sunday night staying up late shaking the sand out until he had a film canister filled with solid gold. In those days, gold was probably worth only 35 dollars an ounce, so it was a lot of effort for the hundred bucks or so they made from it.

When off duty from pre-deployment workups at Fallon Nevada, the pilots spent a lot of time in the casinos of Reno, 60 miles from the air station. Legend has it there was a light in the ceiling of the aviators' favorite casino that would flash if there were a national emergency, to alert them to head back to base. Ed Phelps supposedly had a system for winning on the roulette table and Jay Shower says that he never lost using this system. There was one place that asked him to leave, but he took his winnings over the road to another casino and carried on.

Like Doug's gymnastics team, his squadron was a team made of individuals. Each man could do every discipline but had his own specialty, and his effort would contribute to the final score in the Big Meet.

We would like to introduce you to TICO Tiger, the spirit of Ticonderoga. He is a mover of men, a guiding light and inspiration. A symbol of progress and success. Where you go on Ticonderoga, he will be watching and protecting. In the following illustrations he attempts to warn you of some hazards that lay ahead during your visit.

"First of all, watch your step. On a ship this size you never....

....know what you are going to walk into next."

"Raised hatches can batter knees and shins .. so step warily over them."

"Climbing ladders from deck to deck can sure get you down fast if you do not use the handrails."

Oh... by the way, don't forget to look up now and then or you might bump your...OUCH!

Visitors to *Tico* were given this helpful guide to staying safe on board. (*Ticonderoga* Welcome Aboard booklet)

CHAPTER 4

The Big T

The 14th American fleet carrier began life as *Hancock* in late 1943 at Newport News, Virginia, but the name was swapped for *Ticonderoga* (a much fought-over Revolutionary War fort in upstate New York) after three months' construction because the John Hancock insurance company offered to sell war bonds to pay for a carrier if it was built in their hometown of Quincy, Massachusetts. It was said that right to the end of *Ticonderoga*'s life plates could still be found deep in the hull embossed with the original name.

On February 7, 1944, 53 weeks after the first rivet was hammered, *Ticonderoga* (CVA-14) rolled down the slipway, the sixth of the *Essex*-class to make the same short journey into the Elizabeth River. When the United States entered the war in December 1941, the United States Navy had seven carriers. *Ticonderoga* was the 65th of various classes built since then, illustrating America's massive industrial might and expertise at mass production. On average, an *Essex*-class carrier was handed to the Navy every 90 days. Each of the 16 of the class cost between 70 and 78 million dollars and displaced around 21,000 tons at launch, although they were to put on a lot of extra weight as they aged.

Three months later *Ticonderoga* was commissioned and, after a shakedown cruise to Florida and back, sailed in late June to the Caribbean for work-ups with Air Group 80, equipped with Hellcat fighters, Helldiver bombers and Avenger torpedo bombers.

Ticonderoga's first skipper was Captain Dixie Kiefer. The 48-year-old Idahoan had begun his naval career on a subchaser in European waters at the end of World War I before switching to the new aviation branch. Designated Naval Aviator No.26, Kiefer was the first man to make a night take-off from a ship when he was catapulted in a Vought biplane from the battleship *California* in 1924. Later the same year he ditched a blazing seaplane in Lake Washington. By 1942 he was the executive officer of the carrier *Yorktown* and survived its sinking at the battle of Midway, being the last to abandon ship and suffering serious injuries including a mangled leg. Navy Secretary James V. Forrestal called Kiefer "The Indestructible Man" when he presented him with the Distinguished Service Medal in July 1942.

On September 4, 1944, *Ticonderoga* sailed through the Panama Canal. This was said to be the first time a large carrier did so without scraping the lock sides or losing any major parts. By late September the carrier was in Hawaii and spent some time doing trials of transferring ammunition at sea, not joining Task Force 38 until early November.

Ticonderoga, quickly dubbed "The Big T" by its crew, first saw combat in the invasion of Leyte in November, surviving kamikaze attacks off the Philippines and a typhoon that killed over 800 men on other task force ships. In the New Year, Air Group 80 struck Japanese bases on Formosa and Luzon and at Hong Kong. The next targets were in Indochina, in what would a decade later become South Vietnam. On January 12 *Ticonderoga's* planes hit Japanese shipping in the Saigon River.

Ten minutes after noon on January 21, 1945, while many of the crew were getting chow, an aircraft of the newly formed Niitaka Special Attack Corps from Tainan airfield on Formosa dived out of a blue sky. American reports describe this as a Mitsubishi A6M Rei-sen "Zeke" fighter, and Japanese documents suggest the pilot was either Ensign Yoshihide Hoiguchi or Chief Warrant Officer Yoshinobu Fujinami, the latter aged just nineteen. The aircraft was carrying a 250-kilogram bomb.

Gunner Robert Strother mistook the incoming Japanese aircraft for an American. "A suicide plane came in and I was standing there fat dumb and happy. I thought it was one of our planes and I thought, *'We gotta respot all those planes in order to take that guy aboard.'* All of our planes were spotted aft ready for take-off and then it suddenly dawned on me, *'Hey that's an attack!'* The guns opened up on him about then and he started firing and I jumped into the armored hatch that was there on the island. There were two doors on the island that were locked, but the third door that was actually facing the flight deck—I got in there and there was probably three inches of armor around that and a whole bunch of us huddled on the floor down there pretty low." The kamikaze smashed into the forward flight deck, 12 feet from the centerline. The semi armor-piercing bomb punctured the wooden deck and exploded between the gallery deck and the hangar deck.

Machinist's mate Bill Blythe was on the hangar deck near the aft end of the ship. "I heard the marines firing the 20mm machine guns that were on the starboard side. I started to go over and see what they were shooting at. I suddenly realized there was a war on and I needed to get down to where I belonged." Blythe's General Quarters station was at the water evaporator six decks below.

As the GQ alarm sounded he ran halfway along the hangar to a hatch that led below. "I get down to the hatch, these guys are coming up, eyes askew. Of course that was a down ladder, not an up ladder. Down on the starboard side, up on port side. Up and aft, down and forward. I put my foot on this guy's chest. I pushed him down and said, 'this is a down ladder!' Then I went on down. I got down to the Third Deck and as I stepped out of the trunk where the ladder was—they dropped the bomb up there where I was just standing. Concussion damn near knocked me on my ass. I looked back and kept on going. I got back to the hatch that led down to our department. It was a booby hatch, it had a wheel on it. The large hatches are always secured when the ship goes out to sea, the only way to get up or down through these hatches is through the booby hatch. The hatch was open and Ensign Anderson was standing in that booby hatch on the ladder, waving his .45 yelling 'Calm down! Calm down!' Well, the reason for that was they were arming 1000-pound bombs on the mess hall deck where we all were and we all wanted to get away from them. I told Andy to get the hell down and I went down after him and we were down there until one o'clock in the morning."

Ticonderoga was badly damaged by the kamikaze. Executive officer William Burch manned a hose and directed firefighting efforts in the hangar bay, during which his clothes caught fire twice, before returning to the bridge.

At 1258 a second suicide plane, a Yokosuka D4Y "Judy" flown by Flight Warrant Officer Noboru Fukushima and Flight Petty Officer First Class Kameichi Yasudome flew low up the deck and exploded on the forward gun director just ahead of the island. The director crew survived inside their armored box, but on the flight deck and open bridge, flying shrapnel from the Judy's two bombs caused havoc. The Air Officer Clair Miller and Gunnery Officer Herbert Fulmer were killed and XO Burch was wounded, as were several other officers. Captain Kiefer himself suffered 65 wounds and had a severely injured arm. A seaman was treating a severed artery in Kiefer's neck when the captain said, "I'm sorry I had to bust you." The man had been demoted from petty officer a few days before. Kiefer was being taken below for his safety when he asked about his senior officers. When he was told they had all become casualties, he insisted on returning to the bridge, where he resumed command from a mattress laid on the deck.

Another ship called *Ticonderoga* over the radio, "Are you going to abandon ship?"

"Hell, no!" was Kiefer's legendary reply. Then he set about saving it.

Captain Kiefer ordered the damage control officer to flood ballast tanks to correct the starboard list. This caused a 10-degree port list, draining water and burning gasoline into the sea and tipping damaged aircraft overboard. Then he ordered the course changed to keep the wind from fanning the flames and to keep smoke out of ventilation intakes.

Bill Blythe said: "What the damage control officer did was he looked down and saw the ballast tanks that were down below and flooded them with water. That was on the port side of the ship which had roller curtains all along. You could open those big roller curtains up and that's where the fire was, on the hangar deck. The firemen over here on the starboard side could wash that gas over the side, that's what saved us."

Assigned to damage control, Walter Mallett was cutting holes in the flight deck with an axe to rescue pilots trapped in a ready room when the second kamikaze struck and was knocked down by the explosion, suffering severe injuries to his

Fires raged through *Ticonderoga* for two hours after she was hit twice by kamikazes on January 21, 1945. Heroic efforts by her captain and crew saved the ship. (U.S. Naval Academy, Admiral Nimitz Library)

arms and upper body. Finding himself lying beside a 500-pound bomb, his first thought was I better get up, get out of here before I burn up. That was easier said than done. "I tried to push up my arms but I'd broke my arm. I never did have a broken bone before. So I got up, I started up towards the deck-edge elevator, but I got so weak and I lay down on the deck and there was a fella hanging by his chin from the edge of the flight deck." Mallett thought it was his buddy Joe McMahon. "McMahon! Come help! Come help me!" he hollered. "I thought, poor fella, he's dead, hanging there by his chin but two seconds or so later, he took off running the other way and I guess he got somebody to come and get me." Help soon arrived. "What they did was put me down to the catwalk, which was part of the elevator on the port side and the ship was listing because the captain flooded the tanks." Water from the firefighting efforts was pouring off the flight deck right into Mallet's face. "I was drowning. I called out, 'get something to cover my face' as I was going to drown. Somebody brought a helmet, I believe. I was there for nearly 12 hours. They thought they should treat the ones they could save. It sounds cruel but there's no use letting ten people die to try and save one."

Bill Blythe recalled: "I was fortunate, I had steel over my head. I'm on the 6th deck making fresh water with the evaporator. No one ever told us to quit making fresh water. We continued on while all these activities were going on making fresh water. They put a 10-degree list on the ship. We had heard a few rumblings on the PA system to abandon ship—we didn't know if we were supposed to abandon ship." Then the PA system was knocked out. All they had was a headset that was hooked up topside to the flight deck, which only supplied patchy information, none of it official. "All of a sudden there was a list on the ship. Hell, I guessed she was going down. There was nothing we could do about it, we were down there. All the fire stations pouring water onto the fire, all the water was coming down onto the Third Deck." But the Big T's damage control was good, all the hatches there were sealed and no water came below that level. Meanwhile, Blythe's crew kept doing their duty, producing more water. "What the heck! We didn't have anything else to do!" he recalled. "It was one o'clock in the morning before we got out of there."

Two hours after the second kamikaze hit, the fires were out and *Ticonderoga* was able to launch aircraft again. It was more than 12 hours until Kiefer left the bridge for treatment. With the XO Burch also wounded, command passed to the Engineering Officer Harmon Briner. He sailed the battered carrier back to the anchorage at Ulithi and transferred the injured to the hospital ship *Samaritan*.

"Dixie Kiefer said he was last off the ship, but I don't know if he was before me or after me. I got treated 12 hours later. I had my shoulder shot away, my right arm's four inches shorter than the left, [I was injured in] the throat and the chest. I lost part of the other arm. They said that I was too damn tall! Maybe if I'd been your size, they'd have missed," Walter Mallett told the author. "At that time I was six-foot-four."

As he was transferred to Samaritan on a stretcher, Kiefer spoke to his crew over the PA. "Well, gang, this is the last time I'll speak to you. I have tears in my eyes and it isn't because I am hurt. I always did know that you were a damn good peacetime crew, and the other day out there, you proved to me that you were the best damn wartime crew in the Navy. I did not leave the bridge until 2330 that night, but afterwards seeing how you men kept fighting back, I realized that I could do more good alive when I could come back out here again. I want to thank you men for saving the ship, which I thought was beyond saving. I'm going back to the States soon, and I'll be on the dock when you come in. The captain who takes my place will treat you like I did. Keep up your good work. The 'Big T' still is and always will be the best damned ship in the Navy."

The kamikaze attack left 144 men killed and 202 wounded on *Ticonderoga*. Thirty-nine aircraft were destroyed, pushed overboard or damaged beyond repair. A Judy also hit the destroyer *Maddox*, which would be associated with *Ticonderoga* in a future battle. Among the debris cleared from the carrier's flight deck was a pocket Japanese–English dictionary, a small Japanese flag, a rising sun armband and a pocketknife, personal effects of the kamikaze pilots. Legend has it that a *Tico* crewman identified the knife's owner through an inscription on the handle and returned it to his family many years after the war.

Air Group 80 was transferred to the *Hancock,* and *Ticonderoga* sailed on to Puget Sound Naval Shipyard in Washington for repairs, which took nearly three months. A lip was welded around the bomb elevator openings to stop burning gasoline pouring in again. With Air Group 87 embarked, *Ticonderoga* returned to battle in May 1945. In June her aircraft bombed the islands Minamidaitōjima and Kitadaitōjima to the east of Okinawa and in July Ticonderoga roamed up and down the eastern side of Japan, her aircraft attacking shipping and airfields from Hokkaido to Kyushu.

On July 28, a VB-87 Helldiver ditched in the water off the Kure naval base after a successful strike on the cruiser *Tone.* Pilot Lieutenant Raymond L. Porter and his gunner Airman Third Class Normand R. Brissette were captured by the Japanese and taken along the coast to the Chugoku headquarters of the feared Kempei-Tai military police, where they were held alongside the crews of two Army bombers and two aviators from the carrier *Randolph.* There they were interrogated before being told they were to be moved to a prisoner-of-war camp. At 0815 on the morning of August 6, the B-29 "Enola Gay" dropped the "Little Boy" atomic bomb on the city of Hiroshima. There were no known POW camps in the city, one reason it was chosen as a target for the first atomic bomb used in war, but the Kempei-Tai HQ was 1,300 feet from the hypocenter of the 15-kiloton blast. Raymond Porter and ten other prisoners were killed immediately in the explosion but Normand Brissette and one other man survived, only to die of radiation sickness ten days later. They were the first Americans killed by an atomic weapon.

Before dawn on August 15, Lieutenant Charles W. Gunnels led 15 Air Group 87 Hellcats on a strike to Choshi airfield east of Tokyo. At 0635, the pilots had just pulled out from their bomb runs when a radio message told them to cease the attack and return to *Ticonderoga.* Japan had surrendered. VBF-17's Lieutenant Wally McNab of Quincy, Massachusetts, was credited with dropping the last bomb on Japan in World War II.

Four days after the formal surrender ceremony aboard the battleship *Missouri,* *Ticonderoga* entered Tokyo Bay, joining hundreds of other U.S. and Allied ships. Her air group had already flown overhead in the massive fly past that accompanied the ceremony. In nine months of combat, the carrier had sailed just over 100,000 miles and the two air groups had dropped 4,552 bombs weighing 978 tons on enemy targets. They claimed 45 naval and merchant vessels sunk and 72 damaged, and 81 planes destroyed in the air. The ship's gunners claimed another six aircraft shot down. At least 39 aviators were killed or missing while flying from *Ticonderoga* between commissioning and the end of the war.

As part of Operation *Magic Carpet*, The Big T moved thousands of ex-prisoners and other servicemen back to the United States in a number of journeys. Once the air group had been flown off and some hasty modifications made, up to 4,000 people could be accommodated in the empty berths and hangar deck.

On Armistice Day, 1945, Captain Dixie Keifer was killed with five others in the crash of a Navy transport aircraft near Beacon, New York, the hometown of James Forrestal, who had dubbed him "The Indestructible Man."

Mothballed and Modernized

In January 1947, *Ticonderoga* was inactivated and berthed in Puget Sound as part of the Pacific Reserve Fleet. Technically still in commission, it was not called up for Korean War service. Finally, after five years in mothballs, the carrier sailed to New York to begin a massive rebuild to make it suitable for the jet age. In this new age of jet bombers and nuclear weapons the Navy couldn't get Congress to buy them new carriers, but there was money for "modernizing" them, which in reality was nearly as costly. On *Ticonderoga* steam catapults were installed to launch jets, as was a nylon barrier to catch them when they missed the arrester wires. A second elevator was fitted on the starboard deck edge behind the island, and new radar equipment sprouted on the island.

Lessons were incorporated from wartime experience, particularly about combat survivability. The island was rebuilt taller in height but with a smaller deck footprint. Most of the 5-inch gun armament was removed, having little use against jet aircraft. The aircrew ready rooms were moved from the island to beneath the hangar deck for protection. An escalator was run up the starboard side to take crews in heavy flight gear directly to the flight deck. Aircraft fuel storage was increased, with more powerful pumps to deliver it to the thirsty jets. Electrical generation, fire protection and weapons stowage were improved. Magazines were enlarged and assigned to nuclear weapons storage and assembly.

The weight, or displacement, of *Tico* swelled by 20 percent to over 30,000 tons, necessitating compensating blisters on the hull sides. The beam grew by up to ten feet. This middle-aged spread put it lower in the water and took a few knots off its top speed.

After 29 months and several million dollars, *Ticonderoga* emerged from the New York Naval Shipyard and sailed to its new homeport of Norfolk, Virginia in January 1955. Redesignated as CVA-14, *Ticonderoga* was now an attack aircraft carrier. Somewhere in these years the carrier's nickname evolved from "The Big T" to "Tico," although "Terrible Ti" or just "Ti" were occasionally heard.

As the "newest" carrier in the fleet, *Tico* was used for carrier suitability tests of three new jets, the McDonnell F3H-2N Demon fighter, the Douglas F4D-1 Skyray interceptor and the Douglas A4D-1 Skyhawk attack aircraft. The Demon

Robert N. Miller was the commander of Air Group Three for *Ticonderoga*'s 1955–1956 "Black Cruise" when at least 20 aircraft were lost, wrecked or seriously damaged. A decade later he was the carrier's captain. (1955 Cruisebook)

was underpowered and suffered a terrible accident rate, while the Skyray was too specialized and had some tricky flying characteristics. Both barely lasted long enough to be redesignated under the 1962 tri-service system, but as the A-4, the Skyhawk would become one of the most famous and long-lived U.S. Navy aircraft, only finally retiring in 2003.

In October 1955, *Tico* deployed with a full complement of aircraft for the first time in a decade, but supersonic jets and straight decks were not a winning combination. Crammed with Banshee and Cougar jets and the new supersonic Cutlass, three variants of piston-engined Skyraider and the jet-boosted Savage bomber, plus Retriever helicopters, safety was somewhat marginal. Even today some sailors remember this as the "Black Cruise."

Somehow even before *Ticonderoga* sailed, six pressmen watching from the island were burned and injured by the afterburners of a Cutlass. During the eight-month Mediterranean cruise, 13 men were killed, and this was peacetime. Six died in one landing mishap when a Banshee slid across the deck. The commander of Air Group 3 was Commander Robert N. Miller. After a fatal nose gear collapse, he dumped the Cutlass squadron ashore in Morocco. Miller himself may have ditched a Banshee on this cruise, although records are unclear.

After less than two years, *Ticonderoga* went back in the yard for another major rebuild. The major change this time was to incorporate an angled flight deck. This British invention offset the landing path so that aircraft missing an arrester cable were not faced with an immediate crash into the barrier or worse, into the pack of aircraft parked forward. The angle ended at the port deck edge elevator. Another

British innovation, the mirror landing system was added and pilots now judged their approaches by the relationship of a reflected light to other lights and not the waving paddles of the landing signal officer, something that was becoming increasingly difficult at jet speeds. A new hurricane bow covered openings at the front of the ship and gave better storm protection. The overhanging flight deck on at least one sister ship had collapsed in a typhoon. Most of the five-inch guns were removed as by now it seemed unlikely the carrier would have to fight enemy warships directly. The carrier was now barely recognizable as the Big T that fought Japan in 1944–45.

Over the years *Tico*'s appearance continued to change in subtle ways. Horn-like extensions were added to the forward flight deck in 1962. These were bridle catchers that collected for reuse the bridle cables that pulled aircraft down the catapult. Box-like structures were added under the corners of the flight deck by 1964. Most sailors didn't know they were antennas for a universal radio system, but more than one man rode inside them for a thrill, with nothing ahead but the ocean and all of a 42,000-ton ship pushing them on. These antennas were removed again by the time *Ticonderoga* became an anti-submarine carrier in 1969.

A feature only found on *Tico* and *Intrepid* was a high-frequency antenna mounted on the aft starboard side of the flight deck called the monopole, or more informally, the "pickle fork." It tilted to be out of the way of flight ops and one of the last orders the air boss would give before recoveries started was, "Stand by to recover aircraft. Lower the monopole." Airman George Floyd recalls that one time on the 1964 cruise it started its slow tilt and didn't stop. Evidently the limit switch on the electric motor failed and it kept tilting towards the water, broke off, and fell in. It did not float. Cheers went up but the air boss was miffed.

Now too wide for the Panama Canal, *Ticonderoga* sailed around the Horn to her new homeport at Alameda in San Francisco Bay in May 1957 and rejoined the Pacific Fleet. For the next several years Tico made cruises to the western Pacific (known as WestPac) with progressively more modern air wings. Radar-equipped and missile-armed fighters replaced the early jets. Better helicopters came along that could lift more than just their own pilot and a soggy survivor. The dependable 1940s-vintage Skyraider soldiered on.

In 1958 in a somewhat inglorious incident, *Tico* sank at anchor at the pier at Alameda. The cause was a "stopcock incident," details of which are hazy but seem to involve someone opening a valve or inspection plate and then not being able to close it again as San Francisco Bay rushed in. The incident was hushed up but some say she sank as far as the hangar deck—climbing the gangplank became easier, anyway. There was major damage to engineering spaces and fire rooms and, once refloated, the carrier was towed to Hunter's Point. They had to cut a huge hole in the hangar deck to lift out machinery, then weld it closed after repairs. The opportunity was taken to fit a new "lollypop" TACAN antenna to the highest mast. Someone in navigation either miscalculated the tides or forgot the added height and on the subsequent shakedown cruise the Golden Gate Bridge knocked it off. Back to the yard.

Tonkin Gulf incident

As part of another WestPac cruise, *Tico* was in Sasebo, Japan in early July 1964. Due to stay a week, the carrier went to sea after three days to avoid an approaching typhoon. One sailor missed the sailing, however. He was found in Japan a month later wearing civilian clothes and having grown a beard in the meantime. He was later returned to the carrier via Okinawa and put in the brig. Then while being exercised he jumped overboard off No.2 Elevator, realizing halfway down that this was a bad idea. He was fished out and given six months' imprisonment

Ticonderoga was due to make a port call in Hong Kong but was called to the Tonkin Gulf off Vietnam to relieve another carrier that was having mechanical difficulties. *Tico* would be at sea for 51 days and earn another place in history.

The South Vietnamese Navy had been making attacks on bases in the north in response to infiltration missions, and the U.S. Navy had been supporting them with intelligence-gathering patrols by destroyers and photo-reconnaissance sorties by carrier-based aircraft. Codenamed "DeSoto," these patrols passed without interference until the afternoon of August 2, when, following a South Vietnamese coastal raid, the *Maddox*, 28 miles off the coast of North Vietnam, reported being attacked by P-4 torpedo boats. All torpedoes missed, but the destroyer was slightly damaged by gunfire. Four of *Ticonderoga*'s F-8 Crusaders were airborne at the time and hit the boats with cannons and rockets. While strafing the P-4 nearest *Maddox*, VF-51's Dick Hastings reported that his Crusader had been struck by flak and his CO Jim Stockdale escorted him to Da Nang, where it turned out that he had damaged his wing when dashing at supersonic speed from *Tico* and had not been hit at all.

On the night of August 4, the destroyer *Turner Joy* called for help as it believed it was under attack by torpedo boats. *Ticonderoga* aircraft were soon overhead again but Jim Stockdale later said he saw no sign of hostile boats. The action was confused and despite a lot of radar and sonar contacts and gunfire from the destroyers, no conclusive proof was found of a North Vietnamese attack. The following year, President Johnson was to comment to his press secretary, "For all I know, our Navy was shooting at whales out there."

Nonetheless, Johnson ordered retaliatory strikes on the North Vietnamese torpedo boat bases and oil storage facilities. The next day aircraft from *Ticonderoga* and *Constellation* attacked targets at Vinh, destroying oil storage tanks and numerous boats. The strike, codenamed Operation *Pierce Arrow,* was led by VA-56, commanded by Wesley McDonald. During these attacks two "Connie" pilots were shot down. Skyraider pilot Richard Sather was killed by anti-aircraft fire and VA-144 A-4 pilot

Everett Alvarez was also downed, becoming the first American prisoner of the North Vietnamese.

On August 10, 1964, the U.S. Congress voted for the Tonkin Gulf Resolution. Its preamble stated that naval units of the communist regime in Vietnam, in violation of the principles of the U. N. Charter, "deliberately and repeatedly attacked United States naval vessels lawfully present in international waters, and have thereby created a serious threat to international peace."

The resolution supported the president's determination to "take all necessary measures to repel any armed attack against the forces of the United States and to prevent further aggression." These measures included: "...the use of armed force, to assist any member or protocol state of the Southeast Asia Collective Defense Treaty requesting assistance in defense of its freedom."

Effectively the resolution allowed the use of military force as the president saw fit against communist forces in North Vietnam and surrounding countries. It was later criticized as a blank check that allowed an open-ended involvement with little Congressional oversight.

Meanwhile, *Ticonderoga* was still patrolling the Tonkin Gulf. On Friday, August 13, a VA-56 A-4E lost power after a normal catapult launch. Jay Shower could tell his jet was not going to climb away so ejected five hundred yards ahead of the ship. Smoke floats were thrown into the sea and a whaleboat was launched. Shower himself fired a pen flare as he descended and after splashdown ditched his parachute and got into the one-man liferaft that opened from his seat cushion. So far the ejection had gone as well as he could hope.

The plane guard helicopter was soon overhead. Sea King "Big Mother 54" lowered a rescue harness and Shower jumped out of his liferaft and swam towards it, which is when things started to go wrong. "I actually got into the sling backwards, and that's why I'm still in the hospital today," said Shower 50 years later. "I pulled both my shoulder joints out of their sockets. I was supposed to go into the sling this way and turn around and the cord comes up in front of you, but it came up behind of me and I kept trying to get rid of it." After this struggle the indignity wasn't over. "And then they dropped me on the frigging cat track and burned me!" Shower said. After some medicinal brandy and a day or two off, he was back on the flight schedule.

As a junior pilot, Shower had to share a bunkroom with 15 other officers. To vent the stuffy air and relieve the heat, he and fellow Champ Fred Fox cut a hole in a wall and installed a non-regulation air conditioner that vented into the passageway.

Four officers and three sailors died on the 1964 cruise. Gerald W Taylor's VA-56 A-4E crashed on a night catapult launch off O'ahu. Fellow Champ Donald Vol Hester died when his A-4E crashed in similar circumstances between Okinawa and Japan. VF-53 pilot Thomas B. Fallin died near Subic Bay when his F-8E crashed and exploded after launch. Richard L. Evans died in unknown circumstances. Edward White, a supply chief aged 43, died of a heart attack in his sleep. VA-56 Airman

Joe Lee Williams walked into an aircraft propeller and Wilmer Bolton simply disappeared one night. A search was mounted and all hands searched every bilge, locker and cubbyhole in the ship for the missing yeoman. Sailor Delbert Mitchell had to search a compartment way down on 6th deck between the tunnel for the port propeller shaft and the hull, his way lit only by a battle lantern. The noise and vibration from the spinning propeller shaft were almost unbearable and he was glad when he finished and could crawl back out of the cramped space. The onboard search for Bolton was fruitless, and the helicopter and *Turner Joy* found nothing either. It was determined he most likely accidentally fell overboard and was declared missing, presumed dead. Flight deck supervisor Frank Barrett remembers: "A lot of rumors went around, some said he had some personal issues. I heard others said he was selling leave for money. In other words, someone took two weeks of leave, but he would not reduce their balance and he was about to be found out. I'm not sure if they ever found out what really happened to him."

Nearly 40 years later, Del Mitchell had a drinking session with a buddy who had been aboard when Wilmer Bolton went missing. The other guy told Mitchell that Bolton had refused to pay back money owed to his and another sailor's slush fund and threatened to expose it to the XO. They lured him to one of the starboard sponsons at night to discuss what he owed. The exchange between Bolton and the two sailors got heated, and with that they threw him overboard. Mitchell was profoundly shocked at what this man told him, and from then on he avoided contact with his old shipmate.

Ticonderoga received the Navy Unit Commendation for action in the Gulf of Tonkin and at Hunter's Point was refreshed again in preparation for a full combat cruise, entering dry dock in late January for a five-month overhaul. There were no modifications as major as the angled deck or new island had been, but time was taken to deal with twenty years of wear and tear. Some equipment was renewed for the first time since 1944. The teak deck was mostly torn up and replaced, and the island sprouted many new aerials and antennas including a new main radar. The nonskid surface on the hangar deck was ground off and relaid. The hull was scraped and repainted and both of the 15-foot diameter bronze propellers, each weighing nearly 25,000 pounds, were replaced. Bomb elevators were rejigged and the linoleum floors were redone in part. Berthing compartments were given a makeover, although helicopter crewman Bob Ceccarini is fairly sure they missed his. Some of the work had to be finished in San Diego.

Eighteen-year-old John Lunsford came aboard when *Tico* was in dry dock. He had never imagined how large a carrier was until he crossed the gangplank for the first time and looked down to see the huge screws. He was overwhelmed by everything about the massive ship.

The yard period was originally supposed to take a year or more, but because of the buildup of ground troops and U.S. commitments to the South Vietnamese government, it was cut to six months. Many of the crew, mainly the single men, were kept aboard rather than being housed in barracks as planned. The married men and their families were moved into Quonset huts at Hunter's Point. It wasn't the nicest part of town and sailors were warned not to walk around there. Some men with particular qualifications had their enlistments extended a further six months, to their dismay. Others discovered when they returned from leave in July that the carrier would deploy in September and not later in the year or early the next as anticipated.

Soon after *Tico* entered drydock, ordnanceman Gary Reynolds and a buddy went into town on liberty and were shocked by a movie theater marquee that said "Welcome home *Ticonderoga* baby killers." During the cruise just finished, Joe Lee Williams, another of their friends, fatigued after 12 hours of weapons loading, had walked into a turning propeller and suffered fatal injuries. It wasn't right to say such things. In 2004, through the efforts of VA-56's Randy Wilson and others, Williams' name was added to the Vietnam Wall.

Twenty-seven new members of the ship's Marine detachment (Mardet) came aboard in January. This caused their new CO Captain Donald Williams an administrative headache because none of them came with the clearances required for "participation in the nuclear posture of the vessel."

Finally, on May 7, the plug was pulled on the drydock, and no doubt to the relief of anyone who remembered the stopcock incident, *Tico* floated again. At midnight the captain had all the crew that could be mustered on the flight deck for a stability test. This involved a thousand sailors running around the flight deck, jumping up and down on the spot and then moving the other side of the ship and doing it again. For two hours. Some sailors had just that day returned from leave and were dying for some sleep. Stability proven to someone's satisfaction, the carrier was then towed across the bay to Alameda to prepare for sea trials.

Town at Sea

A carrier is sometimes described as a city at sea, but *Ticonderoga* more closely resembled a small town in middle America, albeit one with its own, very busy, airport with regular jet service to the Far East. It had many of the features of Anytown, USA. There was a tiny hospital, a dental surgery, a library, a laundry, a bakery, a post office, a chapel, a jail, a TV and radio station, a local newspaper, a general store, a hobby shop, a gymnasium and several diners. It had its sports teams and competitions, its ceremonies and celebrations, its bands and movie shows. *Tico*'s 2,900 all-male citizens mainly worked for the one employer. The town's light industries were primarily munitions assembly and aircraft maintenance. Others worked in the service sector including food preparation and payroll. Unemployment was zero in the town of *Ticonderoga*. The town in upstate New York was not all that much larger than its floating namesake, with only 5,600 or so residents in 1965.

Tico's captain could be likened to a mayor, albeit an unelected one granted almost dictatorial powers that were enforced by his own police force and court system. Through his executives he controlled every aspect of the residents' lives from their working hours and vacations to their mail, their entertainment and even their diet. He remained a remote figure that most of them rarely saw, although they heard his voice at least once a day. It was the ultimate company town, with no women or drinking inside its limits with the exceptions of rare visiting entertainers and prescribed medicinal alcohol.

The mayor of *Ticonderoga* since May 1965 was Captain Robert Nicholas Miller III. Born in 1918, he graduated from Annapolis in 1940 where he boxed and played tennis, his classmates knowing him as "Joe" and regarding him as "a man of the South," even though he was born in San Diego. Miller's father and younger brother were also Academy graduates. Miller's first posting dropped him right into the action as assistant navigation officer of the cruiser *Helena*, which survived a hit from a Japanese torpedo in Pearl Harbor on December 7, 1941. As engineer officer of the destroyer *Lardner*, he escorted a convoy to Russia then took part in the Solomon Islands campaign. He then changed career path to become a fighter pilot and instructor, commanding a Hellcat squadron before ending the war as the executive officer of the escort carrier *Admiralty Islands*. By 1949 he was the CO of attack squadron VA-44, which flew the unsuccessful Martin Mauler. The Mauler handled like a truck compared to the similar Douglas Skyraider and could barely get airborne with no load in the same conditions that the Skyraider could with 3,000 pounds of ordnance. The squadron soon returned to flying the dependable Corsair.

Miller missed action in Korea, assigned to training duties in Florida. He made his first association with *Ticonderoga* deploying to the Med as commander of Air Group 3 on the infamous "Black Cruise." He returned to *Tico* in 1959 as Operations Officer of Carrier Division One. Like all prospective carrier captains he was given command of another large ship first, the stores ship *Aludra* in March 1964.

Despite his wide experience, Miller's biography shows little to no association with nuclear weapons or atomic strike planning, nor does that of his XO Earl Godfrey, a carrier pilot in World War II and Korea, and most recently the CO of VA-125 at Lemoore. Participation in pre-deployment nuclear weapons orientation and operational planning training was mandatory for carrier captains, executive officers and operations officers, but seems to have been neglected as Vietnam escalated. In the case of one of *Tico*'s sister carriers in early 1965, the *Bon Homme Richard*, this was not completed and the captain alone attended a one-day briefing the month before deploying.

Officers

Doug Webster shared the junior officers' bunkroom with up to 15 other men including squadron mates Kaufman, Chapman and Phelps and also supply officers

By 1965 *Ticonderoga* was very crowded. There were 500 more men aboard than the carrier was built for. Enlisted berthing was not luxurious. (Gary Loudenslager via Brian Loudenslager)

and other ship's company. Second tour officers like Jay Shower had smaller staterooms with a washbasin and a strongbox.

Located in the A section of 1st Deck between the shafts of the steam catapults, the JO's bunkroom was hot, humid and noisy. In the Tonkin Gulf the mercury was usually at 105 degrees in the "JO's Jungle." The stateroom floor was often so hot the aviators tried to step straight out of bed into their boots rather than put their feet on it. Shavers wouldn't work due to constant sweat. Everyone suffered from heat rash.

Sailors made fire watch patrols in this "officers' country" and found it hard to concentrate in the heat and humidity, stepping out into fresh air wherever possible. The Champs officers normally hung out in the ready room that they shared with the Roadrunners.

The only air-conditioned work spaces on the ship were the ready rooms, the combat information center (CIC), the bridge, parts of GM division where they handled missile electronics, and SASS (the nuclear weapons magazines). When the missile spaces got air con, the gunner's mates moved their bunks in.

Fresh water was made by distilling seawater and was often rationed to preserve it for the steam catapults. Water consumption was calculated at 21 gallons a day per man, to include cooking, dishwashing, laundry and floor cleaning, leaving about two buckets each for personal use. A man was allowed thirty seconds of shower water to soap up and thirty more to rinse off. Clothes would normally be washed in seawater, necessitating a much harsher detergent which greatly shortened their life. Old hands would save their laundry up to have it done during port calls if they could.

Once underway, replenishment fuels were pumped across from an oiler, and the fuel tanks would often overflow and contaminate the water supply. Even the shower water smelled of jet fuel, aviation gasoline or black oil at times. The evaporator intake was located aft of the fuel discharge port. Sailors who many years later have suffered from Barrett's Esophagus Disease and other ailments believe it might be connected to consumption of fuel-tainted water.

Air Wing Five

The Champions were only one unit of Carrier Air Wing Five (CVW-5), which included four other attack and fighter squadrons and several smaller detachments with more specialized roles. Another jet light-attack squadron, VA-144 "Roadrunners," flew the A-4C "Charlie" model Skyhawk. Their radio callsign was "Warpaint." VA-52 "Knightriders" (callsign "Viceroy") were one of a few Navy outfits still flying the piston-engined A-1 Skyraider or "Spad," a nickname that mixed its old designation (AD) with that of the French SPAD fighters of World War I, a gag about the antiquity of this tough attack aircraft. There were two fighter squadrons flying the supersonic Vought F-8E Crusader, VF-51 "Screaming Eagles" (callsign "Screaming Eagle") and VF-53 "Iron Angels" (callsign "Fire Fighter") along with a detachment of VFP-63 "Eyes of the Fleet" (callsign "Corktip") with the unarmed RF-8A photoreconnaissance version. Detachment Bravo of VAH-4 "Fourrunners" brought aboard the massive A-3B Skywarrior, which was the heaviest aircraft to regularly fly from any aircraft carrier. It was so big that *Tico* only had room for two or three of them and then only on the flight deck. Known as the "Whale," the Skywarrior was built as a bomber, but by 1965 was increasingly being used as an aerial tanker.

VAW-11 "Early Eleven" provided airborne early warning for *Tico* with the Grumman E-1B Tracer, based on the antisubmarine S-2 Tracker (previously the S2F or "Stoof"). With its large radar dome on top, it was known as the "Stoof With a Roof." A further Tracker derivative was "everybody's favorite plane," the C-1 Trader or COD (for carrier onboard delivery) from VRC-30, which brought spare parts, passengers and most importantly, mail from shore to ship. VAW-13 Det. B "Zappers" used the EA-1F version of the Skyraider as a jamming platform, flying ahead of the strike force to confuse enemy radars.

Finally, another detachment, HC-1 Det B. of the "Pacific Fleet Angels" flew a pair of Kaman UH-2A Seasprite helicopters for search and rescue and utility missions. The "Angel" plucked downed aviators and men overboard from the sea and delivered people and mail to the escorting destroyers.

Sailors

Del Mitchell remembers *Tico*, on which he made three cruises, fondly. "That ship made me grow up. It's always hard when you are a youngster facing the cold, cruel world for the first time in your life, and a big thing like an aircraft carrier can be very intimidating. You grow up fast when you find out the magnitude of the ship's interior, and the responsibilities you now have to your shipmates and the ship."

Officers and men were in the same boat, so to speak, but the heat was even worse for those sailors working on the lower decks. In the engine rooms men stood for four-hour watches in temperatures up to 130 degrees. The boiler technicians got ringing ears from the noise and many later suffered from asbestos-related ailments. On *Tico*'s sister ship *Bon Homme Richard*, sailing off Vietnam in the same time period, 90 percent of the enginemen suffered from heat rash, there were numerous cases of heat exhaustion and one man died of heat stroke. Things don't seem to have got quite as bad on *Tico*, but it wasn't pleasant.

Some enlisted bunkrooms had six or nine bunks or "racks" in a row, or side by side, stacked four or in some places five high where overhead space allowed. Even then there were not always enough racks and the newest men had to hot bunk. The top bunk sailor, usually the most junior rate, often slept with his nose almost touching the ceiling or a hot pipe. An advantage of the top bunk, however, was that no one would step on you climbing up or throw up on you from above. On the other hand, for those berthed just under the flight deck, colder climates would cause water to drip on the faces of those on the top bunks. In hot and humid environments sweaty clothes never dried out and some compartments permanently smelled like a moldy locker room or a giant used sweat sock. Randy Wilson said, "Talcum powder was our air conditioning. We used to put that shit everywhere to soak up the sweat from the mattress."

Habitability (or the lack of it) was "an extremely critical situation" according to the post-cruise report. The lack of air conditioning and poor ventilation made enlisted spaces "almost unbearable." There was only one 12-inch fan for every six bunks. With 500 more men than the carrier was designed for, bunks and lockers were now in areas previously used for chairs, tables and TVs, reducing habitability by eliminating relaxation space.

On rare quiet occasions sailors heard all sorts of strange noises, particularly as the expansion joints creaked in a swell, and told stories of the many men who had died and now haunted the ship.

When it became unbearable, some sailors got their sleep in gun tubs or in the ship's boats, which were open to the air. Plane captains slept on the wings of their aircraft, something that was easier on a Skyhawk than a droop-winged Crusader or Skywarrior. While they waited for their charge to return from combat a plane captain might catch a "nooner" nap lying along the aircraft tow bars. The round cross-section ones were much more comfortable than the later square ones, recalls plane captain George Floyd. W Division sailors would sometimes take a nap on the floors of their air-conditioned magazine, surrounded by nuclear weapons.

Supply

Like all carriers, *Tico* went through a prodigious amount of food, including 3,000 fresh eggs and nearly 400 gallons of coffee a day, relying on replenishment ships for supplies when on station. Around this time in WestPac there were shortages of canned hams, sterilized milk, dehydrated sliced potatoes and dry beverage base. Lettuce and tomatoes were often unavailable from replenishment ships and were poor quality when they were. A reliable supply of good fresh items was only guaranteed from Japanese ports. Sometimes on *Tico* the only fruit to eat was reconstituted prunes and apricots hydrated using contaminated water.

Sailors insist the water tasted of JP-5 jet fuel and they could see a film of it on top of the "bug juice," a cordial mixed from powder. Bug juice was usually available in three flavors—orange, green and purple. When that paled men drank Coke at 10 cents a can or coffee so strong that they said you could barely taste the jet fuel in it. But Coke machines frequently broke down and there were not enough mechanics trained to fix them, nor was there enough time on port calls to get them repaired on shore. Medicines, particularly an anesthetic called Pontocaine, also broke down in the heat.

The resupply process wasn't all that efficient. So-called priority items often took weeks to arrive. Goods often came aboard from the replenishment ships damaged or wet and sometimes pilfered. Particularly valued by thieves was aircrew flight gear and flight deck clothing. Flight deck shoes wore out at an alarming rate, and replacing them in the right sizes became difficult. Cotton flight deck jerseys shrank when washed and were in rags by the end of deployment. Nylon ones were harder wearing, but too uncomfortable to wear in hot weather.

Sailors learned to sleep through the sounds of jets landing on the deck a few feet above their heads, engines roaring as they went to full power, followed by the bumping of the arrester cable as it retracted. The A-3, which was usually the last to land after a strike had a squeal you could hear when it was downwind. "*Here comes the Whale, finally!*" sailors thought with relief because now it would be quiet for a while.

Those who worked during flight quarters, which were usually 15 hours a day, were in some ways luckier because they didn't have to sleep when the jets were landing, and when they did get to bed could sleep through anything.

Sailing Away

Its hangar loaded with crewmen's cars, *Tico* shifted homeport to San Diego in late June and began preparations for WestPac. On August 9 two Skyraiders flew from North Island to Alameda. One never made it, as it was seen to crash into the sea off San Simeon and explode. Wreckage was recovered, but Lieutenant (Junior Grade) Daniel Wilder Clark was never found. Clark, a veteran of one Vietnam tour, had been flying "a special mission, for which he had volunteered" when he crashed, according to a report in his hometown newspaper in Burlington, Vermont.

In the latter part of August, *Tico* and Air Wing Five took part in a large exercise with a dozen other ships. Exercise "Hot Stove" tested a "friendly" task force led by *Ticonderoga* against everything from submarines to mines, air strikes to torpedo boats. During flight ops on the morning of September 1, Airman Edward Schaller fell overboard but was quickly rescued with the help of the destroyer *Brinkley Bass*. Schaller required treatment for shock on the ward. The next day the destroyer *Waddell* chased a possible submarine contact for 30 minutes until it was determined to be a non-submarine, which meant probably a whale.

On August 18, the XO of VA-144 Charles "Black Pete" Peters crashed his A-4C during night ops. He accidently set his altimeter to zero instead of 1,000 feet and flew into the water while changing radio frequencies. He escaped the sinking wreck but lost his lifejacket and flares and spent five hours hanging onto a floating drop tank despite having a badly broken ankle and internal injuries. He was spotted by two alert signalmen on *Waddell* and picked up by the ship's boat, by now suffering from hypothermia. With a double compound fracture he would not be joining the combat cruise. A less severe but no doubt uncomfortable mishap befell a ship's fire fighter when he hopped out of his bunk and lacerated his scrotum on a bed stanchion.

A few men left the ship and others joined, lugging all their belongings in their heavy seabags up the gangplanks. Five sailors were released from the brig, one of them for psychiatric treatment. At 2100 on September 13, Airman apprentice Joe Logsdon was picked up by the shore patrol on an accusation of petty theft and placed in the custody of the Marines pending action by the ship's legal department.

Captain Miller took two days leave ashore, having received the battle efficiency award from the commander of Naval Forces Pacific in a short ceremony. The Battle "E" was awarded to the outstanding ship in the Pacific Fleet every 16 months and was highly contested for. It joined the Operations "E" and the Communications "C" symbols painted on the island.

Some aircraft were towed from the airfield at North Island and craned aboard from the pier. Tons of aircraft spares, office supplies, cleaning products, food and other consumables came aboard. Munitions were loaded on from the depot at North Island, and these may have included the nuclear weapons, which are known to have been stored in bunkers at the northern tip of the peninsula. On September 14, munitions were both loaded and offloaded in two short bursts of activity.

Stocking the carrier was not without incident. On September 23, while loading supplies by way of Elevator 3, it was found that repairs were needed to the elevator's lock mechanism. The ship's boatswains rigged a net for a crew of six men to work from. Frank Barrett of V3 Division climbed a ladder to start the work but didn't like the look of one of the securing ropes. It looked like a piece of worn-out clothesline and he thought he'd better test it before letting his men on. "When I climbed up to the corner of the net, the bad piece of line snapped and I fell about 30 feet and landed on my chest and head. I was knocked out cold and carried off in a stretcher." When he got out of the sick bay three days later he had a serious conversation with the petty officer responsible. Then he took his crew back up to repair the locks, thankful that he hadn't fallen directly on his head or along with them all.

There was one last excursion when the carrier sailed on a dependents day cruise in the local operating area, treating family members and guests to a taste of Navy life including flight ops. There was an airshow with low-level air refueling and live weapons firing. VA-56 and the two F-8 fighter squadrons flew aboard. Every level of the island was crowded with spectators.

The last thing to do was say goodbye to America in style. Captain Miller hosted a party, described as an informal occasion to acquaint everyone with everyone else, with drinking, dancing and even go-go dancers. There was a ball at San Diego's landmark El Cortez Hotel, which about half the crew attended, and a separate formal ball for officers and their wives.

At 1000 on September 28, as a band played "Anchors Aweigh," *Ticonderoga* slipped its moorings and sailed past Pt. Loma to join four destroyer escorts, which formed an antisubmarine screen around the carrier. Soon *Tico* was in international waters, headed west. The log recorded seven new absentees. Another man who had been missing for a week turned up in Dallas. That evening a minor fire broke out caused by timber laid across a steam line.

Hawaii Bound

The passage from San Diego to Hawaii was not without incident. During night flying operations a moving aircraft forced admin officer Dale Runge and Airman R. A. Partlow over the edge of the deck and they fell into a gun tub. Both were lucky not to fall in the sea and suffered only abrasions. Radar technician Dwayne LeWillen fractured his right wrist in a separate incident. For some offense fireman apprentice Robert Craft was given 24 days confinement and three days bread and water at a summary court martial.

As well as the thousands of sailors and airmen, there were 15 civilians aboard for the cruise to Hawaii, guests of the Secretary of the Navy, Paul Nitze. These

Tico called at Pearl Harbor in October 1965 for Operational Readiness Inspection, the prerequisite final exercise for carriers heading to Vietnam. (Author's collection)

men, given the chance to see their Navy at work, included the presidents of Salinas Newspapers, Humboldt State College and the Audio-Stereo Corporation. On arrival in Hawaii they enjoyed one of the first cocktail parties of the fall season at the home of Admiral Roy Johnson, Commander in Chief of the Pacific Fleet.

Although he was not certain if it was on the 1964 or 1965 cruise, Jay Shower remembered a loading exercise that culminated in flying a B57 nuclear bomb to Barber's Point, Hawaii, conducted under considerable secrecy. "[A number] of us loaded, got to the flight deck and launched—in the dark," he recalled. "That was one requirement. The other was to land within fifteen minutes of sunrise. Actually I probably landed ten minutes before sunrise, but it was bright, and the Marines were there and they had what looked like a hospital curtain and they swung it around on a wheel so that people couldn't see what you were doing and they'd offload [the bomb] onto a cart and throw a rag around the cart and wheel it away. It was safer than taking it from the ship with a crane and taking it over on a barge, tying it down and taking it to a dock and getting trucks and another crane and getting it off the barge, putting it on a truck and driving it through a lot of civilian areas to get to Barber's Point, a 15- to 20-mile drive. It's not as safe as putting it on a plane, launching the plane and flying it to Barber's Point, which is where they are going to store it anyway."

The morning of October 4, with crewmen manning the rails in their white uniforms, *Tico* berthed at the northwest side of Ford Island. Captain Miller no doubt remembered getting the damaged cruiser *Helena* underway in the same harbor during the chaos of December 7, 1941. Unfortunately this time the captain's gig ran aground on a shoal. The brightly painted and polished boat was not significantly damaged but had to return to the carrier for repairs.

This tropical port call continued inauspiciously when somehow one of the tugs maneuvering the carrier got out of sync and the giant ship's bow hit the pier where various dignitaries and a traditional Hawaiian dance group were waiting. The pier rippled from the blow and everyone briefly did an involuntary hula. As they disembarked, some lucky officers got a flower lei and a kiss from a pretty greeter from the tourist office. Such Hawaiian hospitality did not run to all 3,000 men aboard, and unfortunately they did not stay around to greet everyone personally.

Ticonderoga was not in Hawaii for the sunshine, beaches and hula girls. Every WestPac-bound carrier had to undergo and pass an operational readiness inspection (ORI) before entering combat. Over the next 14 days, *Tico* sailed in and out of Pearl Harbor to the local operating area while the crew practiced various drills and procedures including maneuvering the ship in formation, ship's gunnery and evading simulated mines. The air wing launched strikes on bombing ranges and defended against simulated air attacks. On one day alone Jack Kaufman's weapons crews loaded 27 tons of ordnance on the Champs' Skyhawks.

On the night of October 5, a pair of Skyraiders swept in over the tiny island of Ni'ihau, the westernmost of the Hawaiian chain, filling the air with the rumble of piston engines and the sounds of bursting bombs. Unfortunately they were 40 miles adrift of their intended target, the bombing range at Ka'ula Rock. Eight 250-pound bombs fell on a remote Ni'ihau beach, causing no property damage or injuries but waking some of the two hundred or so mostly native Hawaiian residents on the other side of the island. The Navy waited 40 hours to admit the incident but said there would be a full investigation. They later said that in the future, pilots would be required to fly over the bombing ranges in daylight before making night attacks. In Washington, Hawaii's Senator Daniel K. Inouye expressed his anger and demanded all bombing practice be stopped.

Eight nights later, two nuclear-powered submarines collided off O'ahu. The *Barb* and *Sargo* were exercising 15 miles off Barber's Point at night in the rain when the submerged *Sargo* struck the surfaced *Barb*. The two subs limped back into Pearl Harbor. The damage was covered over and the Navy refused to tell the press many details, but they assured Senator Inouye that there was no danger of a radiation leak.

When not engaged in simulated war fighting, the crew marked time with first-aid and VD-prevention lectures with titles such as "Moral Law: Morality in the Far East," and watched a film called "To Be Held in Honor" (from the biblical verse "Marriage is *to be held in honor* among all, and the marriage bed is to be undefiled.")

Sailors on liberty in Honolulu encountered an anti-war demonstration and a simultaneous pro-war counter-protest. (Randy Wilson)

After the exercises, there was a weekend of liberty on Oʻahu. Many crewmen took a chance to see the sights of Honolulu and further afield. At Waikīkī, some sailors encountered an anti-Vietnam War march and a pro-war counter protest along Kalākaua Avenue. The former was held by the Committee to Stop the War in Vietnam and the Political Affairs Club of the University of Hawaii. Their placards read "Vietnam is a Civil War" and "We're Not Draft Dodgers" and they chanted, "Hey, hey, LBJ, how many are you going to kill today?" The university's Young Democrats and Young Republicans demonstrated bi-partisan support for Lyndon Johnson's policies, marching with signs reading "Back Our Boys" and "Peace or Freedom." They shouted, "Better dead than Red!" Both groups marched behind the stars and stripes and sang the national anthem at least once in what was a lively but peaceful event. A bearded youth, seemingly in neither group marched between the groups with a sign reading "Let's Kill" on one side and "Down With God" on the reverse. "There were a number of bearded people in both camps," noted the *Honolulu Star-Bulletin*, evenhandedly.

Not all the *Tico* sailors were impressed with the capital city's sprawl and over-development. Some found more relaxation at the old royal palace and among the forests and waterfalls at the north of Oʻahu.

The second week of ORI was the actual inspection, which included evaluation of individual air wing units. At the end of the exercises VA-56 was graded excellent with an overall 88/100. VA-52's score is not available.

The last days ashore before sailing for the war zone were punctuated by fights, with commissary man L. Smith receiving a cut chin in a fight downtown with an unknown party and boiler technician J. M. Spaulding getting his thumb bitten by another unknown party. This unknown party was busy, also punching Seaman A. F. Salzman in the face as he stepped off the bus back at the ship.

One prisoner was released from the brig for psychiatric treatment, with the order that he would be returned on completion. Seaman apprentice Paul Bruce fell overboard on October 17 but was rescued. John Lunsford tripped and fell into a fan in his berthing compartment, lacerating his hand. Another airman cut his nose when he walked into the tailfin of an aircraft.

Someone accidently activated the fire system in part of 4th deck during a routine check. The Sidewinder warhead and motor magazines and Shrike missile magazines were partly flooded with saltwater. GM Division had been onloading Bullpup missiles from barges and looking forward to liberty on O'ahu when they were done. Now they had to empty everything out, wash all the missiles with fresh water, remove and wash all the deck plates and put it all back. No one in GM got any liberty before *Tico* sailed again.

At 1215 on October 18, the carrier weighed anchor and set sail for Subic Bay. As the ship pulled out, a deserter jumped overboard and started swimming. A helicopter was launched to rescue him but he started running when he hit the beach. Two hours later, with Diamond Head light receding in the distance, *Tico* reset its clocks to X-Ray Time and set course northwest for Southeast Asia.

Sabotage

On October 28, the log recorded that just before 2200 that evening a Condition Three watch was set "because of saboutage (*sic*) causing minor damage to aircraft." The misspelled word was later crossed out and "possible sabotage" written above it. This type of watch was normally used when the ship was in a war zone. Gunner's mate Jim Little wrote that someone "went through the hangar deck with wire cutters and reached up into the wheel wells of many of the jet fighters tied down in the hangar deck and cut as many wires as he could reach!"

A similar story comes from an anonymous chief who was assigned to *Tico* for temporary duty during the transit from Honolulu to Subic Bay. "During the early hours of one morning, about 3AM local, a large pool of hydraulic fluid was spotted underneath the Alert Five bird," he said. This would have been an F-8 parked on a catapult at five minutes readiness to launch. "It was quickly learned that hydraulic

Tico's newspaper tried to prepare sailors for Cubi Point and Olongapo. Articles emphasized the wholesome leisure activities available on base rather than those to be found downtown. (via John Lunsford)

lines had been cut." Subsequently he clarified that he didn't recall if it was a brake or a hydraulic line.

Ordnanceman Gerald Matlock says the flight deck and hangar bays were on lock down and patrolled by pairs of armed Marines. On October 29, Doug Webster wrote in his diary that Captain Miller had come up on the 1MC the night before and warned everyone about the sabotage. Doug listed the damage he knew about: VA-144 had holes punched in the skin of two jets, VA-52 had lost two tool boxes, A VAW-11 Tracer's seats had been slashed and an emergency hatch actuated. A taxi light had been taken from one of his own squadron's aircraft. "I think there's been one or two other instances but I can't think of them now," he wrote. "I imagine people from ONI (Office of Naval Investigation) will board the ship at Cubi for an investigation. I sure hope they get the guy(s). It's rough enough already without having someone on your own ship fighting you."

About two days from Subic Bay a C-1 flew aboard bringing ONI investigators, something the chief also confirms. He adds that, "Repeatedly, the crew that knew were told not to ever discuss the incident, with anyone. Ever."

As with all such things aboard ship, particularly when silence is ordered, rumors spread and details differ. Randy Wilson heard that the sabotage was the work of a particular group of bosun's mates and that there was a trial on ship with the guilty men sent to Leavenworth military prison. Jim Little says the perpetrator was never caught. Del Mitchell remembers someone cutting fire hoses and dismantling ladders, but not aircraft sabotage. Frank Barrett says, "It really happened. As I recall, it occurred several times over a period of months and the ship's captain announced over the speaker that he had ordered Marines to guard all the aircraft, with orders to shoot to kill anyone sabotaging an aircraft."

No flight ops were scheduled on the transit to Subic, but on the afternoon of October 25 condition "Brown Bear Alpha" was set and the Alert Five jet was launched to investigate bogeys (unknown aircraft). Very quickly four F-8Es, two RF-8s and two A-4 tankers were catapulted off. Eight minutes after the first launch the intruders were identified as Tu-16 "Badger" bombers by the F-8s, who escorted them away. *Tico* was mid-Pacific, somewhere southeast of Tokyo, and the Russians had probably flown around Japan on their long-range mission. It was no secret that *Tico* had sailed from Hawaii, but it was quite a feat to find the carrier and its escorts in the open ocean. The carrier's electronic search measures could detect the Russian radar transmissions long before the radar picked up the ship. It would then go to Emcon Alpha, shutting down all electronic emissions and launching fighters that would find the intruders by themselves.

There would be more Brown Bear alerts before *Tico* reached the Philippines, but no more alert launches. On the night of the 28th, the sighting of a comet was noted. On the 31st, the destroyer group's doctor was sent by helicopter to assist a Japanese merchantman aboard which three crewmembers had been burned by steam.

CHAPTER 5

Shore Leave

En route Pearl Harbor, Hawaii to Subic Bay, Republic of the Philippines
Monday November 1, 1965

Tico was due for its first portcall of the cruise. Subic Bay was a major logistics hub and rest and recreation center for the Seventh Fleet, but it had attractions for young sailors beyond the Navy-sanctioned R&R facilities and plenty of things for them to spend their pay on.

Pay Call

Getting paid at sea was an odd ritual. Whether you were an enlisted man or an officer, first you found your initial posted on a bulkhead and stood in line until you reached a table where a disbursing officer had a list and a pile of money. You looked up your name on a list and the amount you were being paid. Tom Hickey, *Tico's* disbursing officer, counted it out then his assistant checked it again. You showed your ID and got your cash. A Marine with a pistol on his hip stood by to make you didn't run off with the lot, and the disbursing officer usually also had a gun. Officers and enlisted queued together in alphabetical order in Hangar Bay 3. Doug Wilson of GM Division used to stand in line behind Doug Webster every two weeks and would always return to the missile shop and say, "Well, I just listened to another one-sided conversation with LTJG Webster. He is so arrogant." Doug Webster was certainly a man of strong opinions, but perhaps Wilson's view was colored by the natural officer-enlisted relationship. Wilson would be a member of the bomb loading team on December 5.

Sailors at sea usually took out only a small portion of their pay to buy things like cigarettes, toiletries and camera film. They kept some on the books to take out in port and spend on shore leave and saved the rest for when they got home. Some bought money orders from the ship's post office and trusted the military and civilian mail services would get the funds home in reasonable time. Others were less prudent with their money and found themselves owing large sums to various slush funds, having borrowed at a 100 percent interest rate. These practices were common but illegal and being caught running one would see the "fund manager" standing at Captain's Mast and reduced in rank for six months.

Shortly before *Tico* arrived at Subic Bay, Doug wrote to his mother from his 105-degree stateroom: "Sorry for not getting this off sooner but Happy Birthday, Mom. We're pulling into the Philippines for some last minute briefings then out on the line for the first of many months. It promises to be a long, dirty tour, but I'm glad I'm here. I've thought about it, and if someone said, 'Webster you can go home tomorrow if you want to'… I'm pretty sure I wouldn't go." He turned to the dangers of his duty, "If something should happen to me, just remember that this is the way I wanted it. I really believe in what the U.S. is doing over here, and I'm glad I'm part of it. I've had a pretty good life, Mom—I figure I owe a few people. Perhaps I can help pay them back by being here."

Tico pulled into Subic Bay on November 1. The carrier *Bon Homme Richard*, helicopter carrier *Valley Forge* and cruiser *Oklahoma City* were all in port, filling the place with thousands of sailors. Nearly 60 *Tico* men were sent on shore patrol detail to enforce rules they would rather be breaking themselves.

Within hours of arriving, electrician's mate William Woodbury had put his hand through a window at the Cubi chief petty officer's club, an act not judged to be due to his own misconduct. Three sailors were treated for facial lacerations after the first night ashore and another for a bruised hip having fallen onto a barge when a line parted. Seaman apprentice E. P. Thompson asked another sailor for a marlinspike and got beaten up for his troubles, suffering a fractured jaw. Working in the galley, machinist's mate Keith Reagan received second-degree burns when a pipe burst, spraying boiling water over his back. Randy Wilson, still on his messcooking duties, tore his fingernail opening a hatch in the galley.

In sunglasses and civilian clothes, officers on liberty rushed ashore to play golf or stake their place at the officers' club. The enlisted men in their tropical whites set out for the city of Olongapo. A map at the base gate showed large areas of the town out of bounds. The more experienced sailors would head there first. The port was separated from the town by a waterway known to generations of Navy men as Shit River. Children would ride small boats near the bridge that met the main drag Magsaysay Drive, shout "Quarter, Mister!" and dive for coins. Cruel sailors would sometimes throw washers into the water. The first bar on the other side was a club called Ocean's Eleven, but there were dozens of others to choose from.

John Lunsford, like many sailors, still a teenager, followed the sailor in front of him to the first bar he had ever been in. He lucked out as it was a good place and came to love Olongapo. Every bar seemed to have a band playing note-perfect covers of western hits. One place would do pop songs, the next one country and western and beside that, rock and roll; a Filipino band belting out The Who or Rolling Stones hits.

Officially the Olongapo River, but marked on city maps as a drainage canal, the waterway separating the city and naval base was known to generations of sailors as Shit River. (Via Del Mitchell)

Tico sailors Gilley, Hodges, Green and Pickens with their dates at the Orchid Club in Olongapo. (Ray Green)

Some sailors saw Olongapo as an adult Disneyland of bars and brothels, but it was not a good place to take shortcuts off the beaten path. The beaten path itself was little more than that. In 1965 sidewalks were a new thing in Olangapo City, but the roads themselves were still dirt, or in the monsoon season, mud. Every corner had a small boy asking "Wanna shine, Joe?" Turning down a shine might result in a streak of shoe polish on the back of your whites. The streets were crowded with brightly decorated jeepneys, taxis converted from surplus jeeps. At the end of the night the jeepney drivers might slip a few washers into the passenger's change.

Street vendors sold a barbecued delicacy on a stick which they called monkey meat when sailors asked, as if daring them to try it. In reality it was likely to be beef, buffalo or pork. On the other hand, the *balut* eggs the vendors sold did contain an unhatched chick. The local water not being regarded as safe to drink, sailors largely stuck to San Miguel beer, or "San Magoo", at a peso a bottle, or spirits although it was unwise to add ice as that was reportedly made from Shit River water.

Subic Bay generally was not the safest place in the world. There was rebel activity in the surrounding jungles, someone known as the Mickey Mouse Bomber was at large and there was occasional mysterious damage to ships. *Tico*'s bomb disposal team sent divers to inspect the hull and screws for signs of sabotage. A squadron story says that around this time a VA-56 airman was kidnapped by AK-47-weilding

Huk rebels at Subic and held hostage in the jungle for three days before making a daring escape, or that's what he told the skipper, anyway.

Even the golf courses had their hazards with cobras and vipers and who-knows-what in the undergrowth. It was best to take a mulligan if your ball went in the trees. A contemporary rumour says a Filipino boy collecting golf balls from a water hazard was eaten by a python.

The shore patrol had their hands full breaking up bar brawls and occasionally fishing sailors out of Shit River. As liberty ended, these over-indulging souls had to get back aboard and it was around a mile from the base gate to the pier. A contemporary post-cruise report described the "cattle car" transport provided as "highly undesirable" and that every effort should be made to discontinue it as a mode of transport for return from liberty. Cattle cars were enclosed trailers, painted Navy gray of course, pulled by a truck. They looked more suitable for transporting prisoners on a chain gang than sailors on liberty and were the scene of numerous fights. Assigned to shore patrol one night, Del Mitchell had the unenviable task of keeping order on one, armed only with a night stick and an arm band saying SP. "Drunken sailors in a confined space, in a moving trailer, filled with San Miguel beer, is not a welcome environment for a shore patrolman, and with everyone wearing their tropical white uniforms, not the cleanest environment either. The smell of vomit, the sight of blood, the bleeding faces from multiple fist fights is not conducive to one's status of military authority," he said.

Not everyone spent the whole time in drink and debauchery. Grande Island in the mouth of Subic Bay was owned by the Navy and used as a recreation area, and although beer was plentiful, there were more wholesome activities to partake in, even if the island itself wasn't one hundred percent safe. When sailors arrived at the boat landing they were warned to stay on the landward side of the island, which was watched over by harbor patrol boats. Supposedly the unpatrolled South China Sea side was the domain of pirates who would come ashore armed with shotguns and machetes to rob any sailors they found. Some ignored this advice and climbed the hill to look at the fortifications built by the United States and occupied by the Japanese during the war. Many of the bunkers had bullet holes from the fighting to recapture the island in March 1945. There were rumours that the last Japanese snipers had yet to surrender. Other sailors played softball or just drank beer in the sun on Dungaree Beach. George Passantonio remembers, "It was kind of a neat place to unwind. You really couldn't get in any trouble. If you got drunk somebody would carry you back. I carried a lot of people."

The enlisted men's Sky Club was a cabana-type building on a hill above Cubi Point air station. It offered a more controlled environment than Olongapo with regular movie showings and bands. Dancing partners were available and all sorts of recreation facilities were supplied, from gyms to water skiing to bowling. The latter was hard for visiting sailors to use, as every night seemed to be league night for the base personnel. Del Mitchell never saw a sailor with a USS *Ticonderoga* patch on his right shoulder at the base library, or at the Youth Christian Center in Olongapo.

Tico's chaplain tried to find healthy activities such as tours, which were "enthusiastically received and well patronized." All were "outstanding" except one Manila Night Tour undertaken in hired civilian buses, which sadly "proved disastrous from the standpoint of control and its relation to the moral leadership program," the chaplain recalled in the cruise report.

It's a Jungle Out There

A song called "The Ballad of Olongapo" included the stanza:

> Silver dollars on my girl's breast,
> She'll go short time with America's best.
> One hundred men she'll lay today
> But only three in a normal way.

All this rest and recreation took its toll. *Tico*'s medical department reported the following statistics for the 1965–66 cruise: 129 cases of gonorrhea and 50 of non-specific urethritis but happily none of syphilis. This "relatively low number" of VD cases (about a third of that treated on *Bon Homme Richard* in the same time period) was put down mainly to a good training program including extensive lectures. Those who found themselves on the medical quarantine list were made to read a chapter of an official publication titled "My Life in the Far East (What About Women?)" and were then tested on it.

Along with over 120 men from the air wing, Doug attended a jungle survival course while *Tico* was moored at Subic Bay. It doesn't seem to have been a very strenuous business, mainly the instructor, a Pacific Islander, teaching what plants can be eaten and which ones can provide water. It didn't involve a night in the malarial jungle or E&E training and Doug ate his dinner in the O Club with Nealon and Smith that evening.

While he was in the Philippines Doug learned that John Worcester, a friend from Lemoore, had gone missing over North Vietnam. John's Skyhawk had failed to rejoin his flight after an attack on a bridge during a night armed reconnaissance mission from *Bon Homme Richard*. John had been at Doug and Marcia's wedding and had often come to dinner at their house. No trace of him has ever been found.

Governors on Tour

On November 3, *Tico* went back to sea. Two days later a Yugoslavian merchant vessel, identified as the *Uckar*, drew near to *Tico* then turned parallel with the carrier, attempting to come closer. *Tico* increased speed to 24 knots and left it behind.

Some of the governors who visited *Tico* in November 1965 on a "fact-finding" tour. Michigan's George Romney (far right) later said he was "brainwashed." (Cruisebook)

The morning of the 7th, a pair of C-1s landed, bringing the governors of Montana, Wyoming, Oklahoma, Hawaii, Maine, Georgia, Michigan and Iowa aboard from South Vietnam. The arrested landing took one passenger by surprise. "No one prepared me for that stop," Michigan's George Romney (father of future presidential candidate Mitt) was heard to say. "I thought we were going to crash!" The governors were part of a fact-finding tour of U.S. bases in Vietnam.

One pressman travelling with the group was somewhat cynical. In an article "GIs Wince When Governors Make Combat Scene," Associated Press reporter Hugh Mulligan noted the governors' propensity to dress up in combat fatigues and pose with the troops. "The fact that some of the gentlemen look ridiculous in jump boots and jungle jackets in no way discourages them," he wrote. Their prime motivation seemed to be to meet constituents and be photographed with them, followed closely by being shot at and missed. Wearing a patterned shirt, Governor Romney unfurled a Michigan flag and draped it over a mess table, inviting men from the Wolverine State to join him for lunch of steak and potatoes. "Michigan men can do anything," he said. "We've got a pilot, a flight surgeon and a cook," Romney exclaimed. "I've got enough men here to organize a carrier of my own!" Governor Henry Bellmon missed a trick with the flag. The Navy had misspelled Oklahoma on the sign over his table.

After lunch the VIPs put on ear defenders, climbed ladders to some unlikely positions on the island (who was going to stop them?) and watched the launch of a mission led by Carl Ray Smith, staying aloft for his return, bomb racks empty, an hour-and-three-quarters later. Smith explained to the visitors how he had flown a hundred miles inland and followed an Air Force forward air controller down a canal to his target.

One pilot took three attempts to land, beginning to run low on fuel before finally catching the number one wire. "Come on down!" and "Get in this time, buddy!" Iowa's Governor Harold Hughes heard other pilots say to themselves as their colleague struggled to land. "That boy's going to catch some hell," observed one officer. "That's too bad," was Governor Romney's response.

Georgia's Carl Sanders, a former Air Force pilot, sat in a bombed-up A-4 before it went up on an elevator for a combat mission. He talked to Crusader pilot Richard Hastings, who described flying combat over South Vietnam as "a ball" but said raids into North Vietnam were "entirely different … there are two different wars." Not all constituents were fans. Render Crayton, who was from Atlanta, burst into the ready room and asked John Paisley, "Where is that governor from Georgia? I want a word with him!"

Romney took part in a worship service with 15 other Mormons in the carrier's library and visited the sickbay with the Champs' flight surgeon Carl Dila, who was a graduate of a Michigan medical school. Several sailors asked what Romney thought about American involvement in Vietnam. "What we're doing here is very vital to our country," he told them. "And it also is consistent with what our founding fathers wrote about personal liberty and man's inherent right to govern himself. That's what we're here for. These rights just don't belong to Americans. Everyone should have these rights, and we're assisting the people of Vietnam in defending their rights. The people back home are proud of what you're doing here."

George Romney had been known as an enthusiastic supporter of the war in Vietnam, on several occasions calling it morally justified and necessary. The 1965 gubernatorial tour seems to have changed his mind. "When I came back from Vietnam, I'd just had the greatest brainwashing that anybody can get," he said in August 1967. (One smart alec suggested all it needed was a light rinse.) "I no longer believe that it was necessary for us to get involved in South Vietnam to

Congressman Torbert H. McDonald chats on *Tico*'s vulture's row with Skyraider pilot James Donahue in November 1965. Donahue was shot down but rescued in January 1966. (NARA)

stop communist aggression in Southeast Asia." This ambivalence hurt his political ambitions and he failed to defeat Richard Nixon in the 1968 Republican primaries.

The governors flew off again in the afternoon for a reception with Premier Ky in Saigon. Continuing the parade of visiting politicians, Congressman George W. Grider from Tennessee, a former submarine captain, arrived on the 9th. He was only one of seven congressmen and women, one senator, seven governors, nine ambassadors, four brigadier generals, numerous admirals and a bishop to embark on *Tico* during the cruise.

CHAPTER 6

All Day and All of the Night

Dixie Station was the carrier operating area off South Vietnam. Whereas flight operations on Dixie Station usually ran from just before sunrise to sunset, two or three carriers operated simultaneously on Yankee Station 400 miles to the north, flying round-the-clock missions. One was always the night carrier, conducting flight ops from midnight until noon. Late in the year the weather was usually poor; from mid-October the winter monsoon brought thick, low cloud over Vietnam, which caused mission cancellations, diversions to secondary targets or drove attack runs to lower altitudes where they were in range of automatic anti-aircraft guns.

Air Wing Five was assigned several different missions in the winter of 1965.

Begun in March, *Rolling Thunder* was the main campaign against North Vietnam. In November it was in Phases 38 and 39, with the Navy assigned mostly bridge targets and surface to air missile (SAM) installations. *Barrel Roll*, *Steel Tiger* and *Tiger Hound* were all interdiction missions on supply routes in different parts of Laos.

November saw North Vietnam divided into six zones called Route Packages or Route Packs. These were designed to prevent Navy and Air Force strikes conflicting and overlapping. The USAF was assigned those to the north and west, and Route Pack 1 above the Demilitarized Zone (DMZ). The Navy's were Route Packs 2, 3, 4 and later, 6B, all bordering the Gulf of Tonkin.

Combat Mission

Before a single turbine or propeller turned on the morning launch, the squadron line crews made sure the aircraft were armed and fueled, the liquid oxygen was replenished and the brakes serviced. The aircraft were spotted on the flight deck in the right sequence for launch. Plane captains sat in the cockpits to operate the brakes as their charges were tugged, pushed or pulled into their spots with canopies open and their "Mickey Mouse" helmets off so they could hear all whistles and shouts from the yellowshirt plane directors. An official guidebook for plane captains warned: "Any delay or slowness in answering 'BRAKES!' might mean a crunch or even running over a man who slipped!" Brake control was essential, "dragging" the brakes would mean the blueshirts would struggle to move the plane; not enough and it could get out of control. A rolling ship could even move a plane that was chocked and partially tied down. "Hold the brakes when the ship heels and you're headed or tailed outboard," continued the guidebook in its chatty style.

The redshirt aviation ordnancemen brought the weapons to the aircraft from where they were stored, be it the magazines, the mess decks or the "bomb farm" on the flight deck. To load a bomb onto an aircraft, redshirts would lift it with "hernia bars" inserted in the nose and tail. When the bomb was locked in place, they unscrewed the bar and replaced it with fuses. An A-1 had 11 weapons stations. Two were usually allocated to external fuel tanks, and the rest were available for single bombs or rocket pods. Multiply this by a dozen aircraft and one squadron's ordnancemen were lifting over 50,000 pounds a day.

The Skyhawks had fewer weapons stations, but triple and multiple ejector racks maximized their lifting capacity. An A-4E might have six 500-pound bombs on the centerline rack, and two rocket pods on the outer pylons. Austin Chapman thought weapons officer Jack Kaufman's crew of young men were amazing, loading the amount of ordnance they could load in a short period of time, all of it by hand. "The A-4s stood pretty high and they had to lift that thing up at least 5 feet off the deck. I saw them load 2,000-pound bombs by hand. It took a lot of them, but they got the thing up."

Ticket to Ride

As one of the most junior pilots in the air wing, Doug Webster was often assigned tanker missions to gain experience. By now, Doug probably had only around a hundred hours in the A-4, and flying the tanker helped build flight time and bag more traps which contributed to his proficiency. The tanker topped up other jets before long-range strikes or so they could launch with heavier loads. As a recovery tanker it flew orbits near the carrier waiting to help out pilots running low on fuel after a mission, sometimes after multiple landing attempts.

On Yankee Station the usual flight cycle between launches and landings was one hour and fifty minutes. Over a hundred sorties (each being one mission by one aircraft) could be flown in a day from one carrier. Pilots often flew two or even three times a day.

Up to two-and-a-half hours before launch on a strike mission, the pilots held group briefings in the intelligence spaces to get the weather, locations of friendly and enemy units rules of engagement and other "big picture" information. Then they broke up for flight briefings in the ready rooms, covering radio frequencies, emergency procedures, weapons loadouts and attack tactics, which were usually down to the individual squadrons.

Half-an-hour before launch, the pilots draw a sidearm and don their survival gear, which, including the helmet, weigh about 50 pounds. As the 1965–66 cruise began, not all the pilots were suitably dressed for combat. The standard flying suit was bright orange, which was great for a sea rescue but not so good in a hostile jungle. They were also cotton and not very fire retardant. "There was a [cotton] khaki flying suit for WestPac, but when Vietnam started we actually flew in Marine fatigues at first until the [fire retardant] Nomex flight suits came out," says Austin Chapman. "Somewhere between leaving San Diego on Yankee Station, or before we left Dixie Station, we got Nomex. I've got pictures of me flying in just Marine fatigues, which were just cotton, but at least they were green." G-suits with bladders that inflated around the legs to keep blood in the upper body during maneuvers were not always available.

A survival package was worn over the life preserver vest. This included shark repellant, magnesium flares, a whistle, a signal mirror, a beeper, a knife, and sundry other gear. "Most of us by the end of our first cruise we wanted our pistol with at least some tracer ammo in it and two radios. [But] the chances of us using any of the stuff [in the kit] were so remote. If you were shot down you would be picked up quickly." Either by the rescue forces or the enemy, Chapman might have added.

Doug grabs an olive-green bag containing his helmet and mask and rides the escalator to the flight deck, a privilege reserved for aviators. He makes a preflight walk around of his A-4, checking for fluid leaks, loose parts and other obvious faults. Walking ahead of the wing he pushes the leading edge slats to check they move smoothly on their rollers. Climbing into the cockpit he removes two pins from the ejection seat and the brownshirt plane captain takes out a third pin, making it live. Drop tank, bomb rack and landing gear safety pins are pulled out and the aircraft is "broken down" or unchained for taxiing. When it was in the right place, or whenever it stopped, a A-4 needed to be chained down to least three tie-down points, and up to nine to secure it in heavy weather. An A-3 needed six, nine or twelve connections to the pad-eyes on the deck. A bag of chains weighed 66 pounds. It made a good anchor to stop a brownshirt being blown into an intake or propeller.

The voice of the Air Boss Warren Carman booms from the loudspeaker over the flight deck. "All unnecessary personnel clear the flight deck and catwalk areas. Check chocks, tie downs, fire bottles and all loose gear about the deck. Put on your helmets, pull down goggles, roll down sleeves. Stay clear of jet intakes, tailpipes and propellers. Stand by to start all jets!"

Ticonderoga turns into the wind.

When Doug's A-4 is lined up for launch a redshirt pulls out the bomb and missile pins and shows the catapult officer. Looking like a latticed gate, a jet blast deflector rises from the deck behind the aircraft. Five greenshirts hook up each aircraft, three at the front and two at the back. The holdback man at the rear connects the holdback cable to the base of the tailhook, slotting a breakaway link into a holder.

Champs pilots Bob Sturgeon and Job Belcher leave the ready room for a mission over North Vietnam. (Cruisebook)

On the low-slung F-8, he has to lie on the deck and let the aircraft roll over him. With the screaming engine about a foot from his head, he makes the connection then rolls sideways under the central fins to get away. For the A-4 he has enough room to crouch and run.

The catapult shuttle moves forward and tightens the bridle. The bridle checker gives it a tug to be sure. On the cat officer's signal Doug pushes the throttle forward to the stop and grips a bar to stop inadvertently pulling it back with the acceleration of the launch. With his other hand he stirs the stick around the cockpit to check the controls move freely. The intakes gulp in the steam that blows back from the cat track.

The breakaway link for an A-4 is a dumbbell-shaped lump of metal about the size of a beer can painted blue with yellow ends. The narrow part is designed to pull apart when the force on it reaches 28,500 pounds, give or take 1,500 or so.

Doug salutes the catapult officer and puts his head back against the headrest, his right hand on the stick and his elbow in his gut. The cat officer drops to one knee and touches the deck. On this signal the operator pushes a button.

From this moment until the A-4 leaves the bow and either flies or does not, Doug is just along for the ride. In a fraction of a second, the steel holdback stretches and breaks. Two seconds of blur. Doug's peripheral vision goes about halfway along and briefly it's like looking through the barrels of a shotgun. In two seconds and 200 feet he goes from zero to 170 miles per hour.

The wet steam clears. The deflector sinks again to allow the next jet to cross. A bow runner dashes across the deck and drops a little ramp on the catapult track to ensure the bridle is dragged smoothly back over the shuttle. The cat operator receives the details of the next aircraft: "Side number four-seven-one, weight nineteen-point-five."

Doug puts the stick in the center, raises his gear and flaps and following the thin smoke trail from his flight lead begins a climb towards the join-up.

When his mission is over, Doug has to land on *Tico*, looking insignificant on the vast ocean. Flying abeam of the ship he enters the pattern at 800 feet and 250 knots with his hook down, signaling that he intends to land. As he passes the bow, he pulls hard left, pops the speedbrakes out and continues his turn, lowering the gear and slowing to 225 knots, dropping 200 feet as he rolls out and straightens up. Now heading in the opposite direction to *Tico*, about one-and-a-quarter miles abeam, Webster completes the landing checklist: wheels down, hook down, flaps down, speedbrakes out. He begins another turn inwards towards the ship, banking at 22-degrees until he rolls out in the groove.

Standing on a tiny platform is the Landing Signal Officer, an experienced pilot. He holds a pickle switch that causes wave-off lights to flash if he lets go. Each squadron or aircraft type has an LSO, so the platform is sometimes crowded with four or five aviators and a couple of enlisted men, who act as spotters and write down the LSO's comments on the approach. One spotter watches the deck to warn if anyone or anything fouls the landing area. Another watches the approaching aircraft with binoculars to see if the hook, wheels and flaps are all down.

Doug's eyes are on the optical landing system which uses a system of colored lenses to project the correct glidepath to the pilot. When he has the central light or "meatball" lined up with the side-lights, the aircraft is "on the ball." If he climbs or descends, the meatball moves above or below the center. All the while the landing area is moving away and to the left.

"Champ 474, call the ball," radios the LSO. Doug replies "474 Roger ball" or "Clara ball" depending on if he can see the meatball or not and, gives his fuel state, "one point five" for 1,500 pounds remaining.

The LSO continues his patter: "Check your line-up … you're a little high … drifting left … the deck is moving up … hold what you've got … don't settle … a little power … steady with it … cut!"

Just before landing the A-4 hits a "burble" as *Tico*'s island blocks the wind. The refueling probe quivers like a knight's lance. When he hits the deck Doug pushes the throttle forward in case he has to go around again. The deceleration brings the A-4 to a halt in three seconds. The nosewheel castors backwards and Doug retracts the speedbrakes. A greenshirt hook runner with a tool like a hockey stick sprints towards the peak of the taught arresting wire, even before the tension releases. His job is to unhook the cable if it didn't disengage by itself. Another man races for the A-4s right wing tip. As the wire releases and snakes back to its battery position, he jumps up and pushes down on the wing, applying just enough force that with a touch of left brake and a burst of throttle, it pivots and turns out of the landing area. Doug follows the come forward signal of the plane director to a parking spot.

The mission's dangers are not yet over. Another aircraft is seconds behind. Tiredness and tension cannot lead to inattention. A flak fragment could have damaged the hydraulics or brakes, which might now choose this moment to discharge their fluid all over the deck. Teak splinters and worn deck planks caused tire punctures on cat shots. Something like this happened to a Roadrunners jet one bright day while *Tico* was simultaneously recovering aircraft and conducting a replenishment, something Captain Miller did with enthusiasm. The Skyhawk pilot applied the brake, the nosewheel spun back to the trailing position and a brake line blew, all in about the time it takes to tell it. The A-4C was now heading in the direction it was heading—which was mainly towards the Tonkin Gulf—with nothing to stop it but the starboard catwalk. Two Champ handlers waiting for their own jets to recover were looking up at the island watching the signalmen do their flag thing when the errant Scooter came bumping towards them. Scattering in the nick of time, they watched the A-4's nosewheel drop into the catwalk and the centerline droptank crunch down on the deck. The tank probably stopped the jet going any further and it settled in an undignified ass-high position with its nosewheel in the catwalk but with little damage. Randy Wilson wished he could have taken a picture of the pilot frozen in the seat with his hands over his head gripping the ejection handle, not ready to let go until someone chocked and chained the aircraft.

At night, before evening prayers were broadcast over the 1MC, Captain Miller would recount the successes of the day's missions. One time he announced a particularly strategic "kill"—one of the air wing's planes had bombed a water buffalo, which was described as "an NVA pack animal." A cheer could be heard through the ship at this news, but not everyone found it amusing.

A Roadrunners A-4C wound up with its nosewheel in *Tico*'s starboard catwalk in November. (Randy Wilson)

Dixie Station

On November 5, 1965, eleven months after earning his wings, Doug flew his first combat mission. For the first three weeks of November, Air Wing Five flew missions over the South in support of ground operations. The strikes were mostly against troop concentrations and targets of opportunity under the direction of forward air controllers.

Doug had caught a slight cold, possibly related to him drying off after showers in front of a fan just to keep cool. Flight surgeon Carl Dila gave him some pills, which helped.

After a restless night the day began with a very early briefing, around 0445, an hour before sunrise for an 0645 launch. The target was somewhere in the Mekong Delta south of Saigon and Doug flew as Bill Nealon's wingman. Jack Holland flew twice this day, each with six old high-drag bombs and two 19-shot rocket pods, so it is likely Doug's A-4 was similarly configured. The air wing recorded 40 targets hit and 35 destroyed, of which VA-56 destroyed 17 and damaged 22, so Doug and the Champions could be satisfied with the results of their first combat mission of the 1965 cruise.

Doug had begun a diary on October 24, probably for the first time in his adult life. He thought it would be amusing to look back on in middle age, or to show the children he one day hoped to have with Marcia. In the entry after his first combat mission he considered what caused him fear as a carrier pilot. It wasn't being shot down and killed or made prisoner. Like all of his fellows he had anxieties about carrier landings on a pitching, rolling deck and performing his assigned mission satisfactorily. He worried that if an important mission was ordered that he wouldn't be chosen to fly it.

What concerned him most was prophetic. "What I hear a lot is that there is the possibility of being blasted from the deck and plunging into the ocean while seated in the Skyhawk's cockpit. Somehow this possibility worries me a lot, although I know it isn't going to happen to me. I think it's stupid of me to worry about this, but nevertheless this unease is always lurking somewhere inside me."

On November 6, Doug flew another tanker mission while the air wing attacked troops in the Mekong Delta. Lou Herzog had a radio problem that kept him from communicating with his flight and the following day mechanical problems of one sort of another kept several Champs A-4s on the deck, including Doug's, much to his frustration.

Looking tired but happy, Doug Webster catches up on some post-mission paperwork in the Champs ready room. (John Paisley via Bill Paisley)

On the second of two missions Doug flew on the 9th, Doug hit a building with a 500-pound bomb that his flight leader Tom Callahan had missed. John Paisley confirmed that the explosion caused the structure to disappear, leaving only a big crater. Doug was pleased with his combat success and with the praise of his comrades at debriefing.

On the 12th, Air Wing Five flew close air support at Ap Bau Bang, 30 miles north of Saigon where troops of the Army's 3rd Brigade, 1st Infantry Division were surrounded by Viet Cong troops. Directed by Air Force forward air controllers in the air and on the ground, the A-4s struck first, followed by Knightriders A-1s. John Mape led a flight of Skyraiders to drop 500-pound bombs, napalm and cluster bombs on enemy recoilless rifles and mortars. Repeated bombing and strafing attacks drove the enemy back, causing many casualties. Unfortunately, to steal a quote about a later battle, this was one of those occasions when it

A Roadrunners A-4C roars down the port catapult in November 1965. VA-144 lost four Skyhawks and two pilots on the cruise. (U.S. Navy)

became necessary to destroy the town to save it, and Ap Bau Bang was left a lifeless, smoking ruin.

On the 13th, Doug flew three times, twice in the morning and the third time at noon. By the time he came back from his last mission he was exhausted. His first landing attempt was waved off because his line-up was poor. So was his second. On the third he missed the cables and went around again—a bolter. A pilot can't keep doing this all day, even with repeated tanking. The deck had to be prepared for the next cycle. Approaching bingo fuel state when he would have to divert to Da Nang, Doug finally caught a wire on his fourth attempt. Then he had to suffer a haranguing from the Air Boss about his poor performance,

Ap Bau Bang was followed quickly by the battle of Ia Drang, one of the first major encounters between the U.S. and North Vietnamese regular armies. Made famous by the book and movie *We Were Soldiers*, airmobile forces led by Lieutenant Colonel Hal Moore of the 7th Air Cavalry landed by helicopter in the Ia Drang valley in the Central Highlands. The Americans were soon encircled by a much larger NVA force at Landing Zone X-Ray. On November 15, American forces came close to being overrun, and Moore ordered transmission of the Broken Arrow signal, which in this context meant that all available tactical aircraft were to come to their aid, bombing extremely close to American positions if necessary. This support included Air Wing Five and other carrier-based aircraft, but it was one of a pair of Air Force F-100 fighter-bombers that dropped napalm on American forces in a tragic "friendly fire" incident.

The next day *Tico* began launching aircraft at 0600. Eighty minutes later a Skyraider returned with a hydraulic leak and ditched off the port bow. Viceroy 393 sank in 150 fathoms, but the Angel plucked Jules Gustie (a native American from the Bishop Paiute tribe) out of the water and delivered him back on deck without any apparent injury. That afternoon Ed Pfeiffer crash-landed his Skyhawk on deck. He made a good landing but then his undercarriage collapsed. Pfeiffer had flown mostly tanker missions on the last cruise, but now he was raring to get at the enemy. Around this time he told a visiting reporter that the "real thing" was much better than doing practice runs and described a mission where a forward air controller had called him in to strafe a VC machine-gun crew fleeting across a clearing after raiding a hamlet. "I dove on them, fired and saw nothing but dust. Later the FAC radioed that I'd got them all." Air support helped defeat the NVA attacks at Ia Drang, but there were over 300 Americans dead by the time helicopters withdrew the last of them from the battlefield on the 18th.

Doug Webster missed all this drama. On the day the Ia Drang battle started he flew an A-4 to the Philippines for fitting out with missile warning equipment. With more and more missile sites being constructed, SAMs were becoming a serious threat and all the air wing's Skyhawks were ferried to Cubi Point over the next few days for urgent modifications. The work seems to have been regarded important enough to take squadrons off Dixie Station even while troops on the ground were screaming for close air support.

On the evening of the 14th, together with Gene Kryger from the Roadrunners, Doug launched for Cubi Point, but learned while airborne that the runway was under repair, and the A-4 section diverted to Clark Air Base, about 50 miles to the northeast. Freed of responsibility for the evening, Doug, Gene and another pilot went out and spent 30 dollars apiece on a meal and a few drinks at a restaurant in Angeles City near the base. Doug returned to his room at the bachelor officer's quarters (BOQ) after 2AM.

The next morning, presumably with delicate heads, the two pilots made the short hop to Cubi and handed their jets over to the depot. There the technicians installed a defensive jammer in each Skyhawk with distinctive cone-shaped antennas that poked out under the wing roots. It worked by manipulating the radar return of the SA-2's "Fan Song" fire control radar so it directed a SAM to a point in space where the jet wasn't, hopefully far enough away from the blast zone. This installation was called "shoehorn" because of the way the equipment had to be fitted into the limited available space. There were different versions, one of which eliminated both 20-millimeter cannon and their ammunition, one that replaced one gun and ammo, and one that kept both, but left space for only 20 rounds of ammunition per gun. The Champs retained both guns, but the ammo was only enough for just over a second of firing.

With no aircraft to fly and no other duties, Doug and his buddies, whose numbers grew as more jets flew in for modification, mainly passed the time drinking. The main hangout was the officers' club housed in a low-slung building on the hill overlooking the airfield. Over time it became decorated with elaborately carved plaques recording the units and pilots who passed through Cubi. After the base closed in 1992, the decorations were shipped to Pensacola, Florida and now grace the Cubi Bar in the National Naval Aviation Museum.

One popular O Club activity was propelling a comrade on an office chair down the stairs between the bar and dance floor, most such missions ending in a crash landing at the feet of the dancers, but occasionally an aviator would arrive upright to the cheers of his launch crew and the other pilots. Admiral Cousins suggested to the base commander that in light of the injuries being done to his aviators that this practice be eliminated. The eventual solution was the "Cubi Cat," which was a mock-up cockpit that simulated a catapult launch and arrested landing, or more likely a ditching in the pool outside. This was a few years in the future, however, and we don't know if Doug ever took a chair ride down the staircase or participated in any of the exploits that the young pilots got up to when they had a chance to let off steam.

One night John Paisley was a little late getting to the bar and somebody at a dice table grabbed him and said, "Get in this roll." They were rolling for drinks. "How many are in the roll?" Paisley asked.

"You'll make seven."

"Well, you can't lose with seven rollers," thought Paisley. He lost, and everybody got their drinks and as he was trying to find money the bartender came over and told him his damage.

"How much?"

"Let's see, seven drinks—that will be 35 cents."

"Whoa, something's wrong here."

"No, this is nickel night."

The club was making money like crazy but they were limited by regulations regarding how much they could make, so once a week mixed drinks were 5 cents while beer was still a quarter. "So you could kill yourself on a dollar and a quarter," said Paisley.

One evening, coming down from his room Doug found Ray Foster, an old friend from Ohio State ROTC sitting at the bar by the slot machines. Another time he spotted a familiar face in the distance across the crowded room but didn't check it out. Later he found the name that matched the face on the club's bulletin board.

It was Fred Guarnieri, a high school friend from Warren. The last time they had met was at the amusement park just after they graduated in 1959 when Doug was on a date with Carole Rigsby and Fred with his buddy Jay Morris. Fred had gone to Youngstown State, served on a transport ship and was now a LTJG running the Cubi O Club and bachelor officer's quarters. Doug popped by Fred's office several times, but always missed him and could only leave a note saying he hoped to see him the next time he was at Cubi.

Together with Callahan, Paisley and Phelps, Doug ventured out into the wilds of Olangapo on their last night ashore. One stop was at an infamous joint called Pauline's on Magsaysay Drive, which had a pool outside complete with a 5-foot long crocodile. Local children would sell drunken sailors live baby chicks for a peso and they would throw them to the crocodile. If the croc was too full to eat any, angry sailors were known to leap the wrought iron fence and wrestle it. Pauline's burned down at the end of 1968 and the croc perished.

After five days they flew back to *Tico*. Doug's aircraft (473, which had his name on the side) suffered several instrument failures. It was only by following Ed Phelps closely that Doug made it back to the ship and a fairly rough landing.

It wasn't unheard of for returning pilots to bring back a few liquid souvenirs from Cubi. Personal gear could be carried in a modified fuel tank or "blivet," and this often included cans of Shasta soda. Champs line crews joked that their operating area off Yankee Station should be renamed "Shasta Shoals" for all the aluminum cans they threw overboard there. Alternatively, six bottles of San Miguel or a couple of bottles of Viejo rum would fit alongside the liquid oxygen (LOX) bottle and a red X marked in grease pencil on the port drop tank was a signal to the plane captain to open the compartment hatch carefully before the carrier's LOX crew found it.

While the ship was receiving ammunition from the *Paracutin* on the 9th, Engineering Officer Richard Bishop was caught between a cargo net full of bombs and a winch. He was sent for observation on the sickbay ward but recovered and would sign the deck log after the search for Doug Webster. Illustrating how stories grow on a ship, the rumor spread on *Tico* that an officer had been killed when a net load of bombs fell on him.

The next day Airman A. J. Carlson was injured in a fistfight, and on the 15th Airman H. R. Burgess was run over by an aircraft, breaking six ribs and damaging his liver. He was transferred to Subic Bay hospital. Even pilots were not immune from injury aboard, although usually less serious ones. Jet blast blew cinder into Jim Halverson's eye, necessitating a trip to sickbay

While maneuvering into the wind to begin flight operations, the destroyer *Ingraham* cut across *Tico*'s bows and the carrier had to put all engines into reverse and apply hard right rudder to avoid a collision.

On the 20th, Doug flew a morning mission and seemed to be overcoming recent difficulties making good landings, landing on the first pass this time. Sometimes this was a matter of luck. Ed Phelps suffered the same indignity as Pfeiffer. "I was coming in for a completely normal landing but instead of the front wheel gently touching down, the thing collapsed," he said. There seemed to be a problem or two with the Champs' Skyhawks.

Nobody doubted that the Knightriders were brave but they seemed to have some problems with navigation. On the 22nd, they attacked a civilian bus near Cam Lo, eight miles to the south side of the DMZ, killing one passenger and wounding three. A military spokesman said the Skyraider pilots had been hampered by low cloud and that a military investigation was underway. A press report noted that this was the fifth time targets had been mistakenly struck below the DMZ.

Early that morning, about 0535, sailor Jim Weber claimed to have seen a damaged B43 bomb on an elevator that opened onto a messdeck, most likely on Third Deck. Weber was a metalsmith and not part of any loading operation, so his knowledge of weapons was limited, but what he saw spooked him. It was not unknown for nuclear weapons to be passed through messdecks, surprising sailors who were eating. On *Tico* usually they were warned beforehand when missiles or special weapons were being moved, so as not to disturb hungry sailors, but on other carriers at other times the procedure seems to have shouting Marines forcing bystanders against walls as the weapons came through.

If a bomb was damaged it should have generated an Unsatisfactory Report that would go to the Defense Atomic Support Agency in New Mexico and appeared in the appendices to their regular Technical Letter publication. In this time period this document records that four B43s suffered pressure sealant failures that were reported to DASA, and connector pins were bent on another four, but these could have been Air Force weapons and this damage would not have been noticeable to an outsider. A B57 was slightly damaged when it fell from a hoist at some undisclosed location on December 2.

In 2000, Weber made Freedom of Information Act (FOIA) requests about the "damaged bomb," the October sabotage incident and Webster's accident, believing that these things were related. In them he wrote that in the days after he saw the bomb he was ordered to sickbay twice and asked how he felt. He didn't specify the nature of the damage, so what he actually saw remains a mystery.

On the 21st, *Ticonderoga* turned north for Yankee Station. As the carrier had sailed towards Vietnam, Doug had written in his diary: "I've heard so often since I got on board this carrier that the Vietnam front had greatly changed in the last several months. The military situation has become more and more serious, and in fact a far greater number of pilots than the American people are told have died in crashes."

He wasn't sure his training was suitable for the real combat missions Air Wing Five were flying. "As things stand now, we are still spending more than half of our flying exercises on those for nuclear attack procedures. It looks as if the flying exercises for the basic conventional weapons are being conducted during the intervals." If the Chinese Air Force entered the war, which an intelligence officer had told him he was worried might happen, he wondered how many of *Tico's* pilots would make it back, not being trained for true air combat. He doubted that much of his own training would be useful in a dogfight.

Get off of My Cloud

The pilots of Air Wing Five soon found out, although Doug wasn't with them. On the 25th there was an Alpha Strike on the Me Xa highway bridge, east of Hanoi. CAG Mac Snowden led the attack with a section of F-8s, firing Zuni rockets to suppress the flak sites. Four A-4Es and two A-4Cs, each armed with Mk 83 500-pound bombs were assigned to strike the bridge. As Render Crayton and Jim Delesie pulled off the target at 500 feet and 450 knots, two silver Russian-built MiG-17 fighters dived out of nowhere from behind and slightly to the right of the Skyhawks. The Roadrunners, circling above at 10,000 feet saw each MiG launch a missile at an A-4E, but neither Crayton or Delesie was aware of the attack and the missiles missed. On the opposite side of the circle the second Champ section, led by Tom Callahan with Austin Chapman as wingman was about to begin their dive on the bridge when Chapman saw tracer shells going by his canopy, the larger cannon rounds looking like basketballs as they streaked past. He called out "Picking up ground fire!" before realizing the shells were coming from behind him. One of the Roadrunners shouted, "MiG behind you!" A third MiG-17 had joined the fray. Chapman looked in his mirror and saw it frozen there, right behind him. The A-4s were doing 350 knots but the MiG had much more speed and as the A-4s broke towards the MiG it overshot, passing between Chapman and Callahan then pitching off high and left. "When the plane passed overhead I could *hear* the guns you know, *Thump, Thump, Thump, Thump!*" Chapman saw the bridge and figuring that he was about to roll in anyway and there wasn't any real reason not to get the bombs on target, rolled to the right, dropped his bombs on it and got away. The MiG made another pass from the right and below on Crayton in the lead A-4, but he evaded and got behind the MiG, tracking it until he was in a firing position. He pulled the trigger … nothing! His cannons didn't fire. The MiG slipped away so Crayton dropped his bombs on target and made good his escape. He started to climb but Delesie called, "Stay low!" He figured they could outrun the MiGs down in the weeds.

Diving into this contested piece of sky, the Roadrunner A-4Cs ran into the first two MiGs again at 3,000 feet. Leading the section was Ronnie Boch with Ed Hotelling on his wing. With his call of "MiG, nine O'clock low!" they dropped their external tanks to reduce weight and drag. Chapman noted: "The A-4 matched up pretty well with the MiG-17 and once we got the bombs off and were stripped down clean, we were a darned good fighter."

Hotelling made three turns with a MiG. His guns didn't work either and he tried to charge them again and again without success. His Skyhawk took a cannon hit in the rudder but he carried on, dropping his bombs and getting out of dodge. Now all three MiGs were chasing Boch, who was doing 500 knots at about 2,000 feet. The first one came in level from the left, firing from long range, then a simultaneous attack by the others from slightly behind on either side. The MiGs reversed to come at him again from the opposite sides. For five minutes Boch was alone, fighting three MiGs with useless cannons, but a clean A-4 could match them for maneuverability. The MiGs made five firing passes on Boch in all, but he evaded the MiGs until they finally disengaged. The Crusaders returned to the scene to find aircraft all over the place, but couldn't target any MiGs and headed home. Radar tracked the MiGs heading north in the direction of China.

A quarter-of-an-hour after this indecisive dogfight two RF-8s flew over the bridge on a battle damage assessment run, taking photos that showed good hits on the approach and east end of the bridge. Orbiting at 25,000 feet they saw two MiG-19s way below them, but the North Vietnamese pilots didn't spot the photo birds and they went on their way.

Back on *Tico* the Skyhawk pilots were debriefed on the air battle. As Snowden handed Delesie a cup of medicinal brandy the CAG said when he got back to the scene there was nobody there and he felt lonely. Delesie was one of those who got to brief the carrier division's commander. Under Defense Secretary Robert McNamara a complex reporting system had been established. For every mission, pilots were expected to record such details as cloud type and cover, altitudes flown, defenses encountered, weapons release altitudes, damage inflicted, damage taken and many other parameters. These would be coded, transmitted and analyzed somewhere in the Pentagon, and then kept secret from almost everybody.

The pilots filled in numerous forms for a daily operational OPREP-4 report that was supposed to be transmitted within three hours, but seldom was. The pilots also needed to report aircraft gripes to the plane captains, fill out flight record forms ("yellow sheets"), debrief within the squadron and grab a bite in the wardroom if possible. It was often two hours before the report reached main communications center for transmission, which took about twenty minutes. If there was a dogfight or aircraft loss there were extra forms to complete. Over time aircrew stopped marking many of the extensive list of routine indicators on the forms, which consequently became almost useless.

The Pentagon's Weapons Systems Evaluation Group made its own reports based on aircrew debriefs and other intelligence. At this time in the war, they seemed unsure about the national insignia used by North Vietnamese aircraft, which seems fairly fundamental. The report on the Me Xa dogfight described the MiGs as having two red stripes around the fuselage and a large star on the vertical fin. One pilot said he got a good look at a dark star with a yellow border on the wing

Seen here with supply ship USS *Sacramento* and the destroyer *Basilone*, *Tico* refueled and replenished dozens of times on the 1965–66 cruise, sometimes simultaneously with flight operations.

of one MiG. These descriptions do not tally with known North Vietnamese Air Force MiG-17 markings.

The Skyhawk armorers looked at the gun failures and found there was a simple reason for them. The cannon were disconnected. When the shoehorn jammers were installed at Cubi Point, the cannon firing circuits had been cut. This mistake may have cost Crayton and Boch MiG kills and came very close to causing *Tico* to lose an A-4. In the same timeframe Air Wing Nineteen complained of aircraft coming back from the shoehorn modification with flashlights and tools lodged in compartments, fouling control cables and causing other difficulties. Enraged over his boys being unnecessarily exposed to danger, Admiral Cousins wrote a "spectacular" message about the gun firing circuit damage. The problem does not seem to have reoccurred.

Chapman walked into the ready room after the Me Xa mission with eyes that were very large. He confided in John Paisley, "Y'know, I'd *swear* I heard that guy's cannon fire!" Paisley just chuckled and later said, "I had towed banners for air-to-air gunnery practice back in my flamin' youth and was able to assure Austin that he did, in fact hear the guns. The most dominant noise in a jet cockpit is the pressurization and air conditioning systems. All the engine roar goes out the back end and machine guns, 20mm cannon and especially 37mm cannon make a lot of racket."

"I never saw a MiG over there. I was *looking* for them," said Paisley. "I didn't know what I was going to *do* with him when I found him because all we had at that time was about forty rounds of 20mm, although I do recall that one A-4 did get a MiG with a Zuni rocket … I have heard of other squadrons being jumped but that was the only incident in my two tours with VA-56. And I missed it! If the assigned mission permitted, we used to go looking for the MiGs. Never found them."

At Me Xa, with the F-8 fighters being used in the defense suppression role, the A-4s were nominally at a distinct disadvantage to the afterburner- and missile-equipped MiGs, which had similar manoeuvrability, but were operating over their own territory and under the control of ground-based radar. The CIA's assessment of the encounter was that the MiGs negated the U.S. "Big Eye" EC-121 radar planes orbiting off the coast by approaching from a relatively low level. There had been earlier reports of unguided rockets fired by MiG-17s, without success, but the weapons fired this day might have been AA-1 "Atolls," a Soviet copy of the AIM-9 Sidewinder. The missile-equipped MiG-17PF had just arrived in Vietnam, along with MiG-21s, but the first of the latter was not spotted on the ground until December 23.

Bridges and Bullpups

On November 28 Doug flew on an Alpha Strike mission against a bridge northeast of Haiphong not far from the Chinese border. The Hà Chanh road bridge was a 150-foot-long steel and reinforced concrete structure and was deemed worth sending 19 A-4s from *Ticonderoga* and *Bon Homme Richard* armed with Bullpup missiles and 1,000- and 2,000-pound bombs against it.

John Paisley says the squadron was qualified in both types of Bullpup missile but it "wasn't our favorite weapon, because we had to maintain a predictable flight path to guide it." Austin Chapman adds, "We had about a week's training on the Bullpup. The problem with the Bullpup is the plane had to chase the weapon down to keep it lined up on the target. You ended up exposed as much as the weapon was to anti-aircraft fire. It was not a giant success or popular to use."

The ordnancemen didn't like the Bullpup much either, particularly their liquid fueled motors. "If one started leaking [in the magazine], it was always the bottom one where we had to remove all the ones in the stanchions before we could get the bottom one," says Del Mitchell. "We had to suit up in a butyl rubber suit, with gloves, boots, and OBA (oxygen breathing apparatus), and with the engine room on the 6th deck, it was hell [with the heat]. The Bullpup had two chemicals separated by a collapsible diaphragm when ignited, UDMH (Undiluted Methyl Hydrozine) and RFNA (Red Fuming Nitric Acid), both pretty deadly and incapacitating. During daily magazine temperature checks and inspections, it was always a bit leery going into B-505-M."

Led by the Roadrunners, the Alpha Strike approached the bridge at low altitude, facing intense anti-aircraft fire of various calibers. Hitting it many times, *Tico*'s A-4s dropped the bridge's center span and damaged the southern span. The *Bon Homme Richard* bombers were left with nothing to hit, so they went onto a secondary target (the Thanh Hóa Bridge) where two of their escorting F-8s were shot down by flak. One pilot was rescued but the other was captured.

Doug was assigned a SAM site as his target. At this time many of the SAM sites were dummies or not yet occupied and no missiles were spotted, although there was plenty of flak. The Roadrunners' skipper Bruce Miller would be awarded the Distinguished Flying Cross for leading this mission through continuous anti-aircraft fire. On return to *Tico* the pilots were each given a two-ounce shot of medicinal brandy.

In response to U.S. President Lyndon B. Johnson's call for "more flags" in *Vietnam*, Philippines' President Marcos ordered the deployment of Filipino troops to join the effort. The day before there was a large anti-war demonstration in Washington, attended by over a quarter of a million people. Organized by the Committee for a Sane Nuclear Policy, it was the first large anti-Vietnam War march on the capital.

The next day Doug flew again on a *Rolling Thunder* mission, albeit one on a smaller scale. The target was another small bridge and Doug dropped his bombs at very low altitude, scoring a direct hit on and destroying some small buildings, which were still burning as the attackers departed. A second night mission was canceled and Doug got some rest. Although he supported the war and America's need to fight communism, Doug was skeptical about the targets chosen and the tactics being employed. He understood that an attack on a "meaningless little country bridge" as he put it in his diary was part of the strategy but that he could foresee that before long one or two of his buddies might fail to return from this type of "stupid sortie."

F-8 Overboard

On November 13, the air wing suffered its first fatal casualty of the cruise.

Steve Richardson of VF-53 returned from a routine combat air patrol with Gail Bailey. Fire Fighter 229 made a good approach and caught the three-wire, but as it pulled out and the jet slowed to 90 knots, the shank of the arrester hook fractured. Too fast to stop and too slow to climb away, Richardson hit the afterburner as he left the angle and kept the wings level and the nose up, in a desperate trade-off between lift and gravity to keep the wallowing Crusader airborne, but it could only struggle another 200 feet before it hit the calm sea and broke up. *Tico* put on full left rudder to avoid the wreckage and then resumed course to continue taking recoveries. The plane guard helicopter arrived overhead immediately, but it was able to do no more than watch the pilot go down with the aircraft and retrieve a few pieces of his safety equipment floating on the surface, including a badly damaged helmet. A search by

The broken tailhook of Steve Richardson's Crusader was recovered from the deck and sent to the manufacturer to be examined for metal fatigue. (Naval Safety Center)

the helicopter and *Turner Joy* failed to find any remains. The plane and pilot sank to 50 fathoms, 100 miles off the DMZ.

The culprit lay on the deck in the form of a broken piece of steel and rubber, quickly picked up to clear the landing area; the tail hook and two feet of steel shank.

That same day VF-53's skipper Robair Mohrhardt wrote to Steve's parents in Seattle, and to wife Nancy, who was pregnant, describing the accident's circumstances and praising Steve's character. "I can attest to his courage and superior airmanship and love of flying. There was never a finer, more dedicated officer than Steve." Mohrhardt added, "As yet, we do not know why the tail hook failed; possibly some internal molecular flaw in the metal was the cause. Please rest assured that I will do everything possible to find out."

The tailhook shank was sent back to the manufacturer for analysis. A stress corrosion crack had worked its way deep into the metal from a poorly applied protective coating and spread gradually with each landing. Whoever was assigned that aircraft that day was fated to crash. The hook had made 46 previous arrestments. Naval Safety Center records showed that hook fractures had happened seven times since August 1964 and three F-8s had been lost. An urgent engineering change was requested to redesign and test the arrester hook shank and supply retrofit kits.

Stephen Gould Richardson was 25 and had flown 49 hours in the last 30 days, out of a total of 618 flight hours. An arts and philosophy graduate and president of his fraternity at Linfield College in Oregon, he was the second of his graduating class to die in Vietnam in ten days.

Doug's first flight of the day, a *Steel Tiger* mission over Laos had been scrubbed when there were not enough available jets and he got some rest. He was in an office below the angled deck preparing for a night mission when Steve's jet tried to take off again after the hook snapped. He heard the bang and roar as the afterburner lit, which was not that unusual if a jet made a bolter and went around again, but the noise quickly turned to silence and Doug thought that cannot be good. He went up to the flight deck, but all there was to see was the helicopter and some floating wreckage.

Doug went back to his stateroom and wrote in his diary. He remembered the rainy day at Meridian when Steve had cheerfully given him a lift in his little black VW. "I have never forgotten his kindness. He was such a good man, but now he's gone." As aviators do, Doug took Steve's accident as a learning tool, analyzing it to reassure himself that in the same circumstances, he would survive. Whichever way he looked at it, however, he could see that Steve had at most two-and-a-half seconds to realize his jet was not stopping and to eject. In that brief window, Steve chose to try to save the jet and probably never began the ejection sequence. Tests proved that the water pressure on a sinking F-8 sealed the canopy shut until it reached 70 to 80 feet and it equalized, but 100 feet was a depth of no return, again giving a window of only two to three seconds for escape. Steve's battered helmet told a story.

Doug knew that Steve had found himself with an impossible task and that the first casualty of this cruise would not be the last. Despite his nerves he got some sleep before his flight, which was to be his first night mission in some time, but he woke up to find it was canceled. The Champs were having trouble with their A-4s again and the maintenance crews worked through the night to have them ready.

On December 1, the air wing launched 17 fighter-bombers on an Alpha Strike against a target deep in North Vietnam, the Hai Duong road and rail bridge between Hanoi and Haiphong. The target was one of six assigned to the Navy under *Rolling Thunder 38*. Cutting the Hai Duong Bridge would isolate Hanoi from the main port of Haiphong. The CO of an F-8 squadron on *Bon Homme Richard* had been shot down attacking the bridge on November 11 and three more Navy jets were lost attacking it on the 17th.

John "Mac" McCormick's A-4C was one of a division of four Roadrunner Skyhawks each armed with only a single 500-pound bomb on the centerline rack so as to improve performance.

A forward air controller (FAC) was orbiting the area and cleared the A-4s to attack the bridge. Heavy flak rose up as McCormick dived on the target and while passing through about 6,000 feet, a 57mm shell struck his Skyhawk. Warpaint 547 disintegrated and the flaming wreckage crashed in rice paddies between the Rang and Thai Binh rivers. No radio transmission or distress beacon was heard and it was clear that Mac could not have survived. He was 11 days short of his 26th birthday.

The Pentagon and White House dictated many of the tactics for striking targets, as well as the targets themselves, often putting areas off limits for risk of hitting civilians or Chinese or Russian advisers. In 1965–66 bridges were one of the few acceptable target types in North Vietnam, but the line of approach was mandated to be at 90 degrees to the bridge, not along its length or at a slight offset because a short or long bomb might hit civilian structures. This massively reduced the likelihood of actually hitting a narrow bridge, and a near miss would only splash it. The North Vietnamese soon realized the Americans would attack from predictable directions

The bomb in the hand cart is a WW II-era M64A1 500-pound bomb with a conical tail, called a "Fat Boy" in the official caption. The A-4C behind was shot down on December 1, 1965 with the loss of John McCormick. (U.S. Navy)

and placed their antiaircraft guns to concentrate fire on the expected approach paths of American bombers.

The North Vietnamese had placed at least five light AAA and five heavy machine-gun positions around the Hai Duong Bridge in early 1965. Mac's single bomb had to be accurate to have any effect. The raid scored a single Bullpup missile hit on the bridge, which would have to be attacked again and again. More aircraft would be lost and more aviators would die but the bridge would never completely fall.

John Vern McCormick was the oldest of six children from Saginaw, Michigan. Average height and skinny, he had blue eyes, prominent ears and a wayward forelock of dark brown hair. A trombone player in the school band and a keen member of the Future Farmers of America, he graduated in chemical engineering from the University of Michigan before joining the Navy. Mac was the only U.S. casualty of the strike and *Tico*'s first combat loss of the war.

Doug's Final Mission

Doug was not on the morning Alpha Strike. He was assigned to fly wingman to Gary Scoffield on an afternoon *Rolling Thunder* mission in Route Package 4 around Nam Dinh. As the Air Wing Five LSO, 31-year-old Texan "Scof" Scoffield was qualified to fly multiple aircraft types, including all A-4 versions and the F-8E. He would sometimes fly with junior pilots to evaluate the training standards of the squadrons and was known for carrying a little beanbag ashtray in a plastic bag so he could smoke in the cockpit.

Their Skyhawks loaded with Mk 82 bombs and Zuni rocket pods, the pair launched a quarter-of-an-hour before sunset. The forecast weather deteriorated and visibility dropped to almost nothing in the target area, so they headed for an alternative target further south in Route Pack 2 near Vinh. Doug flew at around 25,000 feet, trailing a mile behind the CAG's Skyhawk. They were wary of SAMs as they did not have full information about the defenses in the area. Although the weather was clearer, it took two orbits to locate a target, a steel bridge about a mile inland. With rain and broken clouds upriver, Scoffield dived steeply on the target and pulled up at low altitude. Doug followed, but frustratingly, his bombs didn't explode. Around this time, one in forty bombs was a dud. Sometimes the catapult shot would disconnect the arming wires. So far they had not seen a response from the defenses.

Still carrying unexpended rockets, the two A-4s turned south to look for targets of opportunity along the coast. Suddenly Scoffield shouted, "Get the hell out!" There was panic in his voice.

As Doug pulled hard on the stick to climb out of range, an object like a flaming telephone pole flew across his vision. "SAM!" he screamed, redundantly.

Several missiles lit up the clouds as they exploded in orange fireballs behind Scoffield's Skyhawk.

Roaring upwards at half a mile a second, SAMs were terrifying at the best of times, in cloud at night, even more so. If they were coming straight at you they looked just like a red light. Dale Palmer was flying over the North one time and all of a sudden out of the corner of his left eye he saw a red light tracking him coming closer and closer even when he pulled hard. He said to himself "Oh shit ... too late" and closed his eyes for the impact but nothing happened. A second later he looked to the left and realized it was just a navigation light reflecting off the cloud next to him and it was getting closer because he was getting closer and closer to the cloud.

Doug and Scoff escaped with no damage from these particular SAMs and climbed away towards the coast, turning north, looking for a target for their rockets. Although effective against troops and vehicles, they were mostly useless against hardened structures, and flimsier ones would be quickly repaired. They shot them at a small bridge and missed.

As the pair headed back to the carrier, a drama which had begun as the Skyhawks launched played out over the radio.

A pair of Knightrider Spads were returning from a rescue combat air patrol (RESCAP) to Hai Duong when the engine on Paul Giberson's Skyraider faltered.

"It blew a jug. The whole cylinder came out," he told the Naval Aviation Museum Foundation in a 2016 interview. Giberson's Spad was still flying, but it was getting dark and they were a long way from *Tico*. Flight leader Steve McBride asked Giberson, "What do you want to do?"

"I haven't really decided yet," was his reply.

In the growing darkness blue flames could be seen coming from under the Skyraider's cowling. The oil pressure and manifold pressure were dropping. The only way to keep going was in a gradual descent. Giberson finally decided he was going to have to ditch, but he was still 60 miles from the carrier. The cruiser *Gridley* happened to be nearby and Giberson radioed them to say he was going to ditch alongside. Faced with landing on a dark sea with no idea of wind direction, his mind went back to his training.

"Can you tell the captain to put the ship into the wind?" he asked, knowing that would give him the heading to take, but the answer was somewhat surprising.

"Are you kidding? He's not going to do that!"

Giberson contemplated this news for a moment.

"OK, I'm going to ditch alongside the ship and take whatever you've got."

"You're lucky, we're refuelling a helicopter on board at the moment."

It seemed the whole ship's company lined up to watch the Skyraider ditch alongside. It hit the water hard and lurched to the right, banging Giberson's shoulder. It sank right away. Giberson had enough time to prepare for ditching but was worried about the cord that connected his earphones to the aircraft. Again he remembered his training and unplugged it, but as water rushed into the cockpit and he began to climb out, he found the cord was hooked up on something. Panicking, he took his survival knife to cut it and in the dark accidentally slashed his own neck. With blood all over the place his next thought was, *"here come the sharks!"*

The helicopter was overhead and lowered a survival harness. A loudspeaker from above warned of the static buildup that might be on the harness: "Let it touch the water first, because it gives off a charge."

"So now I'm going to get electrocuted!" thought Giberson, but he climbed into it and was hauled into the helicopter where he lay on the floor for a while in (non-electric) shock from the events of the last few minutes.

The Seasprite landed on *Gridley*, finished refuelling and then headed for *Tico*. The whole squadron was waiting on deck to see him and after the attaboys, CO Lee McAdams said, "The skipper wants to see you."

"But I'm all wet!"

"Don't worry, he wants to see you now."

Still dripping, Giberson went up to the bridge and found a jovial group. Sharing a drink with Captain Miller was Senator John Tower, visiting on a fact-finding mission.

The officers of VA-56 on *Tico* posed for a photo as the carrier ended its first line period. This may be the last photo of Doug Webster (top row, third from right). (U.S. Navy)

"Hey boy!" he said in his Texas drawl. "I heard you got rid of one of our airplanes. It's gonna cost you!"

"Yes Sir," replied Giberson, not knowing how to respond to that.

The brass wanted to know what happened and after he had told his story, Captain Miller said, "Go on down to sickbay, get checked over and get yourself a couple of bottles of brandy."

"Yes Sir, I'll take care of that," the soaking pilot replied and went below to see the doc for a couple of the two-ounce spirits. Giberson's wrenched shoulder cost him a couple of days off flying duties, but he had cheated the sharks.

Doug heard of Giberson's rescue as he arrived back at *Tico*. Now he had to concentrate on a good night landing, a task many pilots found more stressful than combat. He didn't hear the LSO report that the wind over the deck was 39 knots, and his descent and approach were a bit too quick. Despite this and a rolling deck, Doug caught the four-wire on the first pass. He felt dizzy.

While Doug ate his dinner in the wardroom, C. Ray Smith came over and told him to expect another sortie that evening, a Steel Tiger mission as the XO's wingman.

Doug shoveled down his food and began mission preparations, but the flight was canceled, to his relief.

He returned to the JO's bunkroom to write up his diary. He noted that in the last month he had flown 22 flights from the carrier and made only three perfect landings. On three others he had caught the four-wire, but in general his landing grades were disappointing. "So my hope is to improve my landing technique after we come back from R&R in Yokosuka, Japan."

Then Doug added a P. S. to his diary: "I keep seeing an image of John McCormick and hearing his voice in my ears. I can't believe that he is gone. At the same time in my head I hear a loud airplane noise as another aircraft is about to be catapulted."

It was to be his final entry. Just after midnight, *Tico* turned towards Japan.

CHAPTER 7

In the Middle of Nowhere

"Man overboard, man overboard, port side!" As soon as the alarm sounded the assistant flight deck officer called down, "Raise the elevator!" which was the procedure whenever the ship went into a turn. Peter House cleared everybody else off the elevator and rode up to the flight deck standing near the edge. He could see the white underside of the Skyhawk floating away but no sign of the pilot. Before he was shooed away, William Smith, who was the man closest to the edge, saw what he believed was the bomb separate from the aircraft, bobbing in the water with smoke coming from it. He thought it would go off and the ship would vanish from the face of the earth. Dave Jaensch and Jim Dunn were having coffee in the port gun tub when they felt the ship list and saw the A-4 hit the water and float past them. Fly 2 petty officer Frank Barrett was supervising the men on the mid-section of the flight deck. He looked down and saw the pilot tightening his straps, then as it hit the rail, reach up as if to grab the ejection handle above him. Also looking from the flight deck, Dave Lesley saw him grappling with his seatbelts and later wondered why he didn't eject. Fifteen to twenty seconds after the A-4 hit the water, Barrett saw a fuel tank bob to the surface.

Weapons Officer Edmond Chevalier ran away from the hangar opening to a phone and reported the accident to the Combat Information Center where CIC Officer Worley Creech answered it. He called the bridge.

Smoke flares were thrown in the water to mark the position of the sunken Skyhawk.

The Oscar (man overboard) flag was hoisted. A signal gun fired six times to alert the escort ships, which were surrounding the carrier in a screen at 4,000 yards distance.

A 42,000-ton aircraft carrier travelling at 20 knots takes ten miles to stop in a straight line, but turning back dissipated some of the enormous momentum.

On the bridge, officer of the deck John McCabe gave orders that a sailor passed to the engine room by ship's telegraph:

"Turn 30 degrees to port!"

"Back engines two-thirds!"

"Port engine back full!"

Navigator Lynn Adams was in the chart room and ran forward to the bridge as the carrier began to turn. He got on the primary tactical frequency and called the destroyer screen commander: "We've possibly lost a pilot overboard off the port side while moving an A-4 ... dispatch a destroyer to our position to help us search."

"Say again."

Adams repeated his message as Captain Miller arrived on the bridge and took the conn.

"All engines ahead standard, rudder amidships. Steady course on 200."

As the carrier turned towards the spot, Adams saw the what he took to be the A-4's drop tanks bobbing in the water but nothing else except some cardboard boxes that had been thrown off *Tico* or some other ship, just part of the normal trash that drifts in the oceans.

"All engines stopped."

"All engines back full, rudder left 30 degrees. Rudder amidships."

It was ten minutes since the accident when *Tico* arrived 660 yards off datum, the marked point of the accident.

"Stop engines."

Ticonderoga stopped dead at sea for the first and only time during its nine-month cruise.

"Lower lifeboat."

Aboard *Turner Joy* to the east, Captain Robert McClinton took the conn, set a man overboard detail and raced at 27 knots towards the floating flares off *Tico*'s port quarter, arriving in ten minutes to begin searching. Very quickly the destroyer located a helmet and recovered it at 1511. Thirty minutes later they lowered a whaleboat to look for other objects, recovering a part of one of the drop tanks. From the west the cruiser *Gridley* under Captain Albert M. Sackett joined *Turner Joy*, and maneuvered at various courses and speeds in a fruitless search.

The Angel was standing by on the flight deck as part of the exercise. When the A-4 went overboard, it was airborne within three minutes and was overhead in probably another minute. Bob Ceccarini was the crewman aboard: "The sea was rough and the plane was partly underwater. I was the swimmer and went in but could not get to the pilot. After a number of attempts, the plane was sinking, [and] sadly I had to call it quits." It was his worst day as an aircrewman, he recalled many years later. (The inquiry report says that the helicopter only spotted the helmet and broken fuel tank, nothing about dropping a swimmer.) The Angel was ordered to search along *Tico*'s track then perform an expanding square search.

Carl Ray Smith was sitting in a Skyhawk further aft in the hangar bay, waiting to be moved into the loading position. He asked his plane captain what happened and sent him forward to find out what. When the man came back and told him, Smith just stared straight ahead.

Captain Miller called Commander Nealon.

Tico's escort ships maneuvered around the carrier in a fruitless search for the Skyhawk and its pilot. The destroyer *Turner Joy* was only able to recover a few items. (Cruisebook)

With two rescue swimmers visible in the door, one of *Tico*'s Seasprites flies past the carrier. The "Angel" was launched quickly, but could not save Doug. (Tailhook Association)

Tico's Marines were a serious bunch, responsible, among other things, for the security of the carrier's nuclear weapons. (Cruisebook)

"Can this bomb explode?"

Nealon covered the phone's earpiece with his hand and asked the same question of Jack Kaufman, who had just run in from the elevator. Kaufman shook his head.

William Smith was in the room when he heard the same question and its answer: "No Sir, no chance it can go off." It was the first time in quite a few minutes that Smith realized everyone was not going to die.

Carl Kernan was one of the Mardet. His shift was over and he would have gone off duty but they called this exercise so he hung around out of curiosity. One of his fellow Marines who had been guarding the bomb with a rifle ran to the Gunnery Sergeant's desk and told him, "I've got a problem, we lost a plane, a pilot and a weapon!"

The gunny said, "You should be with it wherever it is!"

"No, no, I haven't misplaced it, it's gone overboard!

Ed Ofstad was responsible for the fathometer in the chartroom and navigator Adams called him to the bridge and quizzed him about the equipment's calibration record. He wanted to be very sure about the depth at the accident position. The fathometer's records indicated it was calibrated when in the yards in Alameda the year before. "The calibration that can be done is rather minor but I did it and also changed the stylus, which had become carbon fouled," says Ofstad. "It used a high voltage stylus and a thermo-activated paper. As I was changing the stylus and being hassled by all the brass, I was stuck in my right middle finger with the carbon-fouled stylus. To this day I still have a tattoo of where the stylus had stuck me." Ofstad adjusted the voltage for a good quality print out and was about to leave when he was told that he would stay on the bridge until they got orders from Washington. Ofstad spent more than 12 hours on the bridge marking depths and times on the graph.

Lynn Adams observed the fathometer readings and confirmed the depth, which agreed with the charts—2,700 fathoms and no shelves on the seabed below. Meteorology Officer Claude Clower recorded weather observations, noting the cloud cover, swell, wind speed and direction. Admiral Cousins verbally ordered an inquiry to be held when the ship reached Japan.

Bill Nealon said years later that the commanding officer made an announcement over the public address system that none of the ship's personnel should write or say anything about the accident. Nevertheless, he sat down to write the letter every squadron commander hopes he will never have to, but always does:

Dear Mrs Webster,

It is difficult for us here to express our deep sorrow in the loss of your son, Douglas. Mere words are inadequate to convey our sense of grief, but I do want you to know that I and every officer and man in this squadron extends to you our sincere condolences....

John Paisley reviewed the maintenance records of Champ 472 and Render Crayton pulled out Doug's personnel file. The officers assigned to the inquiry made their rounds, looking for witnesses to call for the hearings planned in Yokosuka.

No copy of the Broken Arrow message has been located, but based on the standard message format and other known examples, it would have looked something like this:

FLASH
    Z 0506592Z Dec 65
    FM USS TICONDEROGA CVA 14
    TO NMCC WASHINGTON DC   CNO WASHINGTON DC
    INFO CINCPACFLT NORFOLK   NWEF ALBUQUERQUE
    COMSEVENTHFLT   AEC WASHINGTON DC
    COMNAVSURFPAC SAN DIEGO CA COMCARDIV NINE
    CTG SEVEN SEVEN PT FIVE
    S E C R E T NOFORN/(00000)/CTF (00)/IN/OPREP-3/PINNACLE/
    BROKEN ARROW/001
    A.   (1450I) 5 DEC 65
    B.   27–35.2N, 131–19.3E
    C.   ONE B43Y1 WR
    D.   N/A
    E.   N/A
    F.   LOSS OF ARMED AIRCRAFT OVERBOARD
    G.   A4E AIRCRAFT FELL OVERBOARD FROM USS TICONDEROGA CVA14 DURING LOADING EXERCISE. SEARCH UNDERWAY. AIRCRAFT, WEAPON AND PILOT STILL MISSING. DEPTH 2700 FATHOMS.
    H.
    I.   YES
    J.

The President Has Been Informed

The A-4 went overboard at 1450 Japan time, which was 0050 in the morning in Washington, D. C. At NWEF in Albuquerque the initial report was received at 0659 Zulu (1559 Japan time), an hour and nine minutes after the accident. It may be assumed that the news reached the National Military Command Center in the Pentagon at about the same time, approximately 0200 Eastern Standard Time. It was two-and-a-half hours after that that the phone rang in the White House Situation Room.

In the White House, Intelligence Officer Ken Rosen answered the phone. The National Military Command Council was informing the president of the accident. Rosen's entry in the Situation Room Log seems to have been typed with more speed and less care than others that day:

~~SECRET~~

SITUATION ROOM LOG

DATE __4/5 December 1965__

DUTY OFFICER __Rosen__

TIME	ACTION
1415	Signal Duty Officer reports that the courier plane will not leave Andrews until 2000. Pouch will close at 1800 since courier has to be at airfield at 1900. Informed Nash's office.
1545	William Buffum, State Internat'l Org., called and asked if we could have a letter from Amb. Goldberg to the President delivered to the President at the Ranch. Told him to send the letter and we would get it to the Ranch.
1720	FAA reports a mid-air collision between a TWA 707 and an Eastern Airlines Constellation near Danbury Conn. Informed Maj. Robinson at the Ranch.
1722	Califano's office informed sitroom that they would have material to go to the Ranch by plane but it would not be ready until 1900. Called Col. Cross and asked if it was necessary could the plane be held up for awhile. He said it could be done.
1920	Pouch closed. Califano has released aircraft for the flight.
2030	Will Sparks, press office, asked that we send Mr. Valenti a copy of a messg. sent earlier to the President. Mr. Valenti wants the material at his home in the AM.
2043	Califano says that Jacobsen wants to be kept informed on the investigation of the mid-air collision. Sent a detailed summary of the accident to the Ranch.
2230	Jacobsen said to keep the FAA reports on the collision coming all night During after duty hours com center at the Ranch will hold the reports until OOB.
0430	NMCC reports tha t an A4e Skyhawk has rolled off the deck of the carrier Ticonderoga. The aircraft was carrying a ⌐————————————————┐ └————————┘ Reported this info to Maj. Robinson at the Ranch. He will notify the President when awakens in the AM. NMCC has not notified the Secretary yet. They will do so in the AM. AEC has been notified of the incident. 16,000 ft
0730	Material sent to Valenti's residence. See 2030 entry.

~~SECRET~~

The White House Situation Room log with the report of the Broken Arrow. (Via USS *Ticonderoga* Association)

0430 NMCC reports that an A4e Skyhawk has rolled off the aircraft carrier *Ticonderoga*. The aircraft was carrying a [one line redacted]. Reported this info to Maj. Robinson at the Ranch. He will notify the president when he awakens in the AM. NMCC has not notified the secretary yet. They will do so in the AM. AEC has been notified of the incident.

President Johnson was staying at his Texas ranch near Austin. On December 4, he watched the TV coverage of the launch of Gemini 7 carrying Frank Borman and Jim Lovell and went hunting. That Saturday evening he watched a film *Night of the Dragon* (a controversial USIA documentary about Vietnam, which incorporated faked footage to make its case for American intervention) with guests and retired to his bedroom at 2145 where he had a backrub and a haircut and reviewed some documents with assistant Jake Jacobsen. By the time the message was received via Washington, he was asleep.

The duty officer at the ranch was LBJ's Army aide, Major Hugh Robinson, the first African-American to hold this post. His regular duties included delivering Vietnam casualty figures to the president each morning. Johnson's staff waited until he was awake, which was not early. The log for the ranch suggests that the president slept in until 1030 that Sunday morning before he got up to dress for church. "When they told me he was awake I think I got there without touching the ground, actually. It was a very important message, certainly one that we wanted

Civil rights leaders John Lewis and James Farmer meet with Lyndon B. Johnson and Major Hugh Robinson in August 1965. Robinson was the White House military aide who passed on the Broken Arrow message to the president. (LBJ Library photo by Yoichi Okamoto)

him to see as soon as it was appropriate," remembered Major Robinson in 1998. 1030 Texas time was 0130 the next morning on *Ticonderoga*, nearly 14 hours after the accident.

Johnson returned from the First Christian Church in Johnson City at 1216 and immediately called his Press Secretary Bill Moyers in Washington for 20 minutes. The rest of Sunday passed with social activities such as driving around the ranch with friends and visiting a neighbor's house to see his puppies. Although there were two more calls to Moyers and a short call to Senator Everett Dirksen, a strong Vietnam hawk, in Washington, nothing is recorded to suggest the loss of a nuclear weapon resulted in any action on behalf of the president.

Rumors

With the secrecy surrounding the accident, scuttlebutt spread in the finest naval tradition. Rumors about the accident flourished at the time, and the passage of time did nothing to quell them.

Petty officer Philip Weldon heard that the pilot was reading a book in the cockpit. Chuck Wilber thought he was reading his war plan checklist. Jay Shower believed Doug was wearing his helmet and could not hear the whistles. Bill Nealon's letter to Margaret said that some witnesses thought he was putting his helmet on and got distracted. Jerry Slagle said that it was surmised that the pilot had a heart attack or there was a major brake failure on the aircraft.

Gunner's Mate John Peters, who brought the bomb up in the elevator, believed the pilot had two kids and red hair. Randy Wilson heard that he had only been married three weeks before sailing and his wife was waiting for him in Japan. Bud Dehnert had heard much the same thing.

Ed Ofstad said, "I know the destroyers were required to steam in circles for several days before receiving the okay to leave the area," and Lloyd Frank said, "We heard that the Russians looked for [the weapon] for a while also to no avail."

Meanwhile Gerald Matlock reported, "LBJ came on the speakers that evening and told the crew the accident had to be kept secret as a matter of national security." No corroboration of this has been found. Others thought Doug was sending letters home against the war (none have surfaced) and his CO was relieved right after the accident (Nealon's change of command came at the normal interval). Jim Weber believed that the "damaged bomb" he saw on an elevator was the one that went overboard a fortnight later, but he was never able to prove or disprove his suspicions. At the subsequent inquiry, witnesses had trouble estimating Doug's height. Plane captain Edmister, who was very tall, thought Doug was small, only five-foot-two. Render Crayton, who knew him better, thought he might be five-nine or five-ten. Flight surgeon Dila said he was five-foot-eight and 150 pounds, which seems closest to the mark.

Notification

At Lemoore the officers' wives were planning a lunchtime get-together at Commander Nealon's house to plan the squadron families' Christmas party. It was nearly 1100 and Commander Nealon's wife Maggie had come back from church and was mixing a glass bowl of punch for her friends. Suddenly the bowl, which was in perfect condition, started to develop hairline cracks and shattered, spilling fruit juice over the kitchen floor. With her husband and his men away at war on a distant sea, this seemed like a premonition. Maggie Nealon was mopping up the glass and juice when the phone rang. It was the base commander Captain Howard J. Boydstun with the news that Douglas Webster was dead. Howie Boydstun wanted the wife of Doug's commanding officer to accompany him to visit Marcia. Maggie told him that the wives were coming to her house and Marcia, who lived off base in Hanford, would have left already with Austin Chapman's wife Anne. Maggie then called Carl Smith's wife to ask her to contact the other wives and call off the meeting. Shortly after, Marcia and Anne arrived and Maggie invited them in. A few minutes later, Captain Boydstun and the chaplain arrived in a black sedan. Maggie let them into the reception room where Marcia was waiting alone.

As the war intensified and more Lemoore aviators were shot down (and 168 would be), there would be many more sombre visits on the base and the surrounding communities. There were realtors who whenever they saw the black limousine with the base CO and the chaplain would follow it to see what houses would be up for sale.

Sam Paisley remembers an odd event from her time in Lemoore, which encompassed two more Vietnam tours for John, so may not be strictly contemporary to this cruise. A friend—we will call her Mrs. Jones—was talking on the phone with another wife and someone broke in to the conversation of these two women and said, "This is the Associated Press, Mrs. Jones. What are your thoughts on your husband getting shot down?" Sam Paisley says it wasn't a party line, so how this could happen she doesn't know, but it naturally upset her friend. "She immediately hung up, called the base and the base didn't know anything about it yet. It hadn't gone from Washington back to Lemoore yet. They put a stop to that, to the news people. Casualty news had to be cleared before it left the ship."

The official casualty report was prepared and sent to the Pentagon just before 0400 Washington, D. C. time. It gave Margaret's address as c/o American Cancer Society, 1140 Washington, Warren, which was not where she lived. It also spelled Morey's middle name wrong (as Raymond, not Rayman)—although this was not an unusual mistake and was even on the Websters' marriage certificate.

In Warren, Margaret returned home that evening from New York where she had been attending the Cancer Society's annual meeting. The casualty notification had arrived at the nearest military base, a suburban Naval Reserve training center, at about 1530 in the afternoon. Unable to reach her then, an officer there phoned a

Navy chaplain who lived nearer to Margaret's house and he went straight over rather than going to the base to pick up the official notification. Tired from her travels, Margaret was asleep when the chaplain rang the doorbell. All he did was ask if she wanted someone to be assigned to be with her that evening. Margaret declined, puzzled but no doubt fearing the worst. The chaplain left and she went back to bed but at 0230 was woken again. This time it was a cab driver, holding a Western Union telegram. Presumably the reserve center's duty officer was the only one there at that hour and resorted to sending a taxi with the message. The middle-aged cabbie felt the need to start reading aloud the handwritten message, which announced:

> The U.S. Navy, with profound regret, informs you that your son, LTJG Douglas M. Webster, died in an aircraft accident during operations at sea on 5 Dec 1965. I further regret that your son's body was not able to be recovered. Efforts to recover the pilot or the plane were precluded since it sank in 16,200 feet of water. Since the details of your son's death on duty have been communicated to your son's widow I trust that you will want to hear about them from her.

It concluded with "Your son sacrificed his life for his country. We express our deep regrets. Signed by Vice Admiral B. J. Semmes Jr. Chief of Naval Personnel."

Following this botched casualty notification, Margaret only read the specifics of Doug's death in the next day's newspapers. On December 6, as *Ticonderoga* headed for Yokosuka, The *Warren Tribune-Chronicle* ran the story "Lt. Webster Killed in Plane Spill," saying that Webster; "a popular young Warren Navy lieutenant" had died on a "routine training mission in the Pacific Ocean." The next day, the *Youngstown Vindicator* carried a similar story headlined "Lt. Webster Dies in Mishap Aboard Carrier." The *Vindicator's* main headline that day concerned the deaths of two sailors in the *Kitty Hawk* fire. Both papers wrote: "According to the Navy Department, Webster had just returned to the USS *Ticonderoga* from a routine training flight in his Skyhawk jet fighter when the aircraft slipped from a deck elevator and disappeared in 16,500 feet of water." Already the facts were being muddled, or concealed.

At Lemoore, where VA-56 was based and most of the families lived, a memorial service was held in the base chapel where Doug and Marcia married, conducted by the same pastor who wed them seven months before. Sam Paisley remembered that at the service Marcia had two of her closest friends, wives, holding her up, steadying her.

A week later another memorial service was held in Warren. It was a cool day but warm for December in northern Ohio. A half-inch of rain fell. Marcia flew in from California and Doug's old friend Roger Ailes came down from Chicago where he was now working in TV. Mike Rawl came back from the University of Maryland. The Reverend Arthur M. Sherman, pastor of Christ Episcopal Church where Margaret worshipped took the service, assisted by Reverend Wilbur F. Christy, minister of the first Presbyterian Church of which Doug was a member. Father Sherman told the congregation, beginning with some perhaps unfortunate phrasing: "Doug's life is not at an end—he is gone to a different stage or a different plane." He continued, "As Christians we have hope and we must live in the hope taking advantage of every opportunity of service that is presented to us. One life comes to an end when we're born. Just as this life is so much richer and fuller than prenatal existence, so much richer and full is the life yet to come. Death reminds us of the shortness and uncertainty of life, and since it is so short and uncertain and since we have so little time we must make every moment count."

Doug's belongings, including his diary and helmet, were returned to Marcia.

The letter from Commander Nealon reached Margaret, which explained the circumstances of Doug's death more accurately, but she never received any more information from the Navy itself after the initial telegram.

The White House sent a standard condolence letter. "We believe the danger to freedom has never been so great, and we are all working that his sacrifice will not have been in vain."

Around the same time, Nealon wrote to the "Champs at Home" with a Christmas newsletter. In it he described his pride in the hard work of all his men during the long days and harsh conditions of the Tonkin Gulf. He noted the arrival of 15 new Champions, including Lieutenant Commander Bill Cain and the departure of four others, including Tom Callahan, plus various milestones and promotions.

Only in the fifth paragraph did the letter report with great sorrow the loss of Doug Webster, who was lost at sea when his aircraft went over the side when moving from the hangar deck to the flight deck. "Although relatively new to the squadron, Doug was a proven Champion, having flown some 17 combat missions. Our heartfelt sympathy goes out to his wife and parents."

According to Austin Chapman, Tom Callahan turned in his wings after only a few months in the squadron. Whether this was spurred by Doug's death or other factors is not known. Lou Herzog also quit flying and his next assignment was as a public affairs officer based in South Vietnam, where he witnessed the effects of air strikes at close range.

Doug had been prudent, having taken out four separate life insurance policies. His base pay was 407.40 dollars, plus 125 dollars flight pay and 65 dollars hostile fire pay, for which he was eligible for the months of November and December.

The Packard Electric *Cablegram*, which had once reported Morey and Jean's vacations, now recorded their thanks for messages of support. Marcia left Hanford and moved to Southern California, where she got a job teaching at the University of San Diego.

One day in February 1967, the mailman delivered Doug's Vietnam Service Medal to Marcia to her home in Del Mar. The next day she wrote a letter to President Johnson. "I do not feel that I can accept this medal for myself or in my husband's memory … for it is a mockery of his death and his life; it is a mockery of the country he loved and values both he and I believed in." She went on: "Mr. President, as executive of the United States of America and commander in chief of the armed forces, you owe a greater retribution than this medal signifies. I accuse you with my husband's death, with the death of 21 of his friends—all pilots—and with the bereavement of my friends, young women who now must raise their children themselves and form their own answers to their husbands' deaths." She appealed directly to the president: "I ask that I might be permitted to travel to Vietnam, and as a private citizen not examine the country and some of its people, but learn and perhaps teach what is to be such a people. The danger of our position, I fear, is that we cannot preserve human rights in Vietnam, in our own country, and in the world if we have forgotten what it is to be human. On these grounds alone can I accept my husband's death. The medal is yours, Mr. President. Its emptiness signifies a mockery of all I cherish." She signed the letter, addressed it to the White House and put it in the envelope with the medal.

CHAPTER 8

Enquiry in Yokosuka

Sunday, December 5, 1965, evening
En route Special Operations Area to Yokosuka, Japan

As *Tico* sailed on towards Japan, plans for an enquiry into the accident were being made. A temporary repair was made on the broken guardrail and safety net on No.2 Elevator, but one section of the latter remained missing.

Following Admiral Cousins' verbal order for an informal investigation, two commanders roamed the ship talking to witnesses and getting them to draw sketches of their positions during the accident. Randy Wilson's shop petty officer talked to him about what happened. Once he determined that he wasn't a part of the operation and was just a bystander Wilson was told that he would not need to be interviewed by the investigators. "The next thing I remember was they were talking about how the pilot's wife was in Yokosuka but didn't know where she was in the city." Some of the crew had arranged for their wives and families to join them in Japan as a part of their Christmas vacation. William Smith heard that Webster's wife was coming over for a honeymoon they had not been able to have before sailing.

That night a sailor stabbed himself in the leg while opening boxes. The next day a C-1 arrived from Japan and seven planes were flown off to Atsugi; a fire broke out in an electrical storeroom and was quickly subdued; Airman J. L. Goforth was hit in the eye by a paint flake while chipping paint; and Airman Wallace Lomax cut his nose by colliding with the wing of an aircraft while walking on the flight deck. *Tico* passed a quiet evening with nothing else to report.

Just before sunrise on the 7th *Tico* sailed into Tokyo Bay, took a harbor pilot aboard and maneuvered to moor at Piedmont Pier, Yokosuka beneath one of the giant cranes built to lift battleship turrets for the Imperial Japanese Navy. It was the 24th anniversary of the Pearl Harbor attack.

In bright winter sunshine various divisions manned the rail as *Tico* entered its berth in Truman Bay. Del Mitchell and GM Division were standing aft of the island on the starboard side in their winter dress blues. As the eight mooring lines were thrown across and the carrier berthed, they saw a lone woman in a dark coat and plain-colored dress standing by a taxicab. They wondered what lucky S. O. B she could be waiting for and surmised he must be an officer as no enlisted man could afford to fly his wife or girlfriend out to Japan. When the carrier had been tied up, Mitchell and his friends went back to their division spaces. Randy Wilson later saw more. The gangplanks were lowered and the woman was allowed on board. "When she came up the officers' gangplank there were three or four pilots from the squadron

Ticonderoga tied up at Piedmont Pier, Yokosuka during the 1965–66 cruise. The inquiry was held on board. (Cruisebook)

who pulled her over to the side to tell her what had happened. I can still see her slump and break down." Frank Barrett saw a VA-56 A-4 pilot take her across the flight deck and show her No.2 Elevator and said that later a VA-56 plane captain told him that it was Webster's wife or girlfriend. Del Mitchell adds, "Of course the rumors started flying later that the woman was Doug Webster's wife, but there was no proof she was."

Who the woman at the pierside was remains a mystery. There had been two other fatal casualties by then, Steve Richardson on November 30 and John McCormick—who was unmarried—on December 1. Each family was notified within a day, so it is unlikely, if not impossible, that they would have been en route to Japan or carried on with their travel plans when informed.

Marcia would seem to be the most likely candidate, although the available evidence suggests she was in California and attended a memorial service in Lemoore on December 8. There were fewer than 30 hours between Marcia learning of the accident and *Tico*'s docking in Japan. When sent a college yearbook photo of Marcia, Del Mitchell thought the woman he saw was probably taller than the tiny smiling young woman pictured standing with her friends in front of her snowy Connecticut college three years before. Frank Barrett says the woman he saw was probably taller than average, adding that if she had been short and fat she still would have attracted his notice, not having seen an American woman for some months.

The Honch

Those sailors granted liberty soon fanned out into Yokosuka and beyond. Although Tokyo was not far away by train, many sailors stayed in town and found themselves in the Honcho district, known as "The Honch," a few streets of bars and clubs bordered by open sewer ditches. Sailors would be disciplined for exposing themselves in public, but the locals, male and female, used these ditches openly.

Neon arches bookended Broadway Avenue, also called "Thieves Alley" and "Submarine Alley." Signs on establishments like the Brassrail ("Shitkicker's Bar") enticed sailors with slogans in fractured English like "Welcome U.S. Hero," assuring patrons they had "The best ugly girls and fine music." The Caravan bar had its own variation: "We serve the fleet bad drinks and loud music."

When not drinking, men went shopping in what Ensign John McCabe called "the stereo system capital of the known universe" and bought hi-fi gear to liven up their staterooms. Others bought Christmas presents to send home at the Navy Exchange warehouse. Inside the naval base, the only currency was Military Payment Certificates issued on paydays which had to be exchanged for yen to spend outside, although certain bars and other establishments would accept MPCs or tax-free cigarettes smuggled off base as payment. With few pockets in their uniforms, sailors resorted to stuffing packs in their socks, but at least one fellow was caught leaving *Tico* with a seabag stuffed with cartons of Lucky Strikes.

Del Mitchell says, "Yokosuka was an interesting city, and back then, most sailors never got much further than the Honch. Booze, babes, and brothels were mostly on the minds of sailors in that port, and when you're a young stud duck at 18 to 22 years of age, there is plenty of the aforementioned subject matter to relieve you of your anxieties, loneliness, and frustrations." The Honch was full of "black marketers" who would sell their mothers and daughters for cartons of cigarettes and greenbacks. If a sailor had dollars, he could black market a 20-dollar bill and get 30 dollars for it. The black marketers could double their price.

The day *Tico* pulled in, a 25-man shore patrol left the ship at 1640 and exactly four hours after that the first liberty-related incident was recorded. Fireman apprentice Hitchcock had fallen down a ladder next to the library when returning aboard. Another man, on duty and presumably having had less fun, fell down another ladder while carrying out trash, the can then hitting him on the head. At 0400 VF-53 pilot Jim Hise found a sailor intoxicated at his watch station and sent him to sickbay.

Japan had become the center of "Bond-mania" and December 9 was the world premiere of *Thunderball* in Tokyo at the Hibiya Cinema. One of the most successful of all the James Bond films, the plot revolves around the loss of a nuclear-armed bomber at sea and the theft of its weapons by bad guys. No doubt some *Tico* sailors caught a showing while they were in Japan, but whether they noticed the parallels is unknown.

It was something of a golden era for movies about wayward nuclear weapons. *Fail-Safe* (SAC bomber cannot be recalled from strike on Russia) was released in April 1965, six months after *Dr. Strangelove* (ditto). *The Bedford Incident* (naval confrontation leads to inadvertent ASROC launch) came out in October 1965. The public couldn't get enough of scary stories about atomic bombs in the wrong hands.

The port call was not just for R&R and Christmas shopping. Combat operations had worn out part of *Tico*'s flight deck, and Japanese yard workers beavered away replacing timber sections in the December cold and rain. This opened a hole right down into the staterooms in A Section, and several were vacated for the duration. Roadrunners pilot Bob Maier wasn't so lucky, and he and his roommate shivered in their drafty room. The tarpaulin over the hole didn't stop the weather getting in and there seemed to be no blankets aboard, so they piled everything from their lockers on top of their beds for warmth. When they woke up, their shoes were floating in an inch of icy water.

Inquiry on *Tico*

On December 8, Admiral Cousins opened a formal board of investigation into Webster's accident. Lieutenant Commander Donald Smith was assigned as counsel for the board, although was an aviator and not apparently a trained lawyer. Smith had been on the scene two minutes after the accident and afterwards had directed that another Skyhawk be positioned on the elevator and for sailors to take photos and measurements of its position, the deck markings, the nets and guardrails. For comparison they measured No.3 Elevator as well.

The inquiry began sitting aboard *Ticonderoga* after lunch on the 11th, probably in the captain or admiral's conference room on the 02 Level. The board was presided over by Carrier Division Nine's Chief of Staff, Captain William Hiram "Willy" House, a Texan known to his 1940 Naval Academy classmates as "Wingspan." A wartime Avenger pilot with numerous medals including the Silver Star, House had won the Navy Cross for torpedoing a Japanese battleship at Leyte Gulf. The third board member was Commander William H. Hudson, the operations officer of Carrier Division Nine. Hudson had served with the Naval Weapons Evaluation Facility (NWEF) and later became CO of the nuclear weapons training center in San Diego, so was the only one with significant nuclear weapons experience, although it was not called on in the inquiry. A reservist seaman acted as reporter for the board, transcribing and typing up the proceedings, which formed the basis of the final report, quoted from here.

The board had called 14 witnesses for the first day alone. The first to be sworn was Lieutenant Carl Dila, VA-56's flight surgeon. "Doc" Dila had known Doug only for three or four months and then only slightly. They were not close friends, Dila told the board. Webster had never sought Dila's counsel for anything other than a trivial medical matter and the doctor was sure that he would not have consulted him for any personal problem that might not have had any medical significance. Doug had no physical defects, mental, sociological or psychological problems that would impair his effectiveness as an aviator, Dila said. He had issued a death certificate stating Webster's cause of death as drowning.

Captain Willy Hiram House, Chief of Staff of Carrier Division Nine, chaired the enquiry in Yokosuka. (Cruisebook)

John Paisley was called next in his capacity as squadron maintenance officer. He gave the board a brief history of A-4E 151022. The Skyhawk had accumulated a total of 655.1 flight hours and 715 landings of which 191 were arrested landings. Since the aircraft had been reworked in August it had flown 90.8 hours and made 47 more arrested landings, all but one of the latter since its last pre-cruise scheduled inspection. At the time of the accident there were a few discrepancies on the maintenance "yellow sheet," mainly radio faults, and nothing relating to the brake system. No work had been done on the brakes or landing gear since December 1.

Commander Smith asked Paisley, "Was a preflight inspection performed on this aircraft?"

Paisley replied that since no flight was actually contemplated no pre-flight inspection was required. However, the plane captain and a relief plane captain had been in the cockpit checking the brake system.

"What was the result of their functional check of the brakes?" asked Smith.

"Operable in all respects," Paisley replied.

Paisley described the hydraulic brake system of the A-4E, which was separate from the utility and control hydraulics. It was strong enough to cause a skid on a flight deck elevator and leave visible marks on the surface, he said. Captain House wanted to know if the brakes were independent—if one failed would the other fail also? That depended on where the failure occurred. In other words, if it occurred down at the unit, the other brake would be fine. If it occurred somewhere between the reservoir and the unit then both brakes would become inoperable. Commander Hudson asked if there was an emergency brake or bottle. There was not.

Smith moved on to the escape systems and the pre-requisite steps for ejecting from the A-4E. Paisley explained that three safety pins needed removing and the "headknocker" lever in the headrest raised before the pilot could eject. The canopy could be open or closed, either way it would jettison before the seat fired.

Smith asked Paisley, "What difficulties might be present in ejecting into the water from an inverted position?"

"This is something where there is little known, and I know very little.'

"Assume the canopy was open at the time the A-4E left the outboard edge of No.2 Elevator. What would you expect would happen to the canopy at the time the aircraft landed on its back?"

"I would expect it to come closed as it hit the water. The canopy hit the water first, forcing it closed."

"Assuming we have the canopy in a closed position, what difficulties might be encountered in effecting an escape from the aircraft?"

Paisley explained, "The canopy ... could have been opened manually or could have been opened using the canopy emergency ejection handle." If a pilot had difficulties it could be a pressure differential problem, pressure on the outside being unequal to the pressure on the inside.

Smith probed further into Webster's escape chances. "If the pilot elected to leave the cockpit by his own power rather than ejection, how many attachments would he have to unfasten before he would be free?"

"He can do it one of two ways: he could pull his seat release or his harness release handle and he would have his seat and parachute with him. Or, if he chose to, he could unstrap. He would have to loosen four quick snap release fittings—two on his shoulder and two on his waist."

The next witness was Hangar Bay 2 petty officer Peter House, an experienced airman with four years on *Tico* but presumably unrelated to the grizzled captain sitting across the polished table. The younger man explained to the board how the accident unfolded. Firstly flight deck control called a phone talker on the hangar deck and asked if 472 was ready to be taken topside. "I walked over to the pilot and asked if he would mind getting into the plane because we had to break it down and take the aircraft topside," House testified. He explained that breaking down involved removing and storing all but three of the tiedown chains, letting off the brakes and pointing the aircraft in the direction of the intended move. "So the pilot gets into the aircraft and the plane captain went up with him and started strapping him in. He was only up there five or ten minutes. The elevator was brought down and we commenced to move the aircraft out and onto No.2 Elevator."

"Would you describe the actual movement of the aircraft as you witnessed it?" asked Smith.

House replied, "Well, from what I seen—I was right next to the pilot on the deck—it seems to me at the time as we were pushing the aircraft onto the elevator it appeared to me that he was looking at something between his legs or in the cockpit—his instruments or something, I don't know. But the way I feel, he did not pay attention to the director at all."

An A-4C was positioned where Webster's A-4E should have stopped on the elevator. This Skyhawk was sold to the Argentine Air Force and crashed in 1976. (Judge Advocate General's Office)

Smith asked House what signals and procedures were used in moving aircraft to the elevator. "Either we use whistles or hand signals, sometimes both. In this instance the hand signal was given first to slow the aircraft down, but when the aircraft did not slow down, the whistle was sounded."

"Was the whistle sounded loudly enough?"

"Yes Sir."

"Did more than one person blow the whistle?"

"Yes Sir."

Petty officer House was shown the photographs of the A-4 on the elevator and confirmed it was positioned where 472 should have stopped, a location that gave about six inches clearance between the wingtip and deck edge. He described how, from his position he saw the nosewheel reach the yellow line as the A-4 moved backwards, heard the whistles blow and the chocks hit the deck. "I looked and seen the port chock come back out. By this time the port wheel was almost into the net."

"What happens when a chock is thrown out after being placed in position?" asked Smith. House's reply was indirect but illuminating. "The chocks usually have non-skid on both surfaces. Most of the chocks we have now, the non-skid is worn off. Sometimes with a little oil or grease or anything of that nature the chocks have a tendency to skid. When this happens they'll slide right out. It's happened many times before."

"Why had the chock come out?"

"Everything happened so fast that I have no idea."

Now Captain House asked his namesake to give a chronological story of what he saw and heard from the time the aircraft started to move until it went over the side, as best he could. Petty officer House began, occasionally pointing to the photographs.

"The aircraft was spotted right underneath Hangar Control on the port side, aft of No.2 Elevator. The aircraft was moved out onto No.2 Elevator. We have a small ramp that goes from the hangar deck onto the elevator. Well, sometimes if we don't have enough momentum the aircraft will not make it up the little ramp the first try. So, it took two tries before going up the ramp. The director was on the forward part of the aircraft, moving the aircraft onto the elevator. At this particular time I was standing right in here," House said, pointing at the sketch of the accident scene.

"The aircraft started moving aft on the elevator. I started walking into the elevator where the cables are for the elevator." House paused and indicated another spot on the diagram. "One thing I left out, there was a bomb cart set out here. As the plane was moved on the elevator the director blew his whistle. This is the first time I noticed the pilot was not paying any attention. The bomb cart was in the way of one of the drop tanks—in this case the port drop tank. The director blew the whistle one time and the plane did not slow down. He clenched his fist, which is the stop sign. At that time the bomb cart was already moved out of the way. The director took him off the brakes and the aircraft continued rolling aft."

"Like I said before, the nose wheel was right in here where it is usually spotted, two feet across the stripe. The nose wheel was at that point. The yellowshirt and the director blew the whistle. The aircraft did not stop. At the sound of the whistle the blueshirts knew the chocks must go in. The whistle sounded but he did not stop. The chocks went in. From what I seen over here the port chock came back out. This one here, the wheel rolled over. If the chocks have too much room the wheel has a tendency to run over or just drag the chock along. That is why this chock was thrown out. [The chockman] tried to kick it back in but it was too late and he rolled out of the way. The port wheel rolled into the safety net and broke it. The reason for this is the starboard chock held longer than this one, turning it on an angle and going into the net. At that particular moment, while it was sitting in the net, I think the pilot realized for the first time what was going on. I saw him look up touching the edge of the cockpit. It seemed to be held in midair, then the safety net broke and it rolled over on its top into the water. As it landed into the water I ran over to the age of the elevator. The assistant flight deck officer passed the word to me from topside to bring the elevator up. I cleared the elevator and took the elevator topside. The elevator has to be raised when the ship goes into a turn. Well the elevator was taken topside I was standing on the very edge watching the aircraft go by and float maybe 100 to 150 yards away or maybe less. And I watched all this time and at no time at all did I see the pilot or him trying to get out."

Smith asked House to comment on the deck condition at the time of the accident.

"Well it appeared to me that it was normal, as a ship has a tendency to roll port to starboard but overall it was like a regular move—no difficulties."

'Would you say the deck was wet or slippery?"

"No Sir, not on the elevator."

Smith asked House about the training of the crew involved. "The way I feel, this is a real good crew as far as following orders particularly when there is an aircraft, a life and a lot of money involved in the movement of aircraft. Like the understanding when the whistle sounds that means chocks automatically go in whether the brakes are applied or not. This is a standard rule of the hangar and as far as I can remember it always has been this way. This is a safety precaution."

Commander Hudson wanted to know where the pilot was looking when the aircraft movement began. House said he was looking inside his cockpit at something.

"Could you tell what he was doing?" Hudson asked.

"No Sir. Not from where I was standing. He was up there. We have no idea what's going on inside the aircraft."

Hudson persisted. "After the aircraft went over the hump and started on the elevator, what was the pilot doing?"

"He was still looking inside his cockpit."

"As the nosewheel of the aircraft approached the yellow line what was the pilot doing?"

"He was still looking inside his cockpit."

"At the point of where the port wheel went into the net what was the pilot doing?"

"All of a sudden he looked up like he was startled, his hands gripping the sides of the cockpit as the aircraft went over and commenced falling."

Although the board had finished questioning him, House wanted to make a statement: "I've never heard of both brakes going out at the same time on an A-4. On an F-8 sometimes during the process of sitting still it loses brakes and while the pilot is off the brakes and doesn't know and you tell him to slow down or blow the whistle and the plane does not stop instantly. That is why the chocks are thrown in and this way we save many planes—because of the alertness of the chockmen. If the chocks are thrown in at the same time the aircraft will stop. If a chock is thrown in on one side then the other the aircraft will jerk either way and if the chock is thrown fast on the port side the starboard will jerk. In this particular case, plane 472, we threw them in there and you can easily tell by the sound of the chocks if they both hit at the same time or one before the other. And it seemed to me the chock that was on the after part hit a split second before—*thump, thump* like that—and this is why the aircraft turned to the side and the port wheel went in first instead of both of them going in at the same time."

Elevator operator Joseph Bocklett was the next witness called. He was looking the other way when the aircraft was going over the hump. "I heard the director yell for the pilot to slow it down. I turned back towards the aircraft as it was moving on the elevator very fast. He blew the whistle. I looked down at the chockman. I didn't know who it was at that time, but I found out later it was a friend of mine. He threw the chock in but it came back out. The aircraft kicked the chock out. He tried to put it in again and it came back out of the second time. He was never able to put it in a third time." Bocklett saw the chockman knocked down by the tow bar and get up again.

Airman D. Hall followed Bocklett to the witness chair. A Hangar Bay 2 safety director, Hall was acting as a wing watcher on the A-4's port wing on the day. He expected the aircraft to stop on the yellow line. "As the nosegear passed the center line I started blowing my whistle—blew it hard—and still nothing happened. Each of the men tried to get his chock in. The plane twisted and the port chock came back out. He tried it again—no good! So I told him to get out of the way before one of them got hurt themselves."

Smith asked Hall how many attempts were required to get the aircraft onto the elevator.

"There were two attempts," Hall answered, before correcting himself. "The last was not an attempt. It was half on and all we had to do was lean on it a little more. It rolled back and then went over."

Airman apprentice C. D. Sherman had been assigned to the starboard main wheel carrying an adjustable metal chock. Commander Hudson wanted to know the state of this device.

"The chock you were using, did it have non-skid?"

"On most of the chocks it is all worn off."

Hudson repeated his question. "The chock you were using, did it have non-skid on it?"

"I don't think so, Sir."

"You said you put the chock around the wheel and it held. What did the wheel do?"

"The wheel went over it. There is so much clearance, so the wheel rolled over it."

"Your feeling is that when your chock held the aircraft turned?"

"Yes Sir. The chock only slowed down the aircraft, it did not stop it, but changed its direction slightly."

"Drew" Chevalier, the weapons officer, told the board he was watching the Skyhawk throughout the move. At first he was looking at the pilot, trying to identify him and wondering if it was someone he knew. Then he turned his attention to the moving crew. He had not observed any moves onto the elevator earlier so he had no basis for comparison, but they appeared to not be having any unusual difficulties or show any sign of distress.

"Where was the pilot's attention directed?" Smith asked.

"At the time the plane was rolled onto the elevator he appeared to have his helmet in his hands like he was getting the microphone cord straightened out in preparation for putting it on. He did have it out in his hands at the time the main mounts crossed onto the elevator."

Hudson wanted to know how fast the A-4 appeared to be moving from Chevalier's viewpoint.

"Well," Chevalier answered, "It was a smart movement. It didn't look alarming until the director blew the whistle and he ceased to slow down. The speed continued almost without any deceleration at all until at the last moment the chockmen seemed to be working around the wheels trying to get the chocks under it to stop it. It appeared they slowed down the starboard main mount and got a chock under it and then the port main mount started rotating to the left counterclockwise and the port main mount didn't slow down and finally rolled over the deck edge and into the safety net. That was the only big change in speed."

Captain House asked if the ship's roll or pitch was significant at the time of the incident.

"No, Captain," Chevalier replied. "I had noticed the sea state, and standing in Hangar Bay 2 looking across, I noticed it had a slight port list. It was steady and not moving at all. The sea state was calm and the ship did not make any turns. Compared to some times when we have operated, I would say it was quite steady."

After lunch the board called Airman apprentice Gene Ott, the port wing chockman. He described his job as to get the chock in as fast as he could when the whistle blew. On this occasion he said, "The second time the director blew the whistle I put it in. It was going too fast to stop it and kicked it back out. I grabbed hold of it again and put it back in but just couldn't quite get it." Ott then heard the crack of the wheel as it hit the guard rail and scrambled out of the way. As he stood up the tow bar hit him in the back of the hip, tearing his dungarees, knocking him down and leaving a bruise.

The aluminum chock Ott was using had been extended slightly wider than the wheel to make it easier to place. He didn't think it had any nonskid on it. Hudson asked if the chock was put in properly. "Yes Sir, it was just too much speed on the plane."

"Is there some possibility that the starboard chockman could have put his chock in and caused the plane to pivot before you placed your chock into position?"

'Yes Sir."

Hudson then changed tack. "How long have you been in your position as a chockman?" The recorded response was rather surprising.

"The plane talker and I switch off sometimes," said Ott.

Hudson seemed to ignore this *non sequitur*, which seems like a serious admission of inattention, and carried on pressing Ott about his qualifications.

"Are you experienced in this procedure?"

"Yes Sir."

"You had no doubt what your responsibility was in the movement of the aircraft?"

"No Sir."

Captain House stepped in. "Approximately how long after you heard the whistle blow—could you estimate how long it took you to put the chock in?"

"It was only a matter of seconds before it was around the wheel."

"Was the chock in position in your hand to go around the wheel, or did you have to move it around your body before you could apply it to the plane?"

"I had the chock in my hand ready to slide it in."

"You were expecting the whistle signal?"

"Yes Sir."

Airman apprentice Larry Dasovic helped push the Skyhawk while also acting as nosewheel tie down man. Commander Smith asked him to remember what the condition of the elevator surface was that day. "Was it slick, oily, or wet?"

"I don't know what the elevator was but I do remember that morning they were using fuel by the gas station and there was fuel on the deck mixed with water. This was on the hangar deck where the plane was sitting in the area. Aviation fuel was on the deck," Dasovic explained.

Hudson asked, "Was this JP-5 [jet fuel] or lube oil or what kind of fuel and what quantity of it?"

"Just before the flight (*sic*) I remember them changing nozzles or something and one of the hoses spilled some JP-5 out—maybe a half gallon or more—onto the deck and there was some water on the deck with spray from the waves that came into the hangar bay that morning and it was in the vicinity of where the aircraft was parked."

"Were men engaged in cleaning up this fuel?"

"I don't remember, Sir. I don't remember seeing anyone out cleaning it up."

"Did you observe the aircraft as it continued over the side of the elevator?"

"As I saw it, after the first whistle had blown I tried to put the tie down on it but the aircraft was moving and I missed. I tried again but missed. I didn't try to put it on again. There was nothing I could do to stop it. The chocks didn't stop it. It seemed to have too much weight. The port wheel was the first to go over. I remember seeing the port tank either bend or break—I don't remember which. It broke the stanchion, then it went up in the air, hesitated and went into the water on its back."

"You mentioned that you stopped pushing and started putting on the tie down. What part of the tie downs were you referring to?"

"The chain part that attaches to the deck. I went for the nose strut once and missed. That is when I realized that the plane was going backwards. Usually when the whistle blows this is where I put the chain in and hook it up and get off the elevator fast. But when I put the chain in and hooked it up and tried to put the tie down on, I went for it again and missed. That was when I heard someone yell 'Hey, don't you have any brakes?' Then the director said to 'Slow down, Sir'—and the plane kept going over the side."

"You said you looked at the pilot's eyes at that point, where was the pilot looking?"

"Looking at something—not something specific—just kept on moving from side to side like this. His eyes were moving fast in a pattern back and forth."

House pressed the question. "And what was he looking at—at that particular moment?"

"I don't think it was anything particular just a movement of the eyes. It might have been something in the cockpit or outside the plane, but there was no movement of his head. He could have been reading something or looking at something or that sort of thing. He could've been looking down at the plane director, but he didn't hear him. His mind was blank. His eyes wandered too fast back and forth to be looking at anything specific."

"Did you say the plane director told him to slow the plane down?"

"Yes, I believe his exact words were, 'Slow the plane down, Sir. Slow the plane down, Sir.'"

The next up was Airman R. Martinez. He and Airman Hall were safety watchers on the port wing. Martinez recalled there was a bomb truck, a wheelbarrow-like cart that could carry a single bomb parked on the elevator where the plane was going. Howard ran out and moved it. The plane director or the safetyman on the other wing blew his whistle for brakes before the A-4 even reached the elevator but, "All of a sudden I looked up at the pilot and he didn't seem to be paying any attention to the director I guess he was looking at something in the cockpit because he was looking down—but he was not looking at the director," said Martinez. The A-4 kept moving. "Well I blew my whistle and the other director with me [Hall] blew his—and the plane didn't stop. The chockmen threw their chocks in and the port chock came back out and the man tried to put the chock back in. But it was too late—because of the guard rail." Martinez saw Ott being struck. "As the nosewheel was going up the towbar swung around the port side and hit him in the hip. I looked up at the pilot and he was surprised. He looked like he didn't know what was going on."

Smith asked Martinez, "Can you describe the condition of the deck on the elevator and hangar deck?"

"The conditions were better than usual, I'd say. When we have been operating, the deck has been wet and the ship would be in a big roll—port to starboard list."

"On this occasion how would you describe it? Would you say the deck was dry?"

"Yes Sir."

"Was there any trace of oil?"

"No Sir, none at all."

Martinez said that he first looked at the pilot just before the move and at that time he was watching the plane director. The next time he saw him was just before the aircraft went over the side. Hudson asked if it was normal for a pilot to be looking down into the cockpit while his aircraft was being moved (although the airman clearly hadn't seen this) and Martinez said it was not. After a couple of the by-now-routine questions from Hudson about the aircraft speed, hand signals and whistles, Captain House came in with a new angle. "You mentioned that you were talking to someone during the movement of the aircraft onto the elevator?"

"Yes Sir."

"With whom were you talking?"

"To the safety director, Hall."

"What was his job during the movement?"

"His was the same as mine. We were both on the port wing"

"Were you watching the stern more so than the port wing?"

"Well, he was watching the port wing."

"Were you paying attention to what you were doing during this movement or were you interested in your conversation?"

"I was paying attention to the movement."

House then moved to where the pilot's attention lay. "Did he give any signal to indicate he didn't have any brakes?"

"No Sir."

"Did he say anything, as best you could tell?"

"Nothing at all."

"Did you have a good view of him at that time?"

"Being on the port wing, yes Sir. As a wing walker you are in a good position to watch the nose, tail section and the port side of the aircraft."

The questioning ended, but Martinez wanted to make a statement. He said, "A lot of times as we move the planes from the hangar bay to the elevator pilots tend to pay attention to someone else instead of the director."

'To whom else?' House asked.

"To the fuel crew, the plane captain, or anyone but the director. In the movement of aircraft, we are responsible if the bird gets crunched—nobody else, just us. Especially on No.1 Elevator, they tend to pay attention to everyone else," Martinez said with obvious frustration.

On the elevator with the bomb truck, Airman W. Howard had a unique view of the accident. Captain House asked Howard to estimate the speed of the aircraft.

"I would say fast—extremely fast."

"What do you contribute the speed to? Was there a great many men pushing it?"

"Yes Sir."

"How many?"

"I couldn't say how many, Sir, but there were a heck of a lot of people pushing the aircraft and when the aircraft went into the water, it was packed with people."

"Did you hear whistle signals given by the directors or safetymen or anyone else?"

'The only time I heard a whistle blown myself was when the airplane was about five feet from the guard rail."

"Were you paying particular attention to the signals?"

"No I wasn't, Sir."

Howard last saw the A-4 floating belly-up before a yellowshirt chased everybody off the elevator.

VA-56 plane captain Richard Edmister related how he had moved A-4E 472 across the hangar bay at approximately 1200 hours, and that he checked the brakes when he entered the cockpit and that they worked "in normal fashion."

Smith asked, "Was there any work done on the brakes before the accident?"

"A screw on the bottom of the brakes needed tightening. That was done a couple of days before the accident. It hadn't required further repair since then."

Smith asked Edmister what preflight action was carried out on the aircraft prior to the movement to the flight deck.

"A complete preflight briefing, and the brake reservoir was checked—the pilot's inspection," he answered. This contradicts Paisley's testimony that there was no preflight inspection because flight was not intended this day.

"Did he check the reservoir?"

"No Sir."

"At what time did you check the brake reservoir?"

"About 1000 hours."

"Will you indicate to the board how positive you are of the position of the following items prior to movement of the aircraft onto the elevator: the landing gear handle."

"It was up."

'It was up?" Smith queried.

"No, it was down."

"How positive of this are you?"

"I'm positive it was down. This is really not an item on the preflight check-off."

That confusion over, Edmister confirmed the canopy was open, the actuation handle was in the unlocked position and the ejection seat safety pins were out. He was the first non-officer witness who knew the pilot. Smith asked to what extent Webster prepared himself in the cockpit.

"When he got into the cockpit I pulled the pins and put his starboard shoulder strap on. He already had his leg straps on and told me he would get the rest, then I gave him the helmet." This was inside its carrying bag. "He was fixing his port shoulder strap when I got off the ladder." Edmister took the ladder away and watched the move. As the aircraft began backing onto the elevator, he looked at Doug.

"Could you tell where the interest of the pilot seemed to be located?" asked Smith.

"He was looking out the starboard windscreen and across the hangar deck—maybe at another pilot." The plane director was on the port side.

Edmister saw the bomb truck on the elevator and heard the director's whistle blow, but there was no slowing down or braking action. The A-4 pivoted and went over the edge. The last he saw of Webster was when he looked up and appeared "startled." Before the A-4 reached the elevator Edmister said he may have looked "concerned but not excited."

Hudson asked, "Did the pilot appear to be looking at any other handling crew besides the director?"

"No Sir, he was not."

"Did he appear to be looking at the plane director?"

"No Sir, he did not."

"Was there anything else going on at the time that might avert his attentions?"

'I don't remember, Sir. He might have been watching another pilot or a member of the loading crew." This was the only unredacted reference to a loading exercise in the public version of the report.

Hudson pursued the line that the aircraft handlers were distracted. "Did you observe any of the chockmen?"

"No, I did not."

"Was there any skylarking around the aircraft during this movement?"

"None that I saw, Sir."

"Did you see the pilot do anything to try to escape?"

"No I did not, Sir."

"There was no effort on his part to get rid of his shoulder straps or otherwise disengage himself from the cockpit?"

"No Sir, I didn't see him."

"At that time did he have his helmet on?"

"No."

"Did he try to stand up in the aircraft?"

"No."

"Could you see his hands?"

"Last I saw of his hands they were gripping the side of the aircraft."

"In your opinion was the pilot conscious at the time he went over the side?"

"Yes Sir."

"Was he looking around when it went off?"

"I cannot say."

"Did he make any efforts to grab hold or brace himself or anything of that sort?"

"As the wheel tumbled into the safety netting I could see him gripping the sides of the aircraft with his hands."

"When you strapped the pilot into the cockpit did he seem overly concerned with anything?"

The lost Skyhawk was quietly replaced by another 472. The new aircraft had subtle paint differences and lacked the 'shoehorn' ECM antennas of the original. (John Paisley via Bill Paisley)

"No Sir."

"Did he appear to be normal?"

"Yes Sir he was acting normal."

The board adjourned at 1455.

With Christmas approaching there were a number of parties ashore. Captain Miller joined OI Division for a drink at theirs on the 10th. A sailor managed to lose a wallet ashore, which contained several hundred dollars as well as his ID and liberty card. A couple of hours after the man had returned aboard with this sorry tale, a taxi pulled up on the pier and a young boy and his mother got out. They came up the enlisted men's gangway and the boy handed the wallet to the chief. He in turn had the officer of the deck call the forlorn sailor to and he was reunited with the wallet. In reward all that the boy wanted was to sit in an airplane cockpit and duly he got his wish, sitting in an A-4 and getting his photo in the ship's newsletter.

At Atsugi airfield a shiny new A-4 was assigned to the Champions to replace the one lost. Bureau Number 151079 took over the number 472 and for all intents and purposes was identical to the lost Skyhawk. There were subtle differences—the clean new jet had a black anti-glare panel ahead of the windscreen but lacked the black tip to the nose of 151022. It also lacked the Shoehorn antennas.

On the 13th the investigation board reconvened at 0902. VA-56 Operations Officer, Render Crayton, was first to testify. Crayton had known Doug Webster since approximately the middle of September when he reported to VA-56 from training. At that time he had approximately 470 flight hours—170 in the A-4 aircraft at the time of the accident. Webster was a qualified pilot with no hearing loss or psychological problems as far as Crayton was aware and he never showed any unusual lapses in paying attention.

Commander Smith asked if Crayton was aware of any unusual happenings with regard to the movement of the aircraft on the day.

"No Sir, to the best of my knowledge it was a [redacted] exercise and up until the time of the accident everything was normal in every way." The single redacted word was almost certainly "loading." Crayton explained that the exercise was to take an aircraft to the flight deck to simulate a launch and required a pilot in the cockpit.

Smith wanted to know where a pilot would put his helmet during this evolution.

"In this type of aircraft when it is on the hangar deck, the most likely place is normally up on the canopy bow," Crayton answered. "When the aircraft is on the elevator and the elevator starts going up we normally put our hard hats on."

Smith wondered where it might have been placed so that Webster would have had it ready to put on. "You said most people put it on the canopy bow. Don't some place it on the stick in the cockpit or on their lap, so to speak? If it was placed on the canopy bow it would have been clearly visible to the people who are observing the exercise," he posited.

"Sir, if it was in the cockpit it would not be visible," Crayton answered.

Returning to the subject of escape, Smith got Crayton to explain the ejection system and the necessity of removing the seat pins. Once the pins were out, all a pilot would need to do is pull the face curtain or alternate ejection lever. Oxygen and radio connections would disconnect automatically.

"What special difficulties might be present in effecting an ejection in the water from an inverted position?" Smith asked.

"To my knowledge there are no special precautions that have to be taken in ejecting underwater. Everything seems to work the same underwater as it does in the air. In either case it would be necessary to get rid of the canopy first."

"Assuming the canopy was open, what would you expect to happen to the canopy as the aircraft landed in the water on its back?"

"I'd expect the canopy to close immediately."

"In regards to previous questions about his helmet, if his helmet had fallen on to the floorboards of the cockpit could he have had use of the brakes?"

"It would be very difficult for the hard hat to fall to the floor of the cockpit," Crayton said. "There is not that much room in the cockpit. He may have had it on the stick. To my knowledge, I don't believe it can get between the stick and the instrument panel. I'm positive that if there were any braking action that he might have wanted to take, the helmet would not have interfered. However, if the helmet had fallen off the stick—if that's where he had it—he could have reached down to retrieve it and could have been distracted."

Captain House wanted to know if there was difficulty in adjusting the brake pedals when a tall pilot or a plane captain leaves the airplane and a short pilot takes over control of the aircraft. Crayton explained, "The brakes in an A-4 are certainly not the easiest to adjust and since we have these new soles on our flying boots – the nonslip soles—it's awfully difficult to push the lever with your foot without having the soles hang up on the lever. It has been my experience that it has been a lot more difficult to adjust these pedals with the new soles. However I don't think the problem comes in moving the pedals to adjust them. I don't believe the rudder pedals in the fully extended position are that far away from the seat in an A-4 aircraft."

"In other words no matter what position the rudder pedals were in, Lieutenant Webster could have reached to them with his feet to activate the brakes?" House asked.

"This is my opinion. I think it is much easier for a short person to reach the brakes that it is for a tall person, due to the position of the brakes under the instrument panel. From what I can gather from talking with other pilots in the ready room, the biggest problem for tall personnel in reaching the brakes in an A-4 is that when the seat is up, you can't get your legs up under the instrument panel to reach the top of the brakes. However I don't feel a short person would have this problem at all."

The next testimony was from plane director C. L. Lindsey. He had been doing that job on *Tico* for 21 months. On December 5, his position was about ten feet in front of the nosewheel of the aircraft on the port side. From that position he could see above, under and on both sides of the plane. Raising a hand and making a fist, he signaled for the pilot to hold the brakes while the tie down men broke it down by removing the chains and the chock men moved the chocks. As the A-4 went backwards towards the elevator, Lindsey saw the bomb truck and signaled to keep it slow. The plane pushers rolled the A-4 up the ramp but it rolled back. He shouted for someone to move the bomb truck and Airman Howard pulled it away to the right onto the forward half of the elevator. Lindsey gave the "off the brakes" signal and the pushers pushed again. When the nosewheel reached the yellow line he blew his whistle but it just kept moving. The wing walkers blew their whistles but it kept moving. The chockmen threw their chocks in, but the port chock came back out. The chockman tried to put it back in but didn't have time. It just went over.

"Do you believe the pilot had taken any braking action on the aircraft when it started rolling back into the hangar bay?" Smith asked Lindsey.

"I don't know—I wouldn't say so. The aircraft looked pretty heavy, it was fuelled up and everything, I couldn't say."

Lindsey said the pilot was watching him as the aircraft was pushed forward from its spot, but after that he didn't know as he was concentrating on the tail and wings, the hump, the cart and the yellow line.

Hudson asked, "Did you experience any abnormal problems in getting this aircraft over the hump?"

"No Sir. When it rolled onto the ramp it rolled back. They usually do that when we don't have enough power to push it over. It went over the second time. Sometimes we have to push them three or four times."

Lindsey couldn't recall observing the pilot trying to use his brakes, but "if he had brakes and hit them, it would stop right away." Hudson asked if he would know when they were applied on the A-4.

"Yes Sir" he replied. "Because they must stop. If you apply the brakes you stop."

Hudson repeated a question he had asked Edmister. "Was there any skylarking in your crew during this movement?"

"No Sir. We never skylark when moving an aircraft—too heavy."

The board adjourned at 1021 to reconvene in two days time.

On the 13th there were several changes of command. Lynn W. Adams relieved Earl Godfrey as *Tico's* XO, Jack Snyder took over from Mac Snowden as CAG 5 and John C. Mape became the new skipper of VA-52. Admiral Hartman, commander of naval aviation in WestPac, came aboard to meet with Captain Miller.

The next day *Tico* hosted over 30 guests, including members of the Japan Private Pilot's Association. The ship had a blood drive for troops wounded in Vietnam. First in line to donate to the Army mobile blood bank were Captain Miller and his new XO, who lined up on the hangar deck with the sailors. The total of 1,187 pints of blood donated was reported to be the most collected from any military installation in the Western Pacific area at one time. The blood was flown to Vietnam for immediate use.

Playing basketball in the fleet gym, Marine Lance Corporal James Grattan suffered an eye injury from another player's finger. "Moose" Grattan weighed 200 pounds and won a "battle royale" heavyweight boxing match against four others the following month, so whoever poked him in the eye was a brave man. Another sailor cut his chin roller-skating.

On the 15th, the board resumed with testimony from Hangar Deck Officer Lieutenant Samuel N. Hallmark. Hallmark was a naval flight officer from Lubbock, Texas and on *Tico's* aircraft accident board. He outlined the background of the han-dling crew. One of the supervisors had two months experience. Two other safetymen had six months experience. The other safetyman had over three years' experience on this ship and the remaining safetyman came here from another command but had been an aircraft director and safetyman for over six months. "The plane pushers and blueshirts have had as much training as we can give them," Hallmark added.

Looking at the photos of the elevator, Hallmark noted the broken safety net and guardrail. He said the latter is used to stop a very slow-moving aircraft, but apparently is not strong enough to stop any large force. The safety net was not designed to catch aircraft, only people. He estimated the A-4E weighed about 20,000 pounds.

Hudson asked whether Hallmark was satisfied with the design of the guardrail along the deck edge elevator.

"That depends on the purpose. It has been a sacrifice here. I think we would need something that would actually stop a plane. I think this was a compromise." The elevator "wasn't wet" and nonskid was applied, so normal braking conditions were present as far as the elevator was concerned, Hallmark said. The brakes were the primary means of stopping the aircraft and the chocks were used for an emergency. "I don't think I would move a plane on the elevator if I had only chocks," he said.

Tico's new XO Commander Lynn W. Adams was a former A-3 pilot from Gassville, Arkansas and was the navigator on December 5. He described the search by *Tico* and the escort ships for Webster. "I considered the actions taken by the *Ticonderoga* and accompanying destroyers were prompt—that if he had gotten out he would have been spotted, and would had been picked up."

The board was coming to the end of examining witnesses. It next heard from Claude W. Clower, the Meteorology Officer, who presented the weather and sea conditions. Clower said the two-to-five-second swell at three feet would be likely irrelevant. He said it would take about nine to fourteen seconds to make a pitch or a roll that was out of the normal range. He didn't see the elevator deck surface to judge its dryness or otherwise, but remembered that in the morning the sea had been coming over the bow. Next, Assistant CIC Officer Worley Y. Creech gave a very detailed description of the carrier's movements after the man overboard signal.

Finally the board's own counsel, Commander Smith, was duly sworn and gave his own statement. He had examined the hangar deck and elevator and taken measurements of the guardrail and ramp. He described his findings to the board in some detail, but only a couple of points stood out. There were no skid marks on the elevator to indicate the application of the A-4's brakes. The height difference between the hangar and elevator bridged by the ramp was only two inches. The guardrail, made of four-inch angle iron, stood six-and-a-half inches above the deck when raised and had a support brace every two-and-a-half feet. For comparison, he presented measurements of the rail on No.3 Elevator, which was fixed, rather than moveable as that on No.2 Elevator had to be to allow its use as the extension of the angled deck. The dimensions he gave for the height of the No.3 Elevator rail (six inches) and its construction (two-inch iron), with braces every three feet were all less than that for No.2 Elevator, but he told the board, "In my opinion being permanently fixed and heavier material, the guardrail on number three elevator would stop a moving aircraft if were not going so fast that it would ride over the guardrail."

Smith had arrived on the elevator two minutes after the accident, presumably at flight deck level when it was raised. He told the board it was dry with no gasoline or seawater from spray on it. Hudson asked if the nonskid on the chocks was in good repair. Lindsey the plane director had shown him the chocks used and Smith described them as "the normal type chocks, made of aluminum, the size of which

CHIEF, WOULD YOU BE MAD IF I TOLD YOU I DROPPED SOMETHING AND BROKE IT?

A cartoon from USS *Midway*'s 1960 cruisebook makes fun of the consequences of damaging a weapon. It was printed in the W Division pages. (*Midway* cruisebook)

are adjustable and to which nonskid had been applied. They were in satisfactory condition."

The board closed at 1100 and began to work on its report. That afternoon *Tico* weighed anchor and headed back to Vietnam.

CHAPTER 9

Day Tripper

So why was a U.S. Navy fighter-bomber loaded with a one-megaton thermonuclear weapon in the waters between Vietnam and Japan? The answer is tied in with America's Cold War plans, but is not totally unrelated to the war in Vietnam.

In a response to an FOIA request by the author, the National Nuclear Security Administration (NNSA) released an account of *Tico*'s Broken Arrow that contained the following explanation:

"During the 1960s, the U.S. Navy was assigned a role in the Single Integrated Operational Plan (SIOP), which was the plan under which the United States would conduct nuclear warfare if required. In this plan each carrier/air wing that deployed was assigned specific targets to strike from the National Strategic Target List (NSTL). The plan was very complicated and required precise arrival times at the target and that aircraft be launched in a pre-set sequence."

"In order to stay proficient, regular exercises were required. These training exercises were designated 'TraEx Alpha' and 'TraEx Bravo.' The Alpha exercises involved loading weapons on the aircraft and an actual launch of the loaded aircraft at a Naval Air Station ashore. The Bravo exercises were conducted while the carrier was underway. The weapons were loaded aboard the aircraft and the aircraft moved into position for a simulated launch. The weapons were then returned to the storage magazine. It was during a TraEx Bravo that the accident occurred."

According to Frank Barrett, who was waiting on the flight deck to supervise the movement of aircraft to the catapult, in total there were a dozen aircraft ready to be loaded and "launched" that day. Bill Nealon's letter to Margaret Webster said there were eight pilots assigned, not specifying how many were from VA-56.

Austin Chapman recalled: "In those days the primary mission was SIOP, and to maintain readiness. Timing was a critical issue in how fast you could get the airplanes launched. We all had alert duties that we had to maintain and [loading] speed was an important factor in getting an airplane off the deck. So loading exercises concentrated on certifying teams for doing it, first of all, and to maintain that capability as people left and came into the squadron, and maintain the ability to load the airplane and

A B43 is loaded on an A-4C of VA-146 in 1967 at NAS North Island, San Diego during a WEPTRAEX Alpha exercise, where live weapons would be loaded on aircraft ashore and then flown to another airfield. (SDASM)

launch in a certain amount of time. It took a lot of practice. Most of the loading drills were to hone those skills or reinforce those skills for loading, so the checklist and all the procedures were met as quickly as you could expect to meet them. [Readiness] depended on the location of the ship. If you were further away from the position than you should have been, you'd take different measures. You might be loaded, hooked up, sitting on the catapult with the canopy open and you could sit there and read or whatever. In those cases we manned the ready aircraft and after so many hours the pilot was exchanged for another. If timing allowed, the plane might be positioned behind the catapult or off to one side of the catapult, then you had time to start it up, pull it out on the cat and launch it. It was all designed to meet time constraints."

Through the 1950s the war plans of the different U.S. commands were uncoordinated, making it certain that many strikes would duplicate and interfere with each other. The SIOP came about after President Eisenhower established the Joint Strategic Target Planning Staff in 1960. It was an effort to coordinate the plans of the different unified and specified commands. The former were multi-service outfits like Pacific Command and European Command, and the latter single-service commands including the Air Force's Strategic Air Command (SAC) and the Navy's Naval Forces Eastern Atlantic and Mediterranean.

Photos of Navy nuclear weapons are not numerous, but this 1959 image shows a Mk 7 bomb being loaded on an A4D-2 (A-4B) of VA-34 on the flight deck of USS *Saratoga*. (U.S. Navy via Gary Verver)

The Plan

In the early years of nuclear weapons at sea in the Pacific, the Navy's plan for General (meaning nuclear) war was the General Emergency Operation Plan, the last of which was GEOP 1–58. The first iteration of the new joint plan was SIOP-62, which took effect from April 1, 1961 and involved about 3,500 weapons (by 1972–73 it was about 8,000). The Commander-in-Chief, Pacific (CINCPAC)'s part was CINCPAC Operation Plan 1–61. The plans were subject to periodic revision, particularly as more was learned about potential targets in the USSR and China from satellite reconnaissance. The overall plan in play in December 1965 was SIOP-64 Revision 7, which lasted from November 10 to March 31 the following year.

CINCPAC No. 1–61 described the objectives of SIOP operations as:

> 1. Objectives. Specific objectives of the National Strategic Targeting and Attack Policy are:
>   a. Destroy or neutralize the Sino-Soviet Bloc strategic nuclear delivery capability and primary military and government controls of major importance.
>   b. Destroy the major urban-industrial centers of the Sino-Soviet Bloc to the extent necessary to paralyze the economy and render the Sino-Soviet Bloc incapable of continuing war.

Before SIOP, individual major commands authorized to use nuclear weapons prepared their own target lists, with no coordination between them. This led to the assignment of multiple weapons to some targets and none to others. Attacking and escorting aircraft would probably be caught in the blast from weapons on or near their target, or their pilots blinded by the flash of detonations on other targets as they made their attack runs.

As the nuclear stockpile grew, the problem became worse. By 1961, 22,691 weapons had been produced for U.S. forces, although retirements of older weapons, plus others lost in accidents or expended in tests had reduced the stockpile to 15,743 weapons amounting to about 10,947 megatons of explosive power. By late 1965 the stockpile had doubled to 31,139 weapons. Megatonnage for that year was about 14,900, 90 percent of which was in the strategic stockpile. Obsolete strategic weapons were being retired and replaced with smaller weapons suitable for low-altitude delivery like the B43. In 1964 the number of nuclear weapons assigned to ships in the Pacific increased by19 percent compared to the previous year (it was a 77 percent increase in the Atlantic). At the end of Fiscal Year 1965, the Navy had 3,734 nuclear weapons afloat on carriers, surface warships and submarines, just over a thousand more than a year before.

How many of these weapons were aboard *Ticonderoga*? Respected naval historian Norman Polmar estimated that in the early 1960s, probably 100 to 200 were aboard each attack carrier. In 1989, amid the Greenpeace revelations, the estimate was "30 to 50" weapons brought into Yokosuka.

SIOP required precise timing so that targets could be struck without destroying other delivery platforms that were en route or returning to their bases. For example, the slow but long-ranged Snark cruise missile was deemed unlikely to reach its targets in Russia from the eastern United States, or would arrive so late as to have no worthwhile effect, so was removed from the inventory. The Navy's Regulus cruise missile was also phased out soon after SIOP was implemented.

The role of naval aviation in the integrated plan required the movement of carriers to designated launch points so that their bombers would arrive precisely on time in coordination with strikes by SAC bombers, cruise missiles, intercontinental ballistic missiles and submarine-launched missiles. Chapman says: "We'd assume a certain defense posture from time to time to exercise the air wing. To meet the time requirements of the plan laid out for us, which was basically designed to give us a free route that didn't interfere with someone else's bombs going off, you had to fly to a kick-off point." This was called a Positive Control Turn Around Point or PCTAP. "The carrier's position determined how long it took you to get to that kick-off point and how much fuel you'd need. So they were constantly changing parameters as the ship moved around."

An air wing would be issued its targets before deployment and pilots would study them and fly practice missions against simulated targets. Each pilot had to know his mission and brief it to a board of senior staff officers every quarter. When deployed, carriers had to be able to reach their launch points within a specified time and were only stood down from this requirement occasionally. If unavailable for reasons such as being engaged in conventional combat, the plan would need adjustment, but the planners in Omaha were reluctant to accommodate tardiness due to the vagaries of weather, ship reliability or port calls. Chapman explains: "Each pilot had a series of targets and I don't remember the exact number, but for academic purposes say you have four or five targets and you'd plan your mission into those targets to give you the best chance of survival and there were various conditions and locations that influenced what group of targets would be assigned to the carrier to execute. If it came down to your mission you would fly if you were physically able." Pilots created their own target folders, updating them as necessary with new target information or if the carrier's part in the plan changed.

The Navy's Part in SIOP

None of the many versions of SIOP has ever been declassified. The closest hint of what targets might have been assigned to a contemporary air wing is a 1956 SAC target list declassified in 2015 entitled "Atomic Weapons Requirements Study for 1959," but it covers only strategic targets that would have been assigned to Air Force bombers, as ballistic missiles were not yet in the inventory. They targeted 1,100 airfields and 1,200 cities. Moscow and Leningrad were top priority, but cities in Warsaw Pact countries were not to be spared. The city of East Berlin contained within it 91 worthy targets. It hardly needs saying that West Berlin (population then approximately 2.2 million) would have been devastated by strikes on its eastern counterpart, if not by blast then by firestorms and radioactive fallout. The NSTL target list grew and grew over the years, particularly as ballistic missiles came into service and reconnaissance aircraft and spy satellites detected military and industrial sites deep inside the USSR. Seldom, if ever, was a target removed from the list.

On the proposed 1959 list the most likely targets for Navy aircraft were in the Pacific and Far East, three airfields near Vladivostok: Vozdvizhenka, Khorol and Spassk Dalniy. Undoubtedly the city and naval base of Vladivostok and other targets would soon have been added.

China was regarded as part of the Soviet bloc and targeted for massive attack regardless of whether it was fighting on Moscow's side or not in any conflict.

China's capital city of Peking (now Beijing) was assigned 23 targets or "designated ground zeros" (DGZs) within it, in categories ranging from military headquarters to pig iron production. The adjacent suburban district of Fengtai warranted another five DGZs. More than one weapon would likely have been allocated to each DGZ. Both target zones included "population" as a category. In 1958 the population of Beijing was around 6.6 million people.

Configured with two 300-gallon fuel tanks and a 2,000-pound weapon the combat radius of an A-4E is about 540 nautical miles. From a position east of the Ryukyus where the Crewcut exercise took place, the city of Shanghai and military targets like the Chongming Island airbase were in range. No part of Russia was in range.

CINCPAC's war plan did address the possibility of "alienation of potentially friendly populations in the satellite areas and fringe areas adjacent to the USSR and China" and to avoid this it was "desired to minimize civilian casualties and civil destruction" in those areas as part of the plan's "Constraint Policy." North Vietnam and North Korea were considered Sino-Soviet satellites so were excluded from this largesse.

SIOP dictated that the use of surface-burst high-yield weapons was to be such that the total residual radiation resulting from Navy (non-SIOP) and SAC weapons would not exceed the "expected dose" limits set forth for the key areas. The gamma ray exposure for Seoul, northern and north-central Japan, Hong Kong, Saigon, the Formosa Straits and Nome, Alaska was not to exceed 150 roentgens, an amount likely to cause acute radiation syndrome (ARS) but not usually fatal.

It is usually assumed that the only authority that can authorize the use of nuclear weapons is the President of the United States through the Joint Chiefs of Staff. In the 1960s this was true in theory only. Early nuclear war planners realized that a single "decapitation" strike on Washington could prevent a U.S. response to a Soviet attack. In 1958 President Eisenhower issued a top-secret letter pre-delegating nuclear weapons authority to the heads of the major unified commands with nuclear weapons (SAC, NORAD, CINCLANT and CINCPAC). In the event that communication with Washington was cut off and they had tactical (i.e. imminent) warning of a Soviet nuclear attack, the major commands could proceed with their own plan.

In practice in the early 1960s, radio-based communication across the Pacific was often interrupted by atmospheric conditions for several hours every day. To overcome this, CINCPAC, based at Camp H. M. Smith in Hawaii in turn delegated nuclear weapons release authority to the Commander of the Seventh Fleet in Yokosuka, and, with communications outages between Hawaii and the South China Sea being as likely if not more so than those between Washington and Hawaii, it is more than probable that authority was again sub-delegated, to admirals in charge of carrier task groups, if not further down the chain of command. In 1965-66 *Ticonderoga* had intermittent communications problems with the relay station in the Philippines, particularly at night.

The danger was of course that in a period of crisis, an incident such as—to choose one at random—a weapons explosion on an aircraft carrier occurring during a period of communications blackout, could convince lower levels of command that an attack was underway and cause them to forego the normal process of authentication.

Countdown

Under CINCPAC No. 1–61 and presumably its revisions, in the event of a DEFCON 1 or 2 situation (the most severe national alert statuses), "A Hour" was declared and a signal called an EM-1 War Message containing one of a series of 14 options was sent to nuclear-equipped units. These ranged from Options 1 and 1A (execute immediately) increasing in hourly intervals through Option 14, which gave 14 hours lead-time. The last option was used in the case JCS had full Strategic Warning time, which was required for total SIOP force generation.

For the men of Air Wing Five, the countdown would begin with receipt on *Ticonderoga* of the EM-1 message, ordering preparation for a strike. The timing of A Hour would be given as a six-digit date-time group in GMT or "Zulu" time. For example: 051830ZDEC65. The actual moment to launch was Execute time or "E Hour," which was the common reference time for all SIOP strike forces. The A Hour for different forces was calculated by working back from E hour, depending on the time they needed to come to readiness.

These timings were based on Tactical Warning time, which was the estimated warning time under conditions of surprise that the operational commanders could expect before their alert forces would be brought under attack. The Alert Force was those units that could be prepared and launched under conditions of tactical warning, on strike assignments against the NSTL within fifteen minutes after E Hour, from a fixed base, or two hours from a mobile base (a carrier).

In an emergency, aircraft could be launched under "positive control" if the commander thought his base or carrier was "insecure"—liable to be attacked before E Hour. Strike aircraft were to fly to the PCTAP, which would be outside of enemy territory and the enemy's radar net and wait for a properly authenticated execute order. Commanders were told that every planned sortie should have a planned positive control point. But even with a tanker, there was a limit to how long tactical jet pilots could wait for the execute order. If communications with the carrier were lost because it was destroyed or because of the electromagnetic effects of nuclear detonations or perhaps just because of atmospheric conditions, the decision to execute or return was essentially down to the strike aircraft pilot(s). If they chose to continue with their mission in the belief that war had begun, there was no way to stop them. There was no recall signal.

Plan into Action

Imagine that in late 1965 it has been decided to launch a nuclear strike on a non-SIOP target in North Vietnam, say a bridge bringing Chinese reinforcements into the war, and that *Ticonderoga,* Air Wing Five, VA-56 and a junior pilot like Douglas Webster were the methods by which the strike would be delivered. Every air wing attack pilot, even fairly inexperienced first-tourists like Doug would be capable of striking his assigned target should the order come through.

The actual strike plan is held on the carrier, so the EM-1 contains not much besides authentication and the timing of A Hour. Once the message is received in Message Processing, the Strike Control Center personnel including the Air Intelligence staff initiate the plan and prepare briefings for the strike pilots. At his briefing our pilot receives his target assignment, the weapon to be used, its yield and set burst height and the latest intelligence on the expected defenses. He collects his target folder and a pre-prepared kneeboard card from a safe and takes them to a secure area for study. Untying the string sealing the cardboard folder, he pulls out a thick pile of paper including target mosaics, a target graphic intelligence book, target information sheets, navigation maps and photographs of waypoints.

He studies these documents and chooses his type of weapon delivery and initial point (IP) for the attack run. He makes his choice of delivery based largely on the ability to escape the blast at the given yield and aircraft performance at the time of detonation. The IP is the last waypoint before the pull-up point for weapons release, chosen from the target graphic intelligence book, full of small-scale charts showing the target area and suggested IPs chosen from landmarks that can be identified at high speed and low level. On a plastic overlay he draws an arc showing the weapon burst range in the direction of his approach (if it is to be a loft delivery where the approach and escape are in the same quadrant) or beyond the target for a laydown attack. The low altitude bombing system (LABS) in the A-4 uses a maximum 30-second timer to count down to automatic release, so he calculates how far he will fly in that time at 500 knots and draws another arc. His IP has to be somewhere between the two arcs but not too close to either to allow correction for wind drift. It should be something that won't have changed since the target photos were taken. Small lakes that may have dried up or buildings that may have been removed are not recommended. After the IP he must make a straight run to the pull-up point and calculate his LABS timer setting from there. If time allows before E Hour, the pilot may do the same for an alternative delivery method. He submits his plan to the air wing staff who double check and approve it. At the last minute he might be given a supplemental folder containing the latest aerial photos.

While the pilot prepares his papers and writes updates on his kneeboard card, the Weapons Coordinator calls the Special Weapons Office on the 30MC, one of *Tico*'s lesser-used main circuits: "Execute Operation *Charley*. Provide one 43 for an A-4 to Hangar Deck forward." He then adds details of yield and burst height.

The desk officer replies, "Understand Sir, one 43 Yield 1 groundburst for an A-4 to Hangar Deck forward." A sailor writes it down. Another arrives with a printout of the strike order, authenticating the verbal instruction.

The W Division Officer immediately relays the strike requirement to his weapons assembly officers. "Keep me advised of progress," he orders.

"Aye aye, understand one 43 for an A-4, out," is the reply from SASS where the gunner's mate technicians select a B43 of the requested yield from the stacks of glossy white bombs.

The GMTs unscrew the top half of a weapon cradle and bring over the overhead bi-rail hoist, lowering its adaptor onto the weapon, connecting it and lifting it onto a wheeled handcart. They take a special wrench from a hatch in the rear part of the bomb and use it to insert the strike-enabling plug, which has been brought from a secure safe.

W Division spent a lot of time painting or polishing equipment in SASS spaces and keeping it clean. Sometimes this was as much for a want of useful work than necessary for safety or efficiency. In the Tonkin Gulf many GMTs were detached to GM and other divisions to help with conventional weapons assembly. The philosophy in the 1960s had moved towards the "wooden bomb" concept, with weapons that needed very little maintenance and no handling of nuclear components once issued to units. Those brought aboard ships were almost always in strike configuration and replacement of limited life components such as gas reservoirs, neutron generators and parachutes was only to be done ashore or on tender ships. Maintenance manuals said that periodic waxing of the external surface would improve the appearance and environmental resistance of the bomb. So apart from giving a good polish every now and then, B43 maintenance was mainly a case of regular pressure monitoring and electrical continuity checks.

The "two-man rule" meant that no person was ever alone with a nuclear weapon, with exceptions, as seen below. The secure nature of W Division's spaces meant that no unauthorized personnel were allowed in, even Marines. This resulted in a certain amount of contraband, mainly snack food, going astray during replenishments and finding itself in W Division. At least one SASS had a dartboard and the GMTs became good enough to win their homeport leagues.

B43 transport cradles were bolted to the deck and earthed with a large braided ground wire. Much later, these cradles had built-in radiation shields over the warhead sections. Sometime after 1966 shields were built into SASS spaces themselves. W Division men admit to playing cards or even sleeping on radiation shields over bombs on other carriers. In 1959, the RAND Corporation's Daniel Ellsberg put his hand on a Mk 28 bomb in Okinawa and said it had "a body-like warmth" even on a cool day.

Some SASS spaces had recognized "hot spots" where it was best to stay out of. The GMTs wore film badges to measure radiation dosage, and sending the men elsewhere for a couple of weeks lowered the average. Many years later some retired W Division men have cancers and other illnesses they attribute to radiation exposure from proximity to nuclear weapons, although secrecy and poor record keeping make it hard for them to prove.

Once assembled the bomb is pushed into the elevator, chocked and chained, with care taken that neither the nose nor tail overhangs the edge and is crushed as it ascends. On smaller elevators the tail had to be detached to fit. Operators at the top and bottom of the shaft talk to each other and listen for untoward noises as the bomb travels upward, but in between decks on *Essex* carriers it was so much for the two-man rule. Re-attaching the tail on the hangar deck involves several judiciously placed whacks with a mallet, an action that tended to freak out observers. "I looked at one of the Marines and said, 'I hate this part 'cause you just never know'' then hit it top, bottom and middle. He almost shot me," recalled one weaponsman with a laugh.

Loading the Bomb

Once the bomb is delivered to *Tico's* hangar deck, the gray tarpaulin is pulled off, revealing the sleek white 14-foot long bomb with its anodyne black stencils: "Do not chock on window"; "TEST"; "Pre-Flight Selection"; "Ejection and Sway Brace Area." Only the large "Y1" on each side and small serial numbers prefixed "43" identify it to the initiated as a one-megaton thermonuclear weapon. A large red aluminium cap stencilled "Remove before flight" protects the bomb's Vibrin resin-tipped aluminium nose and the leading edges of the sheetmetal tailfins have their own vulcanized rubber protective covers. A red strap and cap on the tail end prevent activation of the explosive parachute release until removed before flight.

The bomb is now in the hands of a certified loading crew of six men. With a few exceptions, the process of loading a nuclear weapon was similar to that for a conventional missile. Normally conventional weapons weren't loaded on the hangar deck, but for security nuclear ones usually were. The bomb is transferred to an Aero-33D Bomb Truck and is raised up to the BRU-14 suspension rack with a hydraulic-assisted hand pump. When the two are a few inches apart a CF-1506 (Cable, Functional) is connected between the bomb's pulse plug and the rack. The bomb is raised to mate with the rack and its lugs latched in place. Sway braces are tightened to keep it aligned and stable. The lifting pressure is eased and a redshirt gives the bomb a gentle shake to see the braces are properly seated. The rack's ground safety handle is rotated to the locked position.

The position of the bomb's ready-safe switch is checked through a window on the rear left side of the mid-section. A dial shows a green "S" at four positions when safe and a red "R" at the fifth when ready.

The arm-safe plug is removed, clearing a pathway for the electrical signal.

For a parachute-retarded airburst, cockpit switches are set to RETARD and either GROUND BACKUP or PRECLUDE are selected. The timer is set by opening a nose hatch (on the nose of a Mod 1 bomb) and selecting either TA or TB, giving 30 or 60 seconds delay. On the radar-nosed Mod 0 bomb a range plug is inserted to set the desired radar burst height. If FREEFALL is selected the bomb falls without parachute and explodes when the timer runs out.

There is some uncertainty if the coded locks known as Permissive Action Links (PALs) were in use in the Pacific in December 1965, although they became available as a modification kit on the B43 a year earlier. The Category B PAL used on late model B43s interrupted critical warhead electrical circuits until the proper code was inserted either in the cockpit or by ground control equipment and took about 30 seconds to operate. It wouldn't have taken long to crack either; until 1969 the code was four digits with unlimited tries.

When the bomb is connected, the pilot and a W Division technical monitor go through a checklist together and each enter half the PAL code using an encoder device. Once that is disconnected, only the pilot can deactivate the bomb. Finally, the pilot signs an AEC form for the bomb and keeps the receipt.

He climbs into the cockpit and sets his Aircraft Monitoring and Control (AMAC) control panel to the same burst settings as the bomb. Once the A-4 is on the catapult a squadron ordnanceman removes the protective nose cap and the ejector rack safety pins, shows them to the pilot to verify removal, then turns to the catapult officer to show him too. The catapult officer acknowledges the removal, then turns to the airplane for launch. The pilot and the bomb are now on their own. Once again, so much for the two-man rule.

One Man, One Bomb

After launch, the A-4 would proceed either direct to the target or to the positive control point to await authentication. As Daniel Ellsberg learned, there is no way to authenticate a recall message past the point of positive control. After he and a RAND colleague saw *Dr. Strangelove* in 1964 they agreed it was more documentary than fiction.

As the pilot approaches enemy territory he drops his A-4 to 300 feet and accelerates to 450 knots. As the OPLAN says, "Low level capability will be used to the maximum in the areas where the target defenses present the greatest threat." SAC's policy has been described as "bomb as you go," with air defense targets such as radar stations and SAM sites being hit to clear the path to the more strategic targets. The Navy's OPLAN puts it like this: "Peripheral and en route defenses will be degraded to increase the assurance of weapons delivery on selected NSTL targets." A SIOP carrier strike might require escorts to knock out enemy fighters in the air or on their airfields, and destroy radars and missile sites with conventional or nuclear weapons to let the main strikers through. In 1965, anti-radar missiles like the Shrike were only just entering service, so "mutual mass support" was employed as a defensive tactic. This was described as "the timely confluence of forces in designated areas to take advantage of the principles of mass and crossing tracks." In other words, swamp the defenses by coming from all angles at once and know they can't get everyone.

In 1965 A-4 pilots trained to be within two minutes of their assigned time on target. The Navy deemed 300 feet an optimum ingress altitude. Flying lower might reduce exposure to guns and missiles, but gave very little room to maneuver and less time to spot waypoints. The A-4E's radar was of limited use for navigation, but the bridge would have been visible from a distance.

On *Ticonderoga* in 1965, three types of aircraft had a nominal nuclear role. The high-altitude A-3, the nimble A-4 and the lumbering A-1. The A-3 was about to lose its bombing mission and the A-1's nuclear mission was "a joke" according to Austin Chapman. It was just to meet the numbers requirements, boosting the Navy's image in the eternal battle with the Air Force. "Of course, the A-4 was designed for that mission, what we called a one-way trip. We had all-white flight suits, the harness was white, we had gold-plated visors for our helmets and then on top of that we had a clamshell that would come down over you, and all of that was to try and defeat the flash and thermal effects of the weapon going off," Chapman said. By burning the retina, the flash of thermonuclear weapons could cause blindness at 80 miles and the clamshell Chapman speaks of was called the Thermal Radiation Closure or "baby carriage" because it folded down like the hood of a stroller. With it down the pilot would be flying completely on instruments, without autopilot, so it would usually be closed only at the last minute. Pilots could also wear an eye patch as they approached the target. The theory was that if the flash of another bomb blinded the pilot in one eye, he could switch the patch to the other and carry on. The planners had thought of everything, but making a carrier landing with one eye would test even the greatest naval aviator.

Meanwhile, our pilot is running in low and fast. He moves his hand to the left console and turns a switch on the AMAC panel from GROUND to AIR, which applies power to the pulse plug and to operate the ready/safe switch. For the final run from the IP, he pushes the throttle forward and accelerates to 500 knots. He lifts a hinged guard on the AMAC selector switch and turns the knob from SAFE to ground burst (GRD). If the circuits are good an orange light comes on, then he presses the test button, which lights up red. The ready/safe switch is turned to READY, opening the arming circuit, and a signal travels to the bomb, turning on its thermal battery.

If he had chosen to make a loft delivery, the pilot would hold down the bomb release button once he crossed the IP, starting a whistling tone playing in his headphones. He would pull up at a constant 4g, holding the crosshairs centered in the LABS indicator until the tone stopped and the bomb released automatically. The bomb would continue in an arc to the target while the Skyhawk continued on its back then rolled level and dived as fast as possible in the opposite direction. Hopefully it would be five to ten miles away at the moment of detonation.

The loft or over-the-shoulder delivery methods were preferred for a weapon as large as the one-megaton B43, but the bomb was also designed for a laydown attack, which was more accurate. Drop tests in the 1990s achieved accuracy of around 300 feet from low-altitude releases of gravity bombs. They say that "Close only counts in horseshoes and hand grenades," but it's also true for one-megaton bombs.

Having chosen a laydown attack, the pilot lines up the target in the gunsight and presses the pickle switch on his control stick as it passes under the nose. An electrical charge fires two impulse cartridges, causing gas pressure to build up in a breech, activating a linkage that opens the suspension hooks and simultaneously pushes an ejection foot downwards, kicking the bomb away.

As it falls, the CF cable is pulled free, taking with it the pulse plug and opening a circuit. The timer starts. After the safe-separation time elapses, the radar, firing set and neutron generators arm. The velocity sensor detects sufficient airflow over the bomb to convince itself it's falling.

A device called a rotary chopper converts the thermal battery's 28 volts Direct Current into Alternating Current and changes the waveform to rectangular pulses that pass through a transformer-convertor, emerging as 2,400 volts DC to charge the capacitor of the X-unit and send a signal to the external initiators, or neutron generators, also known as "Zippers."

On a radar-nosed bomb set to air burst the reflection of the surface at the chosen height sends a firing signal that triggers the firing set and detonates the bomb. If this fails and GROUND BACKUP was selected before flight, the laydown fuze triggers the bomb after impact.

The pyrotechnic arming delay timer begins its countdown, giving 30 or 60 seconds to allow the A-4 to escape the blast. Detonators set off Primacord detonating cord to shear retaining pins to blow off the aft cap, which pulls a four-foot pilot parachute with it as it goes, this tugging out the main ribbon parachute, packed as dense as an oak log, with a force of over 1,200 pounds. An explosive actuator ensures that the 23-foot diameter main chute opens in 0.4 seconds, while the bomb is still travelling horizontally, slowing the weapon to near zero forward airspeed. The deceleration imparts a force of minus 100g, causing the weighted nose shroud to fly off, exposing a hollow-tipped steel spike. Dropped from low levels the bomb will hit the ground at an angle below the vertical and possibly "slapdown" in a somewhat haphazard manner on its side or tail. Where it would finally come to rest was hard to predict. Tests revealed the need for a shock mitigator to absorb the initial impact and prevent bounce. Stuffing the nose with used computer paper was one idea that was actually tested by the designers. Another suggestion was using cornflakes, offering the possibility that World War III might have been preceded momentarily by a small cloud of breakfast cereal. They chose the spike.

From 500 feet, the B43 hits the ground in under six seconds under its parachute. The A-4 travels about three-quarters-of-a-mile in the time the blast wave travels a mile further. This is why a time delay of 30 or 60 seconds is essential. A longer timer was not incorporated as it was thought to make the B43 vulnerable to enemy countermeasures while it lay inert on the ground, though one would have to imagine only very alert and brave bomb disposal men would attempt to tackle a ticking thermonuclear weapon, unless they ran over it in a tank.

The X-Unit sends the signal to the detonators attached to each PBX 9404 high explosive lens, detonating all the lenses simultaneously. Timing of the firing signal has to be precise to a level of tens to hundreds of nanoseconds. The amount of explosives in a B43 is classified, as is the number of lenses, but the older Mk 7 bomb had 92 detonators. PBX 9404 was not one of the later so-called insensitive high explosives and the B43 was not "one-point" safe, meaning that detonation of one of the explosive lenses could cause a nuclear yield, if not a full explosion.

The shockwave from the detonation of the lenses hits a beryllium tamper then a layer of exotic, high density plastic foam before compressing the hollow core of plutonium 239 to a supercritical mass and initiating a fusion reaction, turning the core to gas at a temperature of billions of degrees. Before it is destroyed the tamper surrounding the core reflects the neutrons back inwards and slows the reaction enough for more generations of neutrons to form by splitting.

When the fusion reaction in the core meets the tritium from the Zipper it generates a fission reaction, releasing more energy and faster neutrons. At the same time the implosion is crushing the core, the neutron generator does what its name suggests, and a huge amount of energy is released from the core. In the space of less than a millionth of a second, the grapefruit-sized core becomes hotter than the center of the sun. This primary device is only a trigger for the uranium-cored secondary, with its own lithium deuteride fusion fuel, which it crushes like a hammer just with its radiation pressure while at the same time heating it up, releasing more energy and neutrons. Fission begets fusion, which in turn begets more fission and so on as the fireball expands at enormous speed, drawing in air at its center to fill the vacuum left by the vaporized core and creating the characteristic mushroom cloud. 4.6 seconds after a one-megaton airburst, the fireball expands to approximately 1.3 miles in diameter, with the blast wave being about 800 yards ahead of its outer edge.

For a laydown attack, the Skyhawk pulls into a 15-degree climb straight ahead, an angle calculated to provide the best chance of surviving the blast. As long as the tail was pointed towards the explosion, the gamma and beta rays would not penetrate the metal of the aircraft and affect the pilot, but travelling at the speed of light, the thermal wave would overtake the aircraft and might cause his fire-retardant flight suit to begin smoking, warned the weapons employment manual, while adding that this was normal.

Attack pilots joked that a nuclear strike mission was "one man, one bomb, one way" although return to the carrier was planned. It was not anticipated that pilots would rearm and strike a second target. "No recycle of a weapon delivery vehicle has been or will be planned in the SIOP," said Operation Plan No. 1–61.

Where Did an A-4 Fit in?

In mid-December, 1960, a briefing was held at Strategic Air Command headquarters in Omaha for an audience of the Secretary of Defense, the Joint Chiefs of Staff and the generals and admirals in charge of all the major U.S. commands.

At the direction of SAC commander General Thomas Power, a briefer ran through all phases of the just-completed SIOP-62 plan on a giant wall map, almost 100-feet wide. The map revealed the first wave of attacks to reach the Soviet Union would come from carrier-based fighter bombers stationed near Okinawa (which may explain why the Crewcut drill took place where it did). As more transparent overlays were dropped over the map, these opening strikes were followed by B-52s on airborne alert, more fighter-bombers from carriers in the Mediterranean, bombers from European and stateside bases and the few ballistic missiles then in the stockpile. John H. Rubel, an assistant director of research and engineering for the Pentagon who attended the briefing, said a total of 7,847 megatons would detonate on the USSR and China. Forty megatons were allocated to Moscow alone. Excluding the blast and fire effects, radioactive fallout by itself would kill around one hundred million Soviets and three hundred million Chinese over time, the audience was told.

The plan was so complex, involving precise times over target for hundreds of aircraft and impact times for missiles, that it had no room for flexibility. It was all or nothing. "The SIOP Alert Force is the same numerical strength in all options." The chances of it coming off with without massive interference or fratricide was extremely slim.

The bombers of non-U.S. nuclear forces (Britain and France), each with their own targets, would have added to the chaos. No matter what role China may have played in the conflict, it was regarded as part of the Sino-Soviet bloc and thus a legitimate target. The "Sino-Soviet bloc" had pretty much ceased to exist by 1962, if it ever really did, but the war plans didn't change.

At the Omaha briefing, a lone voice piped up to say, "What if this isn't China's war? What if it's just a war with the Soviets? Can you change the plan?" General Power's answer suggested they could but that it was preferable there was a unified enemy, otherwise it "would really screw up the plan."

Thirty Seconds over Hanoi?

But was Lieutenant (Junior Grade) Douglas M. Webster's only nuclear target an airfield, factory or military base in southern China or eastern Russia as part of GEOP or SIOP? Doug wrote in his diary on October 24 that from then on he had to study the "Non-SIOP" attack plan in the event such an order was issued by the president. His target would have been a bridge in the suburbs of Hanoi, he wrote, and the weapon employed would have been a B57. Very rarely has any pilot of the

Doug Webster wrote in his diary that his "non-SIOP" nuclear target was a bridge near Hanoi and his weapon a B57, a freefall bomb with yields ranging from five to twenty kilotons. It could be used against land targets like the B43 or as an anti-submarine depth bomb. (*Always/Never*)

era ever revealed his assigned target and weapon, even after the end of the Cold War and the retirement of the weapon (in the case of the Navy, all tactical nuclear weapons) and the delivery platform. They have felt sworn to secrecy and duty bound to the documents they signed. Doug of course was writing for himself and is no longer constrained by secrecy. This is evidence that beyond the general war plans under SIOP and GEOP, the Navy prepared its own target list for nuclear strikes on targets in Southeast Asia and was training for them in 1965.

Under What Circumstances Would a Nuclear Weapon Be Used in Vietnam?

The idea of using nuclear weapons in the Vietnam conflict was certainly considered before and after *Ticonderoga* set sail for Southeast Asia in September 1965.

As far back as 1954, the United States had considered using nuclear weapons to help prevent the French defeat at Diên Biên Phu in what was then Indochina. Operation *Vulture* was never implemented, but could have involved Seventh Fleet carriers, which by that time had a basic light nuclear attack capability with Skyraiders and Banshees using Mk 7 and Mk 8 bombs. At the end of Fiscal Year 1954, the Navy had 91 weapons afloat in the Pacific, Atlantic and Mediterranean.

Vice President Richard Nixon and Secretary of State John Foster Dulles were in favor of *Vulture,* but President Dwight Eisenhower was less enthusiastic and when British Prime Minister Winston Churchill failed to give British backing for United States intervention in Indochina, the plan was dropped.

In February 1965, Lyndon Johnson called in Eisenhower as an advisor on Vietnam. The former president told his successor that if the Chinese entered the war, which he personally doubted would happen, the United States should use any weapon necessary, including nuclear weapons and (if it were still up to him) he would make use of U.S. carrier strength for instant retaliation, with large troop concentrations and supply depots as suitable targets. Carriers should be kept in constant readiness with tactical nuclear weapons, Eisenhower suggested to Johnson.

In March 1966, Abbot Smith, the acting chairman of the CIA's Office of National Estimates wrote a memo to the Director. Its subject: use of nuclear weapons in the Vietnam War.

Smith saw five scenarios in which nuclear weapons might be employed in Vietnam, listed in order from least to most justifiable. The first was that the military situation in South Vietnam remained essentially as it was and the United States employed nuclear weapons out of sheer frustration at its inability to obtain any victory by conventional means. The second was a U.S. invasion of North Vietnam followed by a Chinese communist counter-attack in large numbers, threatening the U.S. forces with destruction. The third was a large invasion of South Vietnam by the North Vietnamese army assisted by Chinese ground forces. The fourth would be an expansion of the conflict by Chinese Communist initiative, involving invasions of Laos, Thailand, and perhaps Burma. Finally, the Chinese themselves first used a nuclear weapon. The first and last of these scenarios were deemed so highly unlikely as to be virtually out of the question.

The memo's conclusions were that: "Use of nuclear weapons by the U.S. in the Vietnam War would be one of the most important events of modern history. World reactions would be affected to some point by the circumstances in which the U.S. resorted to the use, and the targets attacked. But almost independent of these factors would be a widespread revulsion that the U.S. had broken the twenty-year taboo on the use of nuclear weapons."

The fallout of such taboo-breaking would be more than just radioactive. There is a modern concept of the "strategic corporal," a low-level soldier who can affect the course of a crisis or war by his actions or inaction at a critical time and place. The authorized tactical use of a single bomb by a junior officer such as Doug Webster, in the tiny cockpit of one of those "carrier-based fighter bombers stationed near Okinawa" would have ramifications far beyond the immediate battlefield.

"Among the consequences would be intense agitation in Japan, probably leading to a restriction on the United States' use of Japanese facilities and possibly to denunciation of the U.S.–Japan defense treaty," Smith wrote. There would be

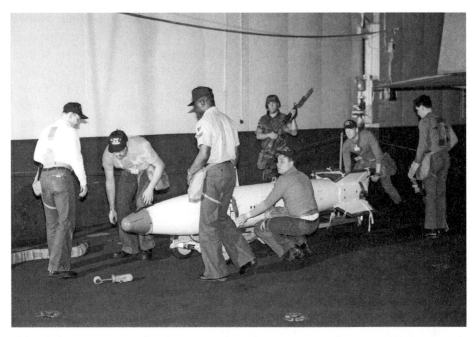

Although from many years after the *Tico* incident, this 1988 image of a BDU-24/C dummy B43 being moved on the carrier *Eisenhower* illustrates many aspects of the procedure, including the marine escort. (NARA)

acceleration towards nuclear proliferation, while at the same time international pressure for nuclear disarmament without verification. Public support for U.S. Vietnam policy would be markedly diminished. After nuclear weapons use it was not even likely the Chinese would move to disengage, the memo continued. It was more likely that they would carry on, using dispersal, "close-embrace battlefield tactics" and intensification of guerrilla warfare to reduce the effect of further nuclear attacks and prolong the struggle. By the time China had intervened, the Hanoi government would be reduced to a secondary role and unable to separate its forces from the Chinese. The USSR would act vigorously against the U.S. on the political and propaganda front but probably wouldn't enter the war or support the Chinese with nuclear weapons.

There was the possibility that use of nuclear weapons, even with "some persistence" would fail to turn back the Chinese or quickly end the war, leaving the United States to pay the political price. The British government would likely fall if they failed to condemn American nuclear strikes and their. use would legitimize nuclear weapons use in the eyes of other countries who would feel they had to have them, destroying U.S. counter-proliferation efforts. The question of *not* using nuclear weapons and accepting a military disaster, perhaps even loss of the war, was deemed outside the scope of the memorandum. These were not the thoughts of a peace group, but the top-secret concerns of an influential group within the CIA.

Despite the misgivings outlined in the CIA memo, the idea did not go away.

Another group to consider the idea was the so-called "Jasons." Formed in 1959, the Institute for Defense Analyses Jason Division was an independent advisory panel named after Jason and the Argonauts of Greek myth and comprised of experts in various scientific fields.

In March 1967, the Jasons published a secret report authored by scientists Freeman Dyson, Robert Gomer, Steven Weinberg, and S. Courtney Wright. "Tactical Nuclear Weapons in Southeast Asia" was inspired by a remark from former Chairman of the Joint Chiefs of Staff General Maxwell Taylor about the war. "Well, it might be a good idea to throw in a nuke once in a while just to keep the other side guessing," Taylor was heard to say at a party, and the Jasons set out to see what effects this might have.

They concluded that the use of tactical nuclear weapons (TNW) would be effective only in stopping the movement of large masses of men in concentrated formations, but that bomblet-canister ordnance (cluster bombs) was more cost-effective against troops in the open.

If used against roads and trails in forested areas, most roads could be cleared of fallen trees and reopened in about a month. After that, further strikes would be ineffective as a tree could only be blown down once. Fallout from a ground burst would provide, at most, a complicating factor in the reconstruction of damaged facilities. Using a study by the RAND Corporation think tank to estimate that one tactical nuclear weapon strike was equivalent to 12 conventional attack sorties, the Jasons judged that a completely nuclear *Rolling Thunder* campaign to interdict lines of communication would require 3,000 nuclear weapons per year.

Experiments had already been conducted in Australia with conventional explosives to simulate a nuclear detonation in tropical forest. Operation *Blowdown* in 1963 saw a sphere of 50 tons (0.05 kilotons) of high explosives detonated in a tower above Queensland rainforest, completely flattening everything in a radius of 200 yards. The trial, run by the Australian military with assistance from the United States, proved that a large airburst detonation robbed troops of cover, but conversely, made the terrain near the explosion's ground zero easier to cross, assuming protective measures against fallout were taken.

In war games simulating TNW use, such as those conducted under by RAND as part of the U.S. Army's Project "Oregon Trail" in 1964, each notional strike against enemy troops engaged in a large-scale fighting with conventional armor and artillery caused, on average, one hundred casualties. It was estimated that several hundred strikes would be needed to defeat a large force even if it chose to fight in this style. Against smaller groups fighting under forest cover, many more strikes than this would have been needed. On the flipside, America's fixed bases in South Vietnam

Under Operation *Blowdown* in 1963, a half-kiloton of explosives was detonated in an Australian forest to simulate the effect of a tactical nuclear weapon in a jungle warfare scenario. (Defense Technical Information Center)

would have been extremely vulnerable to attacks by sappers or insurgents using atomic demolition munitions ("backpack nukes") supplied by China or the USSR were the nuclear taboo to be broken by the United States' unilateral use of TNW.

Whatever the military effects, the Jasons concluded that the political consequences of the use of TNW in Southeast Asia would be highly damaging to the United States whether or not the use remained unilateral. The military advantages of unilateral use would not be overwhelming enough to ensure termination of the war and would be heavily outweighed by the disadvantages of eventual bilateral use.

Despite this, the idea never quite went away. The U.S. commander in Vietnam, General William Westmoreland considered TNW use against the North Vietnamese division besieging Khe Sanh and discussed it with President Johnson in 1968. He told the president he had a small study group looking into the question of using TNW, firstly to destroy any North Vietnamese surge across the DMZ to Khe Sanh and secondly, "to send a signal to China and to North Vietnam."

The fourth president to deal with American involvement in Southeast Asia, Richard Nixon, was a strong believer that a "knockout blow" would defeat the North Vietnamese and that the implied threat of nuclear attack had brought the North Koreans to the negotiating table in 1952. In 1968 Nixon espoused his "Madman theory" to aides. This would involve convincing North Vietnamese leaders that he was obsessed with victory and prepared to go to any lengths, including nuclear attack, to achieve it.

Little was written down about the details of such measures, but a concept of operations paper discussed in the White House dated September 13, 1969 (known unofficially within the White House as "Duck Hook") gave 20 options for escalation from mining North Vietnamese ports to breaching dikes to amphibious landings in the North that would draw the NVA into a "killing zone." Others involved large cross-border land operations into Laos and/or Cambodia or blockading Cambodia's main port of Sihanoukville. Some of these were politically unpalatable or risked starting a wider war. Two stand out as particularly risky. "Clean nuclear interdiction of three NVN–Laos passes" and "Nuclear interdiction of two NVN–CPR [North Vietnam–Chinese People's Republic] railroads." By late 1965 the Pentagon estimated that two divisions of Chinese railroad engineers were helping North Vietnam keep its rail lines open and thus a strike within North Vietnam would have killed many Chinese.

In a memo about these proposals, special assistant for national security affairs Anthony Lake asked, "If we go as far as the (nuclear) interdiction measures … what other actions should we take at this very high level of escalation once the precedent is established? What would we do if these actions fail? What counter-actions would we take in various contingencies?" In other words: would that be it? What if it didn't work? And what if somebody retaliated in kind?

The likely author of the ConOps paper was Captain Rembrandt Robinson, one of the JCS Chairman's liaison officers at the White House. The nuclear interdiction, invasion and blockade plans were discarded. The main option taken up was to mine Haiphong Harbor, and Robinson updated the mining plans, which were implemented in May 1972 as Operation *Pocket Money*. Then-Rear Admiral Robinson was killed when his helicopter crashed into the Tonkin Gulf as he returned to his flagship with the execute orders for the operation.

Of course, neither Nixon or his predecessors ordered a nuclear strike on Vietnam. Nixon told *Time* magazine in 1985 that he had rejected bombing dikes as they would have drowned a million people, and for the same reason he rejected the nuclear option, because the targets he was presented with were not military ones.

The Bridge

There aren't actually all that many bridges near Hanoi that would warrant a nuclear strike. Presumably the purpose would be to prevent a Chinese force heading south if Peking was to intervene in the war. A likely candidate would be the Long Biên rail bridge, also known as the Paul Doumer Bridge, which crosses the Red River in Hanoi's northeast and connects the North's then-capital with Pinxiang, China. An online nuclear weapons effect simulation suggests that the detonation today of an airburst B57 200 feet over the bridge would cause 97,640 fatalities at the B57's maximum 29-kiloton yield and 34,820 at 6 kilotons. The larger yield would also cause over 450,000 injuries and flatten an area just over a square mile in area. These figures are based on the population of today's Hanoi administrative area, which is much larger than its 1965 equivalent and so not directly comparable.

In reality, the Long Biên Bridge wasn't bombed until 1967, when Air Force F-105s damaged one span with a single hit by a 3,000-pound bomb, but it was soon repaired. Hit again twice that year, it was only knocked out for any significant length of time when struck by laser guided bombs in May 1972. Steel truss bridges were poor targets because they have a lot of redundant structural strength and most of the blast from near misses passes through the lattice structure. Designed by French architect Gustave Eiffel and completed in 1902, the Long Biên Bridge stands today.

CHAPTER 10

Hope and Prayer

Thursday, December 16, 1965
En route Yokosuka, Japan to Special Operations Area off Vietnam

Tico rendezvoused with its four destroyers in Kanagawa Bay and set course for Yankee Station. It was back to war, but there was the promise of some light relief before Christmas, with visiting entertainers and other distractions.

Fire Control Officer John McCabe had decided to liven up his stateroom by turning it into JO party central with a new stereo, turntable and amplifier he picked up in Yokosuka. He also sneaked a live pine aboard and all the decorations for a Christmas tree. Unfortunately the stateroom's location underneath the port catapult during constant flight ops meant the record needle gouged new grooves in McCabe's records every time a jet launched, and the vibration, heat and humidity affected the pine needles as well, dropping them all over the floor. By December 24, the JOs had a Christmas twig.

Russian spy trawlers became more aggressive in December, actively interfering with carriers, particularly during flight operations. Sometimes *Tico* had to change course during a launch cycle to avoid these ships. Within the month there was a trawler on both Yankee and Dixie Stations. The trawlers normally followed U.S. ships listening to their radio and electronic transmissions and even collecting trash in the hope of discovering interesting documents. For this reason the Mardet disposed of sensitive papers by burning. Intelligence sources also noted that two Soviet *Whiskey*-class submarines made a deployment to the Philippine Sea in December and January.

As Christmas approached, visitors seemed to outnumber crew. Comic actress and singer Martha Raye and a small band arrived by Army Chinook on the 22nd. The "grand old lady" of the American stage was 50, and her act was probably more suited to the previous generation, but it was well received as a distraction from the war.

The same day *Ticonderoga*, *Kitty Hawk* and *Enterprise* sent 100 aircraft to hit the Uong Bi thermal power plant near Haiphong, destroying the generator hall,

A Soviet Auxiliary, General Intelligence (AGI) ship or "spy trawler" was a common sight shadowing *Tico* and other carriers on Yankee Station from late 1965. (Via Gary Verver)

boiler house and other buildings, greatly reducing its output for several weeks. Two *Enterprise* A-4s were shot down.

That day plane captain Bob Martin of VA-56 had to make the choice between having his own A-4 run over his feet or go over the side. As aircraft were being spotted after recovery the plane director ordered the chock men to chock the jet and Martin was taking pins from hatches and putting them in the bomb racks to make them safe. He was leaning over the drop tank to reach the outboard pylon when he heard the director call "pull chocks" and the engine power increase. The wing was over the water and his feet were braced against the wheel. He chose not to jump up and go over the side as the jet moved. The wheel ran over his foot. "Surprisingly enough I was able to place the ladder and open the cockpit. I gave the pilot his helmet bag and the rest was a blur. I remember being in sickbay and a corpsman asking me what happened. I told him, and he proceeded to pull off my boot and sock and then ran out of the room puking. The skin and meat had come off with the sock." The standard flight deck shoes then in use had no toe protection or arch support and wore out after three months.

"A doctor came in and in true Navy fashion did what he felt necessary and gave me a pair of crutches, 30 Darvon, 30 APCs and a no-duty chit for five days." Darvon is a now-banned opiate-based painkiller, and APC, which mixed Aspirin, caffeine and Phenacetin is also no longer used. As well as coping with these powerful narcotics, Martin still had to negotiate the ship. "Think about this now. Our berthing was three decks down and the chow hall was one deck below the hangar. All this on crutches with the ladders."

The Christmas spirit of goodwill had not spread throughout the ship. Fireman Fielder lost a tooth when he was punched in the mouth after a fire room argument on the 23rd, a day on which *Ticonderoga* and *Kitty Hawk* made coordinated attacks against the Hai Duong Bridge. The Roadrunners CO Bruce Miller was awarded his second DFC for leading the attack in the face of heavy flak and missile fire and inflicting heavy damage while his 40-strong strike force took none. One of the returning jets clocked up *Tico's* 75,000th landing since refit while *Kitty Hawk* headed to Japan.

The Hai Duong strike was the last before the White House declared a 30-hour Christmas ceasefire beginning at 1800 on Christmas Eve. The next day, with no missions to fly, the crew was able to enjoy Christmas dinner. The traditional turkey was served with cranberry sauce, candied sweet potatoes, green beans and corn, with fruitcake and ice cream for dessert. Captain Miller offered Grace: "Almighty God, on this Christmas day we are happy and a joyful because of Thy great gift of love, in that Thou didst come to us in the person of Thy son. Bless us we ask, as we partake of this great abundance of food, and give us mindful of the needs of others always, we pray. Amen."

For George Floyd, memories of Christmas at sea were sitting on the catwalk rail alongside the LSO platform after flight ops listening to Hanoi Hannah play festive music over his portable radio. Floyd and his VA-56 buddies liked "Winchester Cathedral," "Snoopy vs the Red Baron" and other novelty hits.

The next day Cardinal Francis Spellman, the seventy-six-year-old Catholic archbishop of New York and apostolic chaplain for the Armed Forces, arrived on the C-1 to celebrate a late Christmas. His first impression of the sea air was "It smells like Atlantic City." He had hoped to address the crew on deck, but the truce was over and the noise of Crusaders launching on strikes against targets in the South prevented all but some individual greetings. Swapping his life preserver and cranial for his ecclesiastical robes and skullcap he moved on to Hangar Bay 1 where 650 chairs had been set up for mass amidst rows of rockets awaiting the end of the bombing pause. The roar of jets launching overhead sometimes interrupted his words as he took the sacrament.

Cardinal Spellman toured the galley and had lunch with chaplains Joseph Zemites and Harold Symons then visited patients in the sick bay before flying off again to minister to troops in South Vietnam. Spellman was an enthusiastic supporter of the war, so much so that he had been called "the Bob Hope of the clergy" for his frequent visits to Vietnam. This time he was just a warm-up act for the real thing.

President Johnson extended the bombing halt after the Christmas truce in the hope of bringing North Vietnam to the negotiating table. Political support at home was getting thin and the White House was soon to ask Congress for 25 billion

Cardinal Joseph Spellman was known as "The Bob Hope of the Clergy." His visit to *Tico* was a warm-up act for the real thing. (Cruisebook)

dollars to support operations for the next 18 months. They had to be seen to be trying something beyond endless bombing. These pauses were not popular with *Tico*'s fliers. John Paisley says, "President Johnson would show them how benevolent we were by announcing a bombing pause. We hated those, because we would have them [the enemy] beaten down so that we could go anywhere with impunity and this just gave them the chance to build stuff back up."

The war carried on within *Tico*. Armorer Jim Doran slipped off an A-1 while changing ammo cans and injured his elbow and hip. Opening a hatch in the VA-144 line shack, Sullivan Vanway lacerated his scalp on the "darken ship" switch.

Almost as soon as the archbishop had left, the circus arrived. Exactly when the Bob Hope show touched down is a matter of conjecture as somehow the arrival of several helicopters and 85 people escaped the attention of the log writer. The log records a midday position of just over 11 nautical miles from the coast of South Vietnam. Hope's own recollection was the ship was about five miles off the coast. Yeoman Joe Miller says they were five miles off the coast at Cam Ranh Bay, with

Army Chinooks brought most of the Bob Hope traveling circus aboard. The coast of South Vietnam near Cam Ranh Bay can be seen in the background. (Gary Loudenslager via Brian Loundenslager)

the land in clear view when the helicopters arrived. For those concerned that later ailments could have stemmed from exposure to Agent Orange washed down rivers into coastal waters and taken up through the ship's evaporators before being drunk by and showered over the crew, the closest point of approach to Vietnam is not a matter of trivia.

For two memorable days Hope's performers and technicians swelled *Tico's* complement. They included 17 NBC cameramen and technicians, three cue-card flippers, one make-up man, one wardrobe man, two hairdressers, two writers, a PR adviser and a personal masseur for Mr. Hope himself. The female members of the troupe were assigned to squadrons. Dancer Caroll Baker was escorted by Bob Sturgeon of VA-56. Dianna Lynn Batts, Miss World USA, stayed in VF-53's ready room and singer Anita Bryant bunked down with VA-144. Hope's musicians, Les Brown and his Band of Renown, were found space in sickbay. The NBC men had to sleep under the catapult steam chamber.

"They survived a kamikaze attack in 1945, so I guess they are ready for me," Hope wrote in a dispatch to newspapers. "The attack planes take off for Vietnam with all sorts of lethal stuff—bombs, missiles and a few dozen fruitcakes that got here too late for Christmas." Captain Miller had greeted Hope with his own gag; "This is the greatest thing that has happened to the *Ticonderoga* since the last typhoon."

The entertainers found themselves on *Tico* as the result of a conversation Hope with Ted Sally, an illustrator who had often worked with Hope. Hope remarked he'd like to play a "nice, intimate flattop" one day. Sally cabled his son Nick, who was serving on *Tico* and said Bob Hope would like to play the ship. Somehow the message went up the chain. Hope had expected to perform on *Enterprise*, having pre-written a pile of idiot cards with jokes about its nuclear propulsion. He shared some of these in *Five Women I Love*, his account of the 1965 Vietnam tour. "I knew I was on a nuclear carrier … when the captain shook hands with me my nose lit up." "It's amazing the change that comes over a crew when you bring five beautiful girls aboard. We've got more atomic energy on deck than we have below." Little did he know.

Ramp Strike

After dinner, which Hope shared with Admiral Ralph Cousins and Captain Willie House, the comedian and some of his troupe climbed onto vulture's row to watch a launch and landing cycle put on for them by Captain Miller. One account says some of the party watched from the LSO platform. The girls whooped with excitement as afterburners roared and catapults fired. "Boy oh boy!" Hope said to his escort. "This is the highlight of the trip."

John Paisley was skeptical about this particular evolution. "They wanted these people to see flight ops on the carrier, which is natural, absolutely natural, but then they wanted to see *night* ops on the carrier. We didn't want to give the impression that we were just going to go up and fly and show these people, come back and land, so we were going on missions, over North Vietnam at night. But night ops weren't a show, they were deadly serious and far more dangerous than day flying." Paisley wasn't impressed with the idea of flying jets just for show at night: "I just felt like that's fine, but why not just go out on a fine day and put three or four airplanes out of each type and just let them run the deck and see what it's like … and I just didn't feel it was needed. Night ops were different." Austin Chapman adds: "They wanted to see night ops, and I mean they were really frightening in those days because we didn't have flightdeck lighting like you did on later cruises. What you had was two lines, left and right and a centerline and the drop light, which was an extension of the landing centerline and it went down like this, and if you saw an angle, you could correct your line-up, and of course the mirror. That was all you had, it was like landing in a ditch. You followed the ball until you hit something, and you hoped it was the deck and the wires." Working in the hangar deck, Jerry Slagle said it was the only time he can recall jets coming down the forward elevator "hot" (with engines running) and using their own power to move back to Hangar Bay 3.

Bill Brougher's Crusader was having trouble picking up a TACAN bearing. His section leader flew alongside him to give the correct heading then broke off to begin his own approach. As Brougher neared the slightly pitching deck primary flight control became confused as to which aircraft was on approach and called a wave-off. Brougher went around for another attempt. This time he started a little high on the approach, went low, then high again. Half a mile from landing he turned off his approach power compensator and continued in manual. He dropped below the glideslope. The LSO shouted, "Pick your nose up!" Brougher pushed the throttle forward to full military power. The nose pitched up and the jet wallowed. Sensing disaster, he pushed the throttle through the gate into afterburner, but the rear fuselage struck the ramp, shearing off the port landing gear and ventral fin.

The F-8 broke in two. The forward half slid down the deck on fire. As it went off the angle, the ejection seat fired out of the flames. The crash siren wailed. The Angel lifted off and flew low, its searchlight scanning the black sea. On the hangar deck, directing jets aftwards, Jerry Slagle heard the F-8 roar past and off the angle. He thought it was just a bolter but then a man ran past him to the opening of No.2 Elevator and threw a light wand into the sea. More lights rained down from the flight deck and bobbed in the swell.

The Crusader struck the ramp so hard that Brougher saw a white flash, and stars filled his vision. His visor slammed down over his eyes. He pulled the handles above his head and felt the shock as the Martin-Baker ejection seat fired and propelled him into a single somersault, revealing real stars as he briefly faced the night sky. The parachute opened with a bigger shock and swung once before dumping him in the sea.

Brougher fumbled for the new-style Koch fasteners that attached the survival harness to the parachute. He inserted the fingers of his wet gloves under the latches and pulled up. They released without difficulty and the chute floated away. Pulling off the gloves he swam away from the chute and pulled the toggles to inflate his life preserver.

The Angel swept its searchlight over the water. The beam picked out the reflective tape on Brougher's helmet but then lost it again. Believing that the helicopter knew where he was, Brougher didn't switch on the strobe light on his survival harness.

When it found the bobbing pilot again, the helicopter lowered its rescue seat to him, but the swells, rising and falling up to six feet put it out of his grasp. The rotor downwash blew salt into his eyes and made the seat bob away and it took Brougher several attempts to grab the three-pronged device and climb aboard.

As all this went on astern of *Tico*, Bob Hope and his party watched anxiously from Vulture's Row. Joey Heatherton sobbed, Kaye Stephens clung to an officer's arm. Hope's legs felt like they were made of Kleenex. Finally, 14 minutes after the crash, the 1MC announced the pilot was aboard the helicopter. Brougher's only injuries were a sore neck and a bruised left shin from the ejection and bruises to his upper thighs from the rescue seat. A UPI reporter, who misidentified Brougher's jet as a Skyhawk, said that Joey Heatherington ran into his arms and planted a big

It's not certain who the aviator receiving the kiss from Anita Bryant here is, but Bill Brougher definitely got one after being rescued from the sea after his F-8 ramp strike. (Cruisebook)

kiss on his cheek. "Glad to have you back!" she said. "It was almost worth it" was the soaked aviator's purported response.

Jay Shower was in the landing pattern when Brougher hit. "I was right behind him, about three-quarters of a mile. Big explosion. The ship said 'Delta, delta!' [orbit off the port side] and I did that for eight or ten minutes, at the most ten minutes, [until] they had the fire out and I just sort of leveled my wings and landed."

Later that evening Hope's group visited Brougher in sick bay, which he was sharing with two sailors who had struck their heads on hatches, one of them while running to his man overboard station when the F-8 crashed. Hope made a couple of lame jokes "That was pretty good. Now what are you going to do for an encore?" The response was a weak smile, which Hope attributed to shock. "Anyhow, I can't tell you how glad we all are that you decided to stick around for the show."

That night while the NBC crew hammered together a temporary stage on the flight deck, Father Zemites gave thanks in the lights-out prayer for the miraculous recovery of William Brougher.

The next morning there was time for tours and mingling with *Tico*'s crew.

Wearing a flight helmet and drinking from a can of Coke, Anita Bryant sat in a VA-144 Skyhawk. Roadrunners pilot Bob Maier got a kiss from her, adding to the surreality of a 105-degree Christmas at sea.

Hope hit beat-up golf balls off No. 2 Elevator with Willie House, who had headed the investigation into the accident that had happened on that spot 22 days earlier. House knocked a divot out of the wooden surface as he and Hope traded banter with an audience of sailors.

"I was aiming for the thirteenth white cap."

"I've seen water holes before, but *this* I gotta report to *Sports Illustrated*."

Wearing a pink golf shirt, Hope had lunch with the enlisted sailors and sat next to William Smith, asking where he was from, an event the airman would recall as one of the highlights of his Navy career. Wearing a "Miss Iron Angel" satin sash Dianna Lynn Batts ate with VF-53 airmen. The supporting acts enjoyed the hot showers

Bob Hope was never far from a golf club and took several opportunities to swing one on *Tico*. Men watched the show from every vantage point on the deck, island and aircraft and even from other ships sailing alongside. (Author's collection)

and laundry service, a step up from the barracks they had stayed in in Saigon, and watched old Charlie Chan and John Wayne films on the closed-circuit TV.

Finally, at 1330 it was showtime. The *Turner Joy* and supply ship *Sacramento* sailed alongside the carrier, bobbing in the choppy seas. The crew of the destroyer listened to the show on the ship's intercom and many watched through binoculars. A few lucky sailors had been flown over for a closer view.

The ships slowed down to as little as five knots, sailing westward to keep the sun constant for the television lighting and the boiler smoke blowing away from the performers.

On *Tico* men sat everywhere they could. They hung off every part of the island, they clambered on aircraft. Ed Pfeiffer bagged a prime seat in the cockpit of a Champs A-4, although he had to share it in part with Airman Culligan. John Paisley sat on the intake trunk. At least 40 others stood on the wing or sat on the fuselage. Another large crowd clustered on a VF-53 F-8, some of them hanging from a live Sidewinder. Another F-8 was kept on alert on catapult 1 in case the North Vietnamese attacked during the four-hour show.

Although it was his first TV show filmed on a carrier, some of Hope's jokes were probably older than the *Tico*. "I'd like to thank Captain Miller for piping me aboard. I wish he'd let me walk! It was a pretty skinny pipe, I wanna tell you that."

"She really is a beauty. I understand half the whales in the Pacific are trying to get her to go upstream!"

"I'm surprised, I didn't know Texas would float!"

"Very beautiful! It's amazing what you can rent from Hertz these days!"

"What a raft! It looks like Jackie Gleason's surfboard!"

He re-wrote one of his nuclear power jokes that had been intended for *Enterprise*. "It's amazing the change that comes over the crew when you bring five beautiful girls aboard, we've got more steam on the deck then we have in the catapults."

Most of Hope's entourage had arrived by helicopter, but the comedian himself had come aboard on a C-1, letting him use his carrier landing jokes. "I wouldn't say landing on this carrier is dangerous but how come they have a chaplain as landing officer? When the hook grabs you it's like you hit a wall. I flew in this morning on a COD—that's a plane. The pilot asked me if the landing was smooth enough. I didn't answer … I was waiting for my shorts to stop circling around my neck!"

Hope congratulated the crew for donating a record amount of blood to the troops in Vietnam from the Yokosuka blood drive and judged a beard-growing contest. Joey Heatherton danced the watutsi with a small group of sailors. The Nicholas Brothers tried to teach Bob to dance with moderate success and did a duet with Carroll Baker. Hope, Jerry Colona and Jack Jones donned joke-shop Beatles wigs and performed a "swinging England" act as "The Happy Rolling Rockheads."

Not all the sailors appreciated the hokey WW2-era jokes or some of Hope's digs at anti-draft protestors or modern music. Yeoman Joe Miller's group weren't impressed much. John Lunsford and his pals were Beatles fans too, but laughed at all the jokes and appreciated Hope's act as a nice distraction from the seriousness of combat operations. Some were just tired from the effort of launching constant strikes. As Hope and friends did their shtick, one sailor rolled over and mumbled, "Wake me when the broads come on."

Others missed out. Jerry Bright had to steer the ship and John McCabe had to supervise him while watching the show on a black and white TV with no sound. Ed Rizzo had been on the night shift messcooking. He asked a buddy to wake him for the show, but he didn't and Ed only caught the last few minutes. Low-angle photos of Joey Heatherton circulated at a dollar each for those who missed the fun.

Following a request by the captain of *Sacramento*, backed up by a threat to cut off *Tico's* food supply, the girls were flown across for a short visit. They attended a promotion ceremony and collected several souvenirs. Carroll Baker brought back the captain's ashtray. The next morning, just after 0800 the Chinooks departed between jet launches and landings and flew the whole circus on to An Khe in the Vietnam central highlands.

Things soon returned to normal. On the 30th there were two different jet blast accidents. In the morning Airman John Hanens suffered a first-degree burn to his back while sitting on a tractor and was put on the sick list. Airman A. G. Brown was knocked over by jet blast in the afternoon and admitted to the ward. He was joined the next day by Airman J. M. Douglas, who had been injured when a Vacu Blast machine blew up while he was fitting a hose to it. He was the final casualty of 1965.

As the year ended on the home front a light aircraft flew over Long Beach, and leaflets fluttered down over the naval base. On one side were pictured the charred bodies of a woman and a child. On the other was a strongly worded message criticizing the United States' involvement.

A secret Pentagon report concluded gloomily that despite the widening of *Rolling Thunder* to concentrate on Hanoi's industrial capacity through striking its communications and power infrastructure, that by the end of 1965 there was "no indication of any significant decline to NVN morale or of any softening of Hanoi's attitude toward negotiations. Conversely, preparation for a prolonged struggle was indicated."

CHAPTER 11

Keep on Running

Saturday, January 1, 1966
In Special Operations Area, Vietnam

On New Year's Day, 1966 the first entry in *Tico*'s deck log was written in verse, a U.S. Navy tradition since at least World War II. As regulations dictated, it listed the nearby ships, the task group, the formation commander, the carrier's course and speed and its security status:

> 00–04 First watch of the year, holiday cruise.
> No sleep, no broads, no snooze, no booze.
> Out in the night so bright and clear
> *Preston* and *Swenson*, our screen, are near.
> Steaming in company with seven seven point five
> Against the Viet Cong our forces connive.
> The senior officer present afloat
> Is CARDIV NINE embarked in our boat.
> *Tico*'s Commanding Officer is OTC,
> A salty old dog of the seventh sea.
> The captain of the *Preston* is the man in charge
> Of the screen out there protecting our barge.
> Material Condition Yoke is set tonight
> And proper hatches are dogged down tight.
> On course two one zero holding ten knots
> With generators one and four grinding out Watts,
> We've got two boilers making steam
> And the plant is running like a dream.
> Off the coast of Viet Nam
> The wind is high and the seas are rough
> But *Ticonderoga*'s men have grown up tough.
> Although there are those with a better racket
> We know at the very least we can hack it.
> 0130 to zero three zero our course we change
> To keep the wicked catwicks[1] out of range.

---

1 The Catwicks are tiny uninhabited islands at the northern end of Dixie Station.

VA-52 Skyraiders saw heavy action in early 1966. Knightrider 387 at the rear of this formation crash-landed after flak damage on 3 January. Pilot James Donahue was quickly rescued. (National Naval Aviation Museum)

The bombing halt lasted until January 26 but attacks on targets in South Vietnam and Laos continued with over 6,000 sorties flown by Navy aircraft alone during the month, for the loss of ten aircraft and eight aircrew in combat and accidents. Three of the five carriers in WestPac (*Enterprise, Hancock, Kitty Hawk, Ranger* and *Ticonderoga*) were continuously on the line, relieving each other periodically.

Tico's first loss of 1966 occurred on January 3. Attacking a troop concentration near Phú Cúòng, only ten miles north of Saigon, James Donahue's A-1J, the last Spad to come off the production line in 1957, was hit by small arms fire on its ninth attack run. With flames streaming from holes in the fuselage, the Skyraider struggled to stay airborne, but Donahue kept it flying long enough to crash-land without injury to himself about ten miles away. The Viet Cong were around here, too, but an Army helicopter rescued him before they could arrive.

The next day a deck accident claimed another life. Just after 1500 hours on the 4th, Airman Charles Dixon of VAH-4 was working in the bomb bay of a Skywarrior, connecting electrical leads to the bomb racks. These had cartridges that were similar to the starters in very old fluorescent lamps. Plane handler Chuck Wilber was about 75 feet away when he heard an explosion. "I turned and saw him fall to the deck, we stayed back for a few moments until we determined there were no further explosions coming," Wilber said. The cartridge had fired, forcing a bomb ejector foot down which struck Dixon on the left side of the head, and although the fire and rescue crew were only feet away, there was little that could be done other than keep the crowd back. "We could see the side of his face was missing and he was bleeding profusely," recalled Wilber. His skull was fractured and despite emergency treatment including a tracheotomy, he died in the ship's hospital four hours later. Crash crewman Lloyd Frank was tasked with cleaning up.

It seems that at the same time Dixon was connecting the leads, unbeknownst to him another airman was in the cockpit checking the circuits by activating the bomb release switches. This was safe as long as the cartridges were not connected, but once they were, they could be deadly. The day before, Airman Widdop of VF-53 had been injured by an exploding cartridge while loading an aircraft, suffering burns and a chest contusion, although he returned to duty.

Charles O'Neil Dixon Jr., an African-American from Dallas, was just a month past his 20th birthday. The official casualty record describes Dixon's death as occurring in South Vietnam, as the result of an air loss due to hostile causes resulting in a crash on land, although this is clearly in error.

On the 13th, *Kitty Hawk* returned to Yankee Station and relieved *Tico*, which turned for the Philippines. The larger carrier's official history (but not its log) states that nuclear weapons loading exercises were conducted en route from Yokosuka. *Tico* sailed Into Subic Bay on the 14th, mooring at Alava Pier at 0930.

Several new pilots joined the Champions in the last few months of the cruise. Hugh "Tony" Merrill joined the squadron in January and became weapons training officer and safety officer. The line crews called him "Ned Buntline" because he favored a long-barreled pistol for his sidearm like the eponymous Wild West-era author. Van Hough, known as "VQ" or "Huff", and Jim "Maz" Maslowski, a former enlisted man and submariner, joined by the end of March

Subic Bay again brought about almost as many injuries as did combat operations. Groups of up to 50 sailors were assigned to temporary duty with the shore patrol, trying to keep a lid on things. Champ pilot Jim Delesie suffered a cut above his left eyebrow while on liberty, a wound apparently inflicted during an altercation with sailors on the cattle wagon. Seaman Bates fell from a net while painting the overhead on the 02 Level. A strap at the net's corner slipped and he was dumped onto the lieutenants' platform, breaking his left leg in two places and requiring treatment at the Subic naval hospital. Joe Logsdon managed to give himself second-degree burns on his right hand while using a cigarette lighter. That same night a sailor fell down a ladder, another slipped on a sidewalk and a third suffered minor cuts and abrasions in a disagreement with a friend. There were numerous absentees.

Leaving the delights of Subic to the crew of the *Enterprise*, which had arrived on the 17th, *Ticonderoga* cast off on the 22nd. As they sailed past, Ed Ofstad marvelled at the huge nuclear-powered supercarrier. "It [was] so fresh new and clean and our tub which should have been retired was but a back row junker."

When there was no carrier in port the price of everything in Subic ("and I do mean *everything*," said one sailor) was cut 50 percent. It went back up as soon as the next carrier pulled in.

A Happy Sailor Is a Sailor at Sea

The medical officer's work returned to dealing with the usual sober seagoing accidents. Men cut hands and heads on bombs and the sharp edges of aircraft, caught fingers in doors and their hands slipped while working with knives. An airman fell off an A-4 wing and bruised his ribs on a drop tank. The ordnance handling officer suffered skin burns when gasoline splashed on his arm while he was working with napalm bombs. Joe Logsdon was standing near a bulkhead when a grating that was leaning against it fell on his head, lacerating his scalp.

Continuing the stream of VIP visitors, a party of ambassadors to the Republic of Vietnam came aboard on the morning of January 26. Accompanied by General Heintges, deputy commander of the Military Assistance Command in Vietnam, they included diplomats from Argentina, Brazil, Denmark, the Netherlands, New Zealand, Spain, Sweden, Turkey and Upper Volta.

By the last days of January, President Johnson's military and diplomatic advisers were urging an end to the bombing halt and to expand the target list to include Hanoi and Haiphong. A survey of senators found them split evenly for and against the resumption of bombing. On the 30th, Johnson relented and *Rolling Thunder* strikes resumed on the next day with the priority being moving targets and then transhipment points. During the pause, the North Vietnamese had accelerated the transport of supplies southwards and all routes were operating.

The Joint Chiefs of Staff ordered CINCPAC to resume strikes at daylight on the 31st regardless of weather conditions. John Paisley was not a fan of this approach. "North Vietnam did something that really pulled his chain so he said, we're going back in *today* at a particular hour and the weather was lousy but because he said we were going back in, we couldn't cancel anything. We were out there milling around under a two thousand-foot overcast, which is stupid! That's shoot-down city." An official report says that little damage was achieved on the first day of *Rolling Thunder* Phase III because of the bad weather and lack of surprise.

That morning Render Crayton was returning in Champ 466 when he found the landing gear would not deploy. After several attempts he managed to get two legs down but not the third. The decision was made to take the barricade with all wheels up, letting the drop tanks take the strain. Landing on the jugs was a recognized procedure that could be carried off with little airframe damage if done right, at least on a long smooth land runway. It was a different proposition on a carrier deck with just under 200 feet of deck between the ramp and the barricade. On the call "Stand by to rig the barricade!" the crash crews sprang into

Tico's only barrier engagement of the cruise came on 31 January when Render Crayton landed an A-4 with the wheels up after a malfunction. The cut-up straps were useful as painting slings and for other shipboard uses. (John Deasey)

action, removing the arrester cables and rigging the barricade to its stanchions in a well-rehearsed drill.

Crayton made a perfect landing on the drop tanks without the nose pitching forward, kept the refuelling probe clear of the deck and caught the barrier. The nylon engaging straps dug into the leading edges of the wings, fin and tailplane. Randy Wilson was one of the many crewmen watching. "When he hit the barrier the probe hit dead on one of those straps, doubled back and went down the intake, spilling fuel all down the intake." The fuel ignited in the engine and a huge fireball bloomed out of the exhaust and intakes, unseen by Crayton. Randy recalls, "Here he is, being all fucking nonchalant after he knew he was okay. The crash crews are all out there all over trying to get the canopy open and he's pushing them away like *get out of the way I can get myself out.* Then he saw that fire warning light and he got out of there real quick."

Even before Crayton unbuckled, a conga line of sailors dressed only in regular deck gear were thrusting a hose down the intake and aiming two more at the wreck just in case. Lying in a pool of dissolving foam with its paint scorched and a big notch cut out of the fin by the barricade, and more damage where the probe was ripped from its mounts, 466 was done for this cruise.

"Tilly" the mobile flight deck crane lifted the wreck, barricade and all, out of the landing area and onto No.3 Elevator. An hour after the accident, *Tico* was launching the next strike. Pushed to a corner of the hangar deck, 466 was left in Cubi after the next port call but was eventually repaired and served again over Vietnam. The boatswain's mates loved a barrier engagement as it provided them with a great supply of nylon strapping for all sorts of shipboard purposes such as painting slings.

The next day Marine Private Spelger accidentally shot himself in the hand with a .45 pistol. "You've got to be careful with those things," said his buddy Carl Kernan. Spelger's injury was just one of many. A sailor burned his scalp with steam when he turned the wrong shower tap. The gunner's mate who brought the B43 up on the elevator on December 5, hit ordnanceman J. J. Smith, cutting his lip. Fireman apprentice Richard Pitts lost two teeth when he was hit in the mouth by someone or something. Ensign Wayne Wilson, the classified materials officer, cut his head when he stood up from sitting on his bunk. An airman cut his own forearm with a razor and was put under observation. A sailor doing work duties as a brig prisoner received bruises to his chest. On February 4, Joe Logsdon cut his hand on a grinder. He returned to duty after treatment. *Tico* sailed north to relieve *Kitty Hawk* on Yankee Station.

On February 7, a week after his crash landing, Render Crayton flew his last mission. On an overcast day, he led five Champ Skyhawks on an afternoon armed reconnaissance mission over Route Pack 3. The objective was to find and destroy rail cars near Phu Dien Chau in Nghe An Province.

Jay Shower was not impressed with Crayton's navigation. "We flew right past the target which was some rail track and we passed it by about five miles and I'm shouting 'We passed the target! We passed the target!' And he didn't know which way to turn … and people are shooting at us while this guy is lost up there and this is very bad."

As the A-4s dived on the target, they came under fire from 37mm guns. Looking to his left, one of Crayton's wingmen saw an explosion on the side of his Skyhawk's fuselage. Crayton reported a fire warning light and climbed back to 4,500 feet, but Champ 462 was doomed, beginning a roll to the right with the nose falling through the horizon. Crayton ejected and landed in a river, injuring himself in the process, but was able to get ashore.

Finding himself surrounded by water on three sides and facing a village on the fourth, Crayton pulled out his survival radio and called his wingmen. "I'm all right,

Render Crayton, seen here in the Champs ready room on the 1964 cruise, was shot down by light flak and captured a week after his wheels-up landing. (Cruisebook)

except I think I have a broken arm. I can't move very far." In fact he had a broken right shoulder and enemy troops were moving in.

Ed Pfeiffer called in the situation and a rescue effort was launched. The Air Force dispatched an HU-16B Albatross amphibian from its offshore orbit point 200 miles north of the DMZ, but as Crayton had not crossed the coast, the vulnerable aircraft couldn't come inland or pick him up.

A destroyer launched a helicopter, which picked up an A-1 escort. The Champ A-4s remained overhead, using their remaining ordnance to keep the approaching troops away. "The guys on the west bank of the river were getting into little boats and we were shooting at them to keep them away," recalled Jay Shower. "And I shot all my bullets, cut boats in half." Pfeiffer jettisoned his drop tanks on the enemy as the fuel in them ran out and then flew low passes just to keep their heads down. Phelps even added his bomb racks to the mix. William Smith on *Tico* saw aircraft involved in the rescue effort return with mud on their undersides, sprayed up from paddy fields as they streaked overhead firing cannon and rockets. Jay Shower witnessed more bravery from VA-52 Skyraider pilots. "One of the Spads fired all his LAU-3 pods of rockets at this boat that was probably only a few yards, half a football field, away and he was down at five feet above the water and of course they ricochet and these explosions that he flies into completely destroys his engine. He had 250 shrapnel holes in the airplane," Shower said. The Spad story grew in the telling. Randy Wilson heard that the Spad had even killed Vietnamese troops with its propeller and wing leading edges. Shower says that although the battered Skyraider made it back to *Tico*, it was beyond repair and was pushed overboard, but this doesn't tally with any known A-1 losses and VA-52's Jim Doran says none were dumped, but on this particular Spad a Purple Heart medal was painted under the canopy rail. "This was the bird's medal not the pilot's," said Doran. Harvey Browne and Paul Giberson of VA-52 were awarded Silver Stars for their exceptional bravery in the rescue attempt.

The suppressing fire could only hold back the enemy for so long. "They're almost on top of me," radioed Crayton. "They are going to get me, boys. You'd better go home, you don't have much fuel." He was right, the now clean-winged A-4s had only about 15 minutes fuel remaining and reluctantly they had to leave to meet a tanker dispatched by *Tico*. The Spads stayed until they were out of ammo and observed Crayton being led to a hut, then away into the undergrowth.

Where was the helicopter? Fighting its way to the crash scene along with an A-1 escort. Unfortunately, the wrong coordinates had reached the helicopter and it encountered heavy gunfire. When it finally arrived at the right location, all that remained on the site was a parachute. Crayton was beginning the first of 2,562 days in captivity.

CAG Down

On February 9, Jack Snyder, the new commander of Air Wing Five, was on a low-level road reconnaissance 30 miles from Thanh Hoa in a Roadrunners Skyhawk when he became the first victim of a SAM since the bombing halt before Christmas.

Snyder's flight was flying at 500 feet, presumably below the flight envelope of the SA-2, but out of the corner of one eye Snyder glimpsed the missile, which looked to him like a telephone pole with a ball of fire coming out of its tail. In that instant he was able to see it was white with a black band around the middle. He broke hard away from it, but it curved towards him and exploded behind his tail pipe. The A-4 was riddled with shrapnel in the tail and wings. Fuel poured out of holes in the wing tanks, but the jet was still controllable. Snyder's cockpit instruments spun in front of his eyes, making the decision of which direction to head for the sanctuary of the Tonkin Gulf 35 miles away mainly one of guesswork. Whether the plane was on fire or not was another niggling uncertainty. On one hand, the fire warning light which had come on after the SAM hit was now off. On the other, Snyder's wingman Danny Glenn, who would himself become a prisoner of the North Vietnamese that December, was frantically signalling for him to eject. The prospect of bailing out over the North and becoming a member of the "closed officers mess in Hanoi" was enough to spur Snyder to coax as much remaining mileage as possible out of the battered Skyhawk. Hydraulic fluid was escaping along with fuel, and Snyder activated the manual control system, which allowed him to manuever, but with a great deal of effort.

Scooters were famously tough, and Roadrunner 546 held together for another 12 minutes, crossing the coast and getting some distance from the defenses, before the fire restarted and the stick went loose in Snyder's hand. A moment after he ejected the A-4 broke in two and fell into the Tonkin Gulf about 50 miles from the coast within range of USS *England*'s Seasprite. Snyder was only one of 18 aviators the destroyer rescued in the first half of 1966, a feat which won the ship the Navy Unit Commendation.

On Valentine's Day, Airman C. Bilieu knocked himself unconscious walking through a hatch. Seaman D. A. Jordan received a bruised chest while performing duties in the brig, Airman J. T. Oaks suffered a compound fracture of his left big toe when a hydraulic jack fell on it, the Roadrunners lost another Skyhawk and the Champions came close to losing one.

On a *Steel Tiger* mission somewhere over Laos, Jere Durham of VA-144 was hit by ground fire. His A-4C's engine temperature kept increasing but was still producing thrust. Durham attempted to land at Da Nang but was thwarted by worsening weather. He headed out to sea and ejected from Roadrunner 543 twenty miles off the coast where he was rescued by a Marine Corps helicopter without apparent injuries.

The same day, Jay Shower got a flak hit while attacking a target north of Vinh. He recalls: "I did a 4g pull up and I got hit and all my fuel ran out the wing. The hole was this big around and it was just outboard of the wheel but inboard of the drop tank. So my fuel went immediately down to 600 pounds, which is in the sump tank, a rubber bladder behind the pilot's seat. So I climbed out to 35,000 feet, and figured out where I was, and I was about 120 miles to Da Nang and 90 miles to the ship but I couldn't make it to the ship because I'd be out of gas so I headed for Da Nang and I started an idle descent from about 80 miles out and it was taking me down real nice and as I went through 10,000 feet the gauges were reading zero and by this time I was about ten miles out and the book says the glide ratio is about one in one—one mile distance for every thousand feet altitude and so 10 in 10 meant I was going to make it to the field, gliding."

Shower called for an emergency landing and the tower said, "You are number three in the pattern," meaning he would have to wait his turn.

Shocked, he replied, "No, you don't understand!" Bizarrely, they were playing a joke on him and he went ahead. "I made a beautiful landing and as I got to the end of the runway I turned off and cleared the runway and stopped. They hooked me up and towed me off."

At Da Nang Jay met Dick Taylor, an old college friend, who had a motorcycle so they went off on it and bought bandoliers of ammunition, pistols and other stuff to take back to the ship. Then they went to the Da Nang officers' open mess (known as the Doom Club) for a few drinks. The base was in range of Viet Cong mortar positions. "We were drinking beer and I'm putting it down and pretty soon mortars started coming in and there were sand bags up and down the walls and across the ceiling and when the mortars went off right outside the door I dived underneath the bar and these Air Force officers were just standing there with their hand over the glass and they said, 'Hey Jay, you're getting sand in your beer!' Boom, boom! These guys didn't even flinch."

Jay got off the floor and said to Dick, "We gotta get out of here!"

They went over to the control tower where Jay got on the high frequency radio and talked to the ship, saying, "My airplane is perfectly OK. There's no electrical problem. My pop-out alternator is working, all hydraulics are working. This hole in the wing blew the slat out so the lift I lost in the hole is counteracted by the extended slat, so I don't have to change trim or anything. Can you send me an A-3 tanker overhead that can fly and refuel me for an hour?" and they replied, "Yes."

"I'm taking off in about twenty minutes," Jay said.

Back on the flightline Jay and Dick ran into an Air Force safety officer.

"You can't fly that plane with that hole in the wing" he told them.

"I know I can, I just landed it."

He was insistent that Shower not fly the plane.

"Call the base commander and get him to tell me that a Navy guy can't fly a Navy aircraft."

"OK, I'll go get the CO."

While the safety officer walked a hundred yards down to the ops building, Jay showed Dick the ground starter cart and told him, "All you have to do is turn this switch and that switch and when I get the engine running you just yank the hoses out."

Jay kicked the chocks out and said to Dick, "There you go." Jay got in the cockpit so quickly he even forgot to strap in.

"Dick got me cranked up and I taxied out and I saw this A-3 circling at about a thousand feet and I thought this is great, and I only had about 600 pounds of fuel, that's all, and I can barely get it airborne with that but the guy timed it right and as I took off he came right over at the same speed and I pulled up and plugged in and I said 'give me some gas' and of course within a minute it was coming out the hole so I told him stop." The A-3 gave Shower gas for a minute and then they shut it down for a minute and doing this for an hour they got all the way out to the ship. When it was his turn to land, the A-3 lined up both jets on 3-mile final approach, leveled his wings, gave the A-4 one last shot of fuel and just gunned it, climbing away as Shower went in and got an OK 2-wire. "So I got shot down and saved the airplane and a week later they'd repaired it with a top-to-bottom patch," Jay said.

Back in Japan

On February 21, *Tico* pulled alongside Akasaki Pier at Sasebo, where it spent nine days. During this extended port call, a group made a trip to Nagasaki.

In Sasebo, Seaman John Viegers was treated for abrasions after being subdued by the shore patrol. Boiler technician James Williams somehow caused his leg to bleed profusely with a fishhook. On the last day in Sasebo, Bill Nealon handed over command of the Champs to Carl Ray Smith and left for his next assignment, Air Officer of *Ranger*. The JOs thought Smith was less formal and more approachable

The "Whale" was the largest aircraft on *Tico*. With room for extra crew, non-flying officers (including Captain Miller) were known to fly on A-3 missions to earn Air Medals. (NMNA)

than his predecessor. Pete Sherman, a tall redhead from Bay Village, Ohio became the XO. In turn he would become Champ One and be killed by a SAM in June 1967.

Randy Wilson was heading to his berthing from the hangar deck when someone coming the other way bumped into him and he turned his head to see who it was. He kept walking and turned his head back only to walk straight into a hangar queen F-8 that was parked by the hatch. The nitrogen that pressurized the landing gear had leaked away and the nose was lower than normal. The pitot head jammed into the middle of Wilson's forehead, making a nice three-quarter moon shape and necessitating a trip to sickbay

When *Tico* returned to Dixie Station even the Whales were getting in on the action. Although the Skywarrior was coming to the end of its career as a bomber, Heavy Four went out on March 18 for attacks on Viet Cong training areas near the Cambodian border. A camera in another A-3 filmed Charles Siegwarth's Whale as it bombed the jungle and it is possible Captain Miller was in the cockpit with him, working on his Air Medal for flying ten combat missions. *Tico's* flight surgeon Nenad Buktenica certainly got his by riding along in Whales on the last few months of the cruise. Roadrunners added cluster bombs to the mix this day and were employing another controversial weapon two days later when they lost another A-4 and its pilot.

Jerry Pinneker had just completed a successful napalm run on a Viet Cong company near My Tho in Dinh Tuong Province 30 miles south west of Saigon when he was hit with automatic weapons fire. Roadrunner 553 disintegrated and crashed into a coconut grove. Del Mitchell says Pinneker was a great guy, and when they reported him killed in action, there was a big sigh throughout the ship.

His body was recovered from the crash site and two memorial services—one Christian, one Buddhist— were attended by hundreds of villagers. Shortly afterwards, district chief Nguyen-Van-Tien wrote to Jerry's widow Kay in Moline, Illinois to express his community's appreciation for Jerry's sacrifice. Annapolis graduate and ex-submariner Jerald Lee Pinneker, 25, had learned to fly with his father and uncle in Nebraska. His Uncle Harry had been a Navy flight instructor and bought one of his old planes as post-war surplus in which he flew his nephews until gas got too pricey. In 1971, Jerry's widow Kay visited while travelling across America with a friend. The friend liked Scottsbluff and Harry so much that she stayed there and married him.

As April began, there was some good news for one of the VF-51 pilots. Landing from a mission, Ron Evans was called to the ready room where Captain Miller read out a letter from NASA. Evans had been selected to become an astronaut and would join the Apollo program. The next time he touched down on *Tico* it would be on return from the far side of the moon.

Tico was relieved on Yankee Station by *Hancock* and after a brief stop at Subic Bay went straight on to a four-day port call in Hong Kong, anchoring in the harbor of the British Crown Colony. While sailors went ashore to buy bargain Bulova watches with Timex workings inside or Rolexes with mechanisms made of paper, John Mape, the new CO of the Knightriders, and his XO Bob Worchesek had a meal in a floating restaurant. Mape wrote to his family that he turned down the bird's nest soup and eels, sticking to shrimp and lobster.

Like the cattle cars in Subic, the liberty boats operating to the carrier were the scene of numerous fights, but the only notable incident was a man overboard at 0440 one morning. Six others jumped in to save him and all were picked up by a picket boat. This then fouled its propeller and in turn needed to be rescued by the Captain's gig.

One of Hong Kong's characters was a woman that sailors knew variously as Sally the Painter, Mary Soo or Garbage Mary. She was a widow who had worked out that if she took away kitchen garbage from visiting warships and used it on a pig farm that she had a share of, she could produce pork at a profit. In return her team of female workers would paint the ship's hulls and take over mess hall and scullery duties while the ship was in port. This saved the captain a few dollars from his budget and allowed sailors more time off, giving a morale boost. Before long she had a fleet of sampans to service visiting ships, eventually acquiring a water taxi company and a ferry line and retiring to a mansion overlooking the harbor.

Five Days, Six Losses

All too soon *Tico* was back on Yankee Station, and about to suffer the toughest period of the whole cruise. The new CO of VA-52 was John Mape from Dublin, California. Six-foot-four and slim with sandy hair and a ruddy complexion, he had planned to become a priest, but changed his mind in college where he was studying for a philosophy degree. Nevertheless, he attended Catholic mass every day aboard *Tico*. One day after graduation in 1948 he walked past a Navy recruiting office and decided to look in. "What have you got for me?" Mape asked. Confirming he had a college degree, the recruiter suggested he might like to be a pilot. Mape was very popular with the squadron personnel and said to be devoted to his men. The CAG called them "Mape's Apes."

On the morning of April 10, Plane Captain Gerald Silvia strapped Mape into his Spad, patted him on the shoulder and saw him off on an armed reconnaissance mission over the North.

In Viceroy 381, named "The Whip," Mape led two other Spads towards a location known as Na Pe Pass, inevitably called "Nape Pass" by the Americans. The three Skyraiders were spread out 1,000 to 2,000 feet apart. About 15 miles southwest of Vinh, Mape's wingman looked across the formation, when without warning, a SAM shot up from below, struck The Whip and blew it to pieces. What was left spiralled through cloud in a near-vertical dive to the ground. The other A-1s circled the burning wreckage, but there was no parachute, no beeper and no chance of survival.

It was no place to hang around either. Another SAM was fired at the Skyraiders, but it burned out without detonating.

John Clement Mape left behind Patricia and seven children, five daughters and two sons, aged between two and fourteen. Mape's was the first A-1 to be shot down by a SAM. Flying at 7,500 feet and 180 knots as Mape's formation was, the North Vietnamese radar operators had plenty of time to acquire the Skyraiders, and the A-1s had no missile warning equipment or chaff to confuse SAM guidance.

Another sigh was heard on *Tico*.

Another Ramp Strike

When not in combat, *Tico* maintained two fighters on five-minute alert, waiting on the catapults. A pilot had to be in or near near the jet at all times. Every couple of hours they would start the engines and simulate launch. Frank Barrett remembers sharing flight deck control watch with an F-8 pilot one night who was in a very talkative mood. "I remember him telling me, that when we are on Yankee station, everyone was very focused, but now that we are off Yankee Station, we are slacking off and losing focus and when we lose focus, only bad things can happen."

Tico was back on Yankee Station now, but bad things were still happening. On the night of April 14, the Screaming Eagles' Gary Riese was having trouble getting aboard. He made two bolters then struck the round-down (the extreme aft end of the flightdeck) on the third pass. He ejected as his Crusader slid off the angle, scattering flaming parts down the deck. Riese was recovered from the sea unhurt by the Angel, but LSO Richard Hastings was not so lucky. Jay Shower remembered: "The [F-8's] wings are way out there and when he hit the round-down the wings came down and hit the flight deck and the LSO couldn't get out of the way fast enough and the wing took the top of his head off. How he kept breathing, I don't know, he was in bad shape." *Tico*'s doctors judged he needed more care than they could provide and a helicopter transferred him to the hospital ship USS *Repose*. The remaining parts of Screaming Eagle 106 were cleared off the deck and 11 aircraft were recovered. Californian-born, Youngstown, Ohio educated Dick Hastings was a recently qualified LSO. He had flown with VF-51 in 1964 Gulf of Tonkin incident when he overstressed an F-8 and had to land at Da Nang. He was Gary Reise's roommate and the pilot who warned Frank Barrett that bad things happened when you lost focus.

Four VA-56 aircraft were on a mission searching for SAMs. The plan was to meet up with an Air Force flight but they were late so the Champs headed for their alternative target, a bridge. The Skyhawks were flying fairly low under a 4,500-foot overcast. Van Hough was leading Jim Delesie in the second section and had radio problems—he could receive but not send. Tracer fire suddenly arced up in front of

Hough, then rounds hit his belly. Fuel streamed out and the gunner switched to Delesie's A-4, missing by 30 feet although at the time it seemed to him more like five. "We're too far from the coast, but I can try to get you to Thailand," radioed Delesie as he headed west. Hough turned to follow him but after some miles a fire broke out in the rear of his A-4, then went out, then started again. After several cycles of this, it started to burn continuously. "Get out now! Get out now!" yelled Delesie.

Austin Chapman, number two in the first section, looked over his shoulder and saw Hough's jet, Champ 463, stream fuel from wingtip to wingtip and then burst into flames. "I think the tail of the aircraft burned off pretty quickly and I don't know if he ejected before that or what," Chapman recalled. "I can remember seeing what looked like a tailless wing going down, but I was trying to stay focused on whether or not he had a chute." Delesie climbed and called Invert, the rescue center at Nakhon Phanom, who told him they were number five in the rescue pattern and did the equivalent of putting him on hold. Eventually two A-1 "Sandy" rescue escorts turned up. Delesie pointed out where Hough had gone down and said he had to go as his fuel was low. They replied that so were they, but they would be back in the afternoon. The weather was packing in and Delesie reluctantly left for *Tico*, landing with less than 600 pounds of fuel remaining.

Hough did have a good parachute but lost most of his survival gear during the ejection or landing, including his radio, but managed to hang on to a pen flare gun and a location beeper. The PRC-49A radio was usually stored in the seat pan survival kit, which hung below the pilot as he descended, but this often came adrift or cost valuable time to open. Some squadrons found space on the pilot's harness for the radio so he could hit the ground running so to speak. Landing near a stream, Hough could see a little village on a slope and could hear voices. He had strong motivation to stay free. He had two daughters, aged seven and six, and his wife Alma was eight months pregnant with a third. He looked around, saw the nearest mountain and decided to run up it.

A football star in high school, Van Quillian Hough was short but strong as a bull. Even for a fit man, the climb was tough in the thick jungle. It began to rain, making things worse. Clambering over a rocky outcrop, Hough came face to face with the skeleton of a monkey, which scared him half to death. The Sandys returned and picking up a weak signal from Hough's beeper they relayed the approximate location to a pair of HH-3 "Jolly Green Giant" rescue helicopters. Arriving on the scene, Jolly Green 56 went into a high orbit while Jolly Green 52, flown by Captains "Skip" Cowell and Dave Henry hovered over the trees, but crewmen LaVerne Kellerman and Mike Halvorson in the cabin could not see through the thick jungle canopy and were not picking up a radio signal. The higher helicopter started picking up small arms fire and had to move away. Jolly Green 52 circled over the jungle for 15 minutes until Hough judged it close enough to risk firing a flare. Seeing red smoke drifting out of the treetops, Cowell called to Henry if he could see the survivor, but the canopy was too thick. Flight engineer Bob Watson lowered the rescue penetrator into the jungle and waited to see if anyone got on. Normally the rescue helicopter would authenticate the survivor using a series of code words to avoid a trap, but there was no time. Parajumper Kellerman shouted over the intercom that they were taking hits from ground fire. A couple of tugs on the cable indicated someone was aboard the rescue seat and Watson reversed the hoist. On the way up through the jungle canopy Hough became entangled in a large vine, which caught around his neck. At this point nothing was going to make him let go of the hoist and the vine stretched as he ascended, almost strangling him. Finally it snapped and he was hauled out of the treetops and aboard the helicopter, which could finally move to avoid the gunfire.

Jolly Green 52 flew back to Nakon Phanom, Thailand with a grinning Van Hough, who had spent four hours on the ground. He was able to phone Alma and tell her of his safe recovery. Their third daughter, Dawn, was born the next day. It was three days before he made it back to *Ticonderoga*. The Champs had followed the rescue on the ship's radio and were glad to see him back. Hough told then the first thing that had happened when he was pulled aboard the Jolly Green was that a kid who looked about seventeen handed him a cigarette and a glass of gin. Hawaiian native Cowell's crew had already made several combat rescues and in July would pick up A-1 pilot Dieter Dengler, who had been on the ground in Laos since February.

As well as Hough, three *Kitty Hawk* aircraft were shot down that day. One was a VA-115 Skyraider, flown by LTJG William Tromp, which was last seen somewhere off the mouth of the Song Gia Hoi River. The next day, Knightriders pilot Allen D. Wilson, known as "A. D." or inevitably, "Spad," was searching for Tromp near Hòn Gio (Tiger) Island, a fortified island about 15 miles off shore on the northern side of the Seventeenth parallel, the North-South border. U.S. aircraft were authorized to dump unexpended ordnance on the island as they headed south, and Wilson may have been shooting it up for sport, having been unsuccessful in his search. After five passes over the island he was hit by ground fire. Wilson ditched his Skyraider and was rescued by a USAF helicopter. Tromp was never seen again, although the wreck of his aircraft was discovered underwater in 1973.

On April 19, the last day on the line, *Tico* lost two Crusaders in combat. Led by skipper Robair Mohrhardt, the Iron Angels provided escort for a strike group tasked to strike the Haiphong highway bridge, a reinforced concrete structure nearly 1,500 feet long but only 12 feet wide and one of the major links between Haiphong Harbor and Hanoi. Captain Miller later told reporters that this strike was "the real climax of the tour." Neither the air force nor any of the other carriers had been able to knock the bridge out "so they asked us to take one last whack at it and we loaded up all our airplanes with all the ordnance they could carry," Miller said. Strike leader Bruce Miller, VA-144's skipper, took that order seriously, leaving off external fuel tanks to fill every station on his 11 A-4Cs with bombs, a 2,000-pounder on the centerline and 1,000-pounders on the wing pylons.

Climbing to acquire the target, the Skyhawks' missile warning equipment lit up and Miller dove his flight down again, avoiding two SAMs. As soon as they popped up near the target, they ran into a heavy concentration of flak of all calibres and a 37mm shell blew a hole through his fin. Despite this damage and two more SAM launches, Miller maneuvered the formation to line up on the bridge. His own three bombs struck dead on the western support, dropping the centre span of the bridge, and the other A-4s knocked down four more of the bridge's 21 spans. Hanoi was isolated from its port for a while and Miller received the Silver Star.

It was not a one-sided battle, however. Over the target the explosion of an 85mm shell peppered Robair Mohrhardt's Crusader with shrapnel. The right-wing fold hinge pin was damaged and the outer wing bent up as much as 45 degrees. The Crusader rolled inverted and only the New Yorker's sharp reflexes stopped it becoming part of the landscape. Lighting the afterburner and leaving a dense cloud of black smoke behind him, Mohrhardt headed for the coast, accelerating to nearly 600 knots despite his control difficulties. The broken wing was constantly causing the fighter to roll right, which could be corrected with rudder, but how it would handle on the landing approach was anybody's guess.

Morhrardt's radio transmitter was broken, but he could hear his wingman Paul Gillcrist calling for help as the two F-8s went feet wet and turned south. The *Kitty Hawk* was the nearest carrier and offered to ready its deck for the struggling Crusader. A tanker was sent up, but Firefighter 226's hydraulics were damaged, and the refuelling probe wouldn't extend. Neither would the landing gear. With only a couple of minutes fuel remaining, Mohrhardt accepted that all he could do was "step out of the machine." He stowed loose gear in the cockpit and pulled the handles above his head. His ejection was clean and Gillcrist circled his parachute as it descended to the Tonkin Gulf to be met by one of *Kitty Hawk*'s helicopters.

Mohrhardt's Crusader was the last aircraft *Tico* lost on this cruise, but he wasn't the last pilot to come back without one. Earlier that afternoon VFP-63's Ron Ball was photographing Cát Bà Island, looking for a flak site that had shot down another aircraft. He certainly found one. Ball's RF-8 pulled up from just above the waves to make its photo run over the island when tracer fire streaked out and went straight into his fuselage. Flying escort, Iron Angel Hal Loney called Ball, telling him he was on fire and to accelerate before radioing for a rescue helicopter with its own escort. Ball managed to climb to three thousand feet, but Loney could see right through the hole in his jet. The hook dropped down, and so did the main landing gear, on fire. Loney recommended that Ball get out and the photo pilot agreed, noting that his temperature gauge was climbing through 1,000 degrees before adding a confident "See you back at the ship" and ejecting. Cork Tip 937 exploded a moment later.

With his life preserver inflated, shot-down RF-8 pilot Ron Ball is hauled up into Sea King "Big Mother 68." Enemy fire was coming close and a MiG was in the air. When he was returned to *Tico* the carrier could head for home. (*All Hands*)

The RESCAP Skyraiders picked up Ball's rescue beacon and peeled off in different directions so as to triangulate his position. Soon they located him bobbing in a one-man raft only half a mile offshore. There was a light fog, which played to the advantage of the A-1s as it obscured them from the gunners on land, but it was thin enough to look down through and see the survivor and the red smoke from his flare. They could also see North Vietnamese boats racing to the scene and drove them off with cannon fire.

Eighteen minutes after ejecting, Ball was rescued by Big Mother 68, a Sea King from the USS *Yorktown* flown by Bill Terry and Dick Benson. Enemy bullets were splashing in the water as Ball jumped from his raft and swam to the rescue hoist. Charles Eggleston, a photographer from the Navy's publicity arm was aboard and the first thing he said to Ball after he was hauled aboard was that he had just made him famous. In fact this was the first combat rescue to be photographed as it happened, and the pictures appeared in many newspapers.

There were radar indications that a MiG was in the area and the helicopter left as fast as it could go for the safety of the missile screen of patrolling destroyers. The MiG turned back and Big Mother 68 dropped Ball off on the USS *Coontz* where he was dried off and fed.

Ron Ball had a premonition he would get "bagged" as he sat on the catapult before his final flight of the cruise, but it could have been much worse. *Tico* and 3,000 men had to wait until he was returned before they could leave the line. *Coontz* ransomed Ball for a tub of ice cream.

Ticonderoga's war was over, for the time being.

CHAPTER 12

Homeward Bound

Tuesday, May 3, 1966
Inport, Fleet Activities, Yokosuka Japan

Before returning to California, *Tico* stopped for two more days in Yokosuka, which was barely enough time for a sailor to be pushed through a window. The carrier left Japan on May 3, and headed eastwards toward California.

Just before 0400 on the 6th, General Quarters was sounded as a suspected Soviet bomber was detected on a heading towards *Ticonderoga*. The Alert Five Crusader was launched to shadow it and other aircraft were prepared as backup.

Two more contacts were picked up at 0844 and an E-1 radar plane was launched, followed by four jets, including Jay Shower's A-4. In all there were four "Bear" turboprops and three "Bison" jets. Shower intercepted a "Bear-D" maritime reconnaissance aircraft around 3,000 nautical miles from its base at Khorol near Vladivostok. In company with a Crusader, Shower spent 50 minutes shadowing the giant turboprop patrol plane.

"I wanted to get a close-up picture and I told this guy in the F-8 to get out of the way and I went right up behind one of the inboard engines and the guy [in the Bear] had his mask hanging down—we were at 23,000 feet and the cabin pressure was like 8,000 feet and we were waving at each other and the guy kept going like this, *come in closer, come in closer*, and I picked up my little camera and I showed it to him, took a picture of him and he picked up his little camera and took a picture of me." The Bear crewman kept beckoning Shower to come in. "I was probably five or six feet away, I could see the whites of his eyeballs, I was that close and he dropped the camera, reached down below the window and pulled up this thing on rails … the lens was as big around as the square window and there was a big camera behind it, a huge box and he went *click* and I could see the shutter go and he put it down, and his face – he was just laughing his head off." It was all very jovial, but the rules of engagement were that if the bomb bay doors opened, you were ordered to shoot. If the tail guns pointed at you, you could shoot. "The Russians knew this

Jay Shower photographed this Soviet "Bear" patrol aircraft with VF-51 Crusader escort as *Tico* sailed across the Pacific. (Jay Shower)

too, otherwise we would have had World War III." Shower later had his photos confiscated by an intelligence officer on the ship, but saved one for his logbook.

California, Here We Come

In warmer waters, with Bears finally out of range, the captain held a deck party with a barbecue and a shirtless band playing drums and guitars in front of Tilly the crane. Men sunbathed on the round-down. As they stood in a chow line that ran around most of the deck, sailors appraised the collection of battered aircraft *Tico* had picked from *Kitty Hawk*'s air wing in Subic. There was an A-4 with no engine, a Spad with no prop, an Intruder and a Phantom wearing an unsuccessful experimental green camouflage, the latter on its belly with its nose and tail missing, and a Whale that looked like it had been in a fire, which it probably had. These wrecks would be carried back to the Navy's depots and rebuilt or junked.

The remainder of the transit home was mostly uneventful. Another boxing smoker was held and Airman K. V. Hawes suffered injured ribs. Captain Miller held inspections of all the air wing personnel on the 9th, touring each squadron in turn.

Finally, on Friday the 13th, *Tico* passed Point Loma and moored at 0900 at North Island under an overcast sky. Four thousand dependents eagerly awaited the

With the Goodyear blimp *Columbia* circling overhead, families of *Tico*'s crew wait for gangplanks to come down and their men to come ashore. (Doug Wilson via Del Mitchell)

carrier's docking. A Navy band played "Hold That Tiger," the ship's theme song. The Coronado High School Band contributed to the festive atmosphere. A Goodyear blimp flew overhead flashing welcome home messages.

Just before *Tico* tied up, the music stopped and a voice came over the ship's loudspeakers. Chaplain Harold Symons called on the crew to "raise our voices in thanksgiving for our safe return to the support and our precious families and loved ones." A prayer was said for those who did not return.

The first men given permission to debark were the 62 who had become fathers since the *Tico* had left San Diego nine months ago. At midday Joe Logsdon was reported absent.

Not everyone was quite so desperate to be back on American soil, but Del Mitchell had somewhere to be as soon as he disembarked. "After nine months in the Orient, a round-eyed girl was something we all looked forward to seeing; that and a big tall, cold milkshake. God, I missed those. First day back in San Diego, I would go to the YMCA soda fountain and order two large vanilla milkshakes, and I would savor every delicious ounce of it. Funny how your body craves something like that."

The Crusader squadrons had already flown off to Miramar. Eighteen aircraft launched, but the landing gear on Jack Eppinger's jet wouldn't retract. Waiting for the VF-51 pilot were his wife Alicia and Michael, his five-month-old son he had not yet seen. After the rest of the squadron broke into the landing pattern and taxied in, Mrs. Eppinger tapped her foot impatiently and said, "This is incredible." Almost exactly the same thing had happened at the end of the previous cruise in December 1964, when Alicia Eppinger waited in the same place with Danny, Michael's older brother, also five months old at the time. Then, as now, with his Crusader slowed by the drag of the stuck landing gear, he diverted to Point Mugu, north of Los Angeles for a gear check and fuel top-up. He arrived 45 minutes after his squadron. "I couldn't believe it," Jack Eppinger said sheepishly when he finally arrived.

VA-56 flew off to Lemoore. A while back somebody had taxied Champ 469 into *Tico*'s island and bent the refueling probe. The A-4 flew perfectly well without it, but was restricted to flying tanker missions. During the transit from Japan the corrosion control crew sanded off rivet heads and liberally sprayed zinc chromate primer until 469 seemed to be mostly yellow. Jim Delesie flew the shabby Skyhawk back to Lemoore, but skipper Smith made him keep it outside the formation flyby over the waiting families. On landing Alma Hough hugged and kissed Delesie for his part in her husband's rescue. Of all his flying, Delesie says he was most proud of his efforts on that mission.

Meeting with reporters on board *Tico*, Captain Miller said that it was a very successful cruise and he was particularly proud of the loss rate of the carrier's squadrons. Four pilots were killed and one captured, he said, but the losses would have been much worse if not for the air-sea rescue techniques that had saved many others who had to ditch. While it was true that only four had died while flying, Webster and Dixon had died in deck accidents, and Dick Hastings died on *Repose* off Vietnam the following day. He left a widow, Violet, in Sanford, California.

Miller related how *Tico* had knocked out the Tam Yuan Thong Highway bridge. "The real climax of the tour came just a couple of days before we left the line.

John Paisley with his sons Bill, seven (left) and Bob, eight on return to Lemoore. Bill would follow his dad into naval aviation, becoming an F-14 Radar Intercept Officer. (via Bill Paisley)

There was a particular bridge between Hanoi and Haiphong that neither the Air Force nor any of our carriers have been able to knock out. They asked us to take one last whack at it, so we loaded our planes up with as much ordnance as they could carry," Miller said. "Well, we did it, we lost two planes, but got both of the pilots back."

Statistics

In nine months, Air Wing Five had flown 10,122 combat sorties and expended 8,065 tons of bombs, rockets and missiles on Southeast Asia. In nine months of combat in at the end of World War II, *Ticonderoga*'s two air groups dropped 978 tons of ordnance. In nuclear terms the 1965–66 figure equates to eight kilotons, or less than 1 percent the power of the lost B43. Sixteen planes were lost or wrecked in 1965–66 compared to about 39 lost in 1944–45, including those destroyed in the kamikaze attack. In very round figures, the Champs had flown over 2,000 sorties and 5,000 hours and had expended 2,000 tons of ordnance. They had lost three A-4s and two men.

Ticonderoga had its own statistics. In the course of 13,353 catapult launches and 12,826 arrested landings in 1965–66, there were eight significant aircraft accidents related to aircraft handling, launch or landing, including engine failures shortly after take-off. The medical officer had conducted 25 operations and there were 12,775 visits to the medical department for lesser reasons, with 381 men placed on the sick list, 47 of whom needed treatment ashore. The ship's laundry had washed a million t-shirts, with 11,500 sold in the ship's store.

The day *Tico*'s return was reported in the San Diego newspapers, other headlines told of draft protests at the University of Chicago, China threatening war over the shoot-down of a Chinese MiG by an Air Force F-4, and that radiation from a Chinese nuclear test was approaching the U.S. West Coast, although the AEC described this as "insignificant."

Render Crayton was the one *Tico* man who was still to come home. With an untreated broken shoulder he was taken by his captors on a nine-day march, ending up in Hanoi, but was moved numerous times, including a year spent in a camp called "The Oven." For a time he was the ranking prisoner at the Són Tây camp west of Hanoi. The six-footer was down to a ghostly-looking 100 pounds by 1970. In November that year, a daring helicopter-borne raid was launched to rescue the prisoners at Són Tây, and while skillfully planned and executed, took place four months after the camp had been closed and the prisoners moved to other camps. For a few months in 1971–72 Crayton shared a large bunkroom with his old flight student John McCain.

Crayton was finally released in February 1973 along with 120 other prisoners. In seven years the world had changed. One of the first things he noticed was that men were wearing long hair.

There was a welcome home parade for the PoWs and Texan billionaire H. Ross Perot threw a party at a fancy San Francisco hotel with some of the Green Berets who took part on the Són Tây raid. Other guests included actors John Wayne, Clint Eastwood and Ernest Borgnine, and Nancy Reagan. Crayton would have preferred to just have a get together with his fellow ex-prisoners, but was happy to acknowledge the men who tried to rescue them. Crayton returned to his wife Patsy, to whom he had been married less than a year when he was shot down. Patsy and Render's mother Mary Jane had been stalwarts of the POW's families during the many years he had been in captivity.

Report

The report into Doug Webster's accident had been completed at the end of December 1965 but had to go to various parties for comment and endorsement, a process that took at least until October the following year.

The report's first Finding of Fact was that on the afternoon of December 5, 1965, USS *Ticonderoga* was engaged in a [two words redacted] exercise, a phase of which required the movement of aircraft. A-4E 151022 was manned by Lieutenant (Junior Grade) Douglas Morey Webster, USN, who was a qualified pilot and who inspected the aircraft prior to movement. Its brakes were inspected by personnel of VA-56 the previous day and operated satisfactorily by a plane captain during a previous movement of the aircraft that morning. An experienced handling crew, monitored by properly positioned supervisors conducted the movement. The plane director gave hand signals and blew his whistle for the pilot to apply brakes as the aircraft approached the desired parking spot, but no braking action was discernable by the witnesses and attempts to stop it with chocks proved ineffectual. The elevator guardrail also failed to stop the aircraft and a section was torn off as the aircraft went over the side. Lieutenant (Junior Grade) Webster's hands were clutching the fuselage sides as it went over and the A-4 struck the water inverted. It sank at a depth of 2,700 fathoms and a search only found a helmet and two sections of drop tank.

The board offered several opinions:

- That Lieutenant (Junior Grade) Douglas Morey Webster was well qualified by training and experience to carry out the responsibility of manning and controlling the A-4E during the movements it was scheduled to make as part of the exercise.
- That, in so far as can be determined, Webster was in good health and was adequately rested at the time he manned the aircraft for the scheduled movement.
- That Webster was conscious of his actions at the time he entered the cockpit of the aircraft and that he was aware of the intended movement of the aircraft from the hangar deck to the flight deck.

The report made three recommendations:

1. That pilots flying from aircraft carriers be reminded frequently of the importance and necessity to focus attention on the part of the pilot to the signals of the plane director during the movement of aircraft on board.
2. That plane directors be required to frequently observe the pilot during the movement of aircraft and if, either by the pilot appearance or by his failure to react immediately to given signals, the plane director believes the pilot is not devoting his full attention to the ongoing movement, that the director bring the evolution to a halt until he is assured of the proper cooperation of the pilot.
3. That the removable guard railing on the outboard edge of number two elevator be redesigned to incorporate additional strength and such additional height if

possible within the limits imposed by the necessity for adequate clearance of the guard rail by the underbody of any embarked aircraft.

Essentially, it was the pilot's fault, but it was also the plane director's responsibility to correct him. The board found that the accident was the result of three factors: the pilot's inattention, the lack of application of brakes and the failure of the guardrail to stop the aircraft.

The *reasons* for the first two causal factors were harder to pin down. No reason was established for *why* Doug was inattentive, or why, when he did seem to hear the safety whistles, he made no apparent effort to brake. With no answers to those questions, there was little to be done to address them.

On the other hand, the deficiencies of the guardrail offered the possibility of a technical solution to prevent further such accidents. Such remedies are sometimes called "tombstone technology" because they are implemented only after people die. One example might be the lip welded around *Ticonderoga*'s flight deck openings in 1945 to prevent burning gasoline pouring into the hangar below. Now it was recommended that the guardrail be enlarged from six inches in height to twelve. The guardrail had been designed to stop sliding tractors or forklift trucks, or an aircraft that—at best—was moving no faster than one knot, not a loaded runaway jet.

Naval Ship Systems Command determined that as carrier aircraft were designed to rigid specifications to ensure aircraft and external stores did not interfere with ship structures, and as these only allowed for six-inch clearances, these specifications would have to be changed to allow higher guardrails and that the cost of modifying aircraft and their loading configurations would be prohibitive. NAVSHIPSYSCOM ended its report to the Chief of Naval Operations: "It was therefore concluded that the deck edge coaming height would be restricted to 6 inches."

In his endorsement of the report the Chief of Naval Personnel stated that there was no evidence of malfeasance or gross negligence on the part of the handling crew or any other naval personnel contributing to the accident and so no further administrative action was contemplated.

In other words, nothing was done.

So What Happened?

In light of the investigation's findings, how did a nuclear-armed bomber come to be pushed into the Philippine Sea?

Brake Failure?

One possibility is a failure of the Skyhawk's brake system, which prevented Doug Webster from stopping when he heard the whistles. Plane director Lindsey testified that an A-4E's brakes would stop it dead even if a crew were pushing it. If the brakes were on the verge of failure, whoever sat in that cockpit was doomed, like Steve Richardson landing his F-8 with a cracked tailhook, there was nothing that could save him once things suddenly went wrong except the aim of young men throwing battered chocks.

The last check of 472's brakes on December 4, conducted as *Tico* moved from warm to cold conditions showed no brake problems. Plane Captain Edmister told the enquiry the brakes had been inspected at 1000 on the 5th and worked in normal fashion around midday.

Nevertheless, Randy Wilson says of his friend Bob Redding, who passed away in 2013, "When Bob and I reconnected in about 2003 one of the first things he told me about the incident was that when he rode the brakes earlier that day to move the aircraft to that spot for the load it did not have any brakes." Redding was not interviewed by the board and Edmister, who then took over from the trainee plane captain, did not apply the brakes himself. *Tico*'s catapult officer (and former A-4 pilot) George Fenzl says that since the aircraft had a war reserve weapon on it, a pilot was assigned to ride the brakes for the next step of the drill rather than the plane captain, which was "certainly in this case a mistake as the PC was likely a better brake rider than a pilot."

Sabotage?

The sabotage incident of October 1965 was reported to have occurred while the carrier was in transit rather than combat, as it was on December 5. It seems that no one was caught, despite an apparent investigation. It is theoretically possible that the brakes were tampered with in the hours *after* the last inspection, but any such evidence went to the bottom of the Philippine Sea.

The fire that occurred after Crewcut started could have been a distraction to allow a saboteur to do his work, but fires were not uncommon and only a few men were needed to deal with this one, which they did quickly.

The number of witnesses to the accident is unclear. One account says "about 50" men were in the vicinity of the move and petty officer Howard said there were "a heck of a lot of people pushing the aircraft" and that when it went in the water the elevator was "packed with people." Despite this, only some of them were called to give evidence. Witnesses called were only those who were directly involved in the movement onto the elevator and then only a selection of those.

The preamble to the report claimed that "all witnesses to the accident had been interviewed in an effort to undercover every last detail which might bear on the accident. The witnesses who appeared before the board were selected from those who had specific responsibilities in the movement of the aircraft and those who either observed the accident or participated in the attempted recovery of the pilot. Many people were interviewed who were not called as witnesses because they were unable to add any information of a significant or unique nature." Among those not called were Bob Redding, the loading crew, the Mardet or those waiting on the flight deck for the A-4.

Although restricting the number of voices heard reduced repetition—of which there was plenty—it also helped keep the nature of the exercise out of the official record. The bomb was not mentioned, although a couple of references to a "loading exercise" were made (and all but one redacted in the publicly released report.)

The same questions were asked over and over again—where was the aircraft supposed to stop? When did you hear the whistles? How fast was it moving? Was the pilot wearing a helmet? Where was he looking? These all produced very similar answers from the witnesses.

Fatigue?

Doug was declared rested and in apparent good health by Carl Dila. Dila didn't seem to know Doug well, and the rest of the squadron didn't seem to know Dila well either, despite his apparent designation as their flight surgeon.

Like all of *Tico*'s pilots, Doug was subject to the heat and humidity, the stress of carrier operations and combat over Vietnam. He had recently got over a cold and didn't make a diary entry after December 1. The dangling kneeboard seen by one witness is perhaps telling. Was Doug roused from a nap and got dressed quickly?

Distraction?

Perhaps Doug was simply distracted. Larry Dasovic said, "His eyes were moving fast in a pattern back and forth" when the whistles blew and "his mind appeared blank." Martinez said, "He looked like he didn't know what was going on." Martinez complained that pilots often looked anywhere but at the plane directors, but admitted this was not the case during Webster's move. As the plane began moving backwards, plane captain Edmister thought Doug was looking to the right, through the starboard side of the windscreen, perhaps at another pilot or one of the loading crew.

It is possible that while preparing to put on his helmet Doug dropped it on the floor or his helmet bag fell on the floor and became entangled in the pedals or his kneeboard snagged on something. The last two items were not recovered, despite being likely to float. The seat may have been adjusted for the very tall Plane Captain Edmister, although Doug had plenty of time to notice this, and as Crayton testified, a short pilot would find it easier to use the brakes (when the pedals were in their normal position) than a tall one. Around this time other pilots noted the new type of soles on the flying boots made it harder to adjust the pedal position with the foot lever.

Lack of a Tractor?

Frank Barrett, who watched the accident unfold from the flight deck, believes that Doug may have thought the A-4 was still connected to a tractor, which would provide the braking action and he didn't spot the yellowshirt's signal to hold brakes. If a tractor had been used for the move, the A-4 would not have gone over, even if the brakes had failed, says Barrett.

Skid or Non-skid?

No skid marks were found on the elevator, which would have been expected if the brakes were locked but the surface was slippery. The elevator was declared dry, but witness Dasovic saw oily water on the hangar deck. Martinez said the deck conditions were better than usual. According to Sherman and House, the non-skid surface had worn off the chocks with constant use, which was no doubt critical in their failure to stop the aircraft, despite several tries. Donald Smith described the chocks that plane director Lindsey showed him as "satisfactory" and the board didn't regard them as a contributing factor.

Intensive flight operations would wear the centerline paint off the flight deck and elevator after about a week. A new coat took two days to dry properly so could only be applied during non-operating periods. The *Bon Homme Richard's* contemporary cruise report noted that a film of JP-5 fuel, hydraulic oil and lubricating oil would build up on the flight deck after long at-sea periods. The available degreasing substances available through the supply chain were not effective with salt water, but a commercial product called Aquasolve was, or at least until it ran out.

A Surprise Turn?

Randy Wilson remembers a 1MC announcement to stand by for a turn. William Smith was certain *Tico* listed to port as the A-4 began to move. George Fenzl says the ship took a roll to port. Both Chevalier and Lindsey told the accident investigation board there was a slight port list, but there was no turn. Chuck Wilber remembers the list but says it was unusual in that the ship almost never listed to port with the No.2 Elevator down. Lindsey said that aircraft were sometimes moved to this elevator when the ship was turning (although regulations called for the elevator to be up in a turn). Worley Creech remembered a swell, but thought it was too small to be relevant. Samuel Hallmark said there was a slow roll, but the conditions were very good for the movement of aircraft. Navigator Lynn Adams also remembered some swells but to the best of his knowledge the ship was not turning.

The investigation concluded that the list, weather and sea conditions were not significant factors in the accident.

Seat Adjustment?

William Smith recalled in 1989 that the very tall plane captain (Edmister) had been in the cockpit during preflight "when the electricity was hooked up" and had adjusted the seat all the way to the back "which would make it a little difficult for a man who was a foot shorter to reach the pedals that when depressed activate the braking system." Edmister himself told the inquiry that Doug (who he thought was five-foot-two) could reach the pedals but admitted he couldn't actually see him do so from where he stood on the ladder. The A-4's seat adjustment motor required AC electricity generated by an external power cart or the engine in order to work, and without it Doug would not have been able to move the seat from its previous setting. Smith described Edmister as six-foot-six and Webster as five-foot-four, which is about four inches shorter than reality, but nevertheless, the height difference was significant. This simple variation in the height of two young men and the failure of one of them to put something back the way he found it is perhaps the single most critical factor contributing to the accident.

Procedures?

Certain ways of operating on *Tico* had become routine but were not tested and standardized, leading to some potentially unsafe procedures and habits. The stopping point of the A-4 was decided by eye in relation to a yellow line on the elevator, which was not intended as a stopping marker, it being just the centerline of the angled deck.

The two safety supervisors were on the same wing, which was perhaps not the best place to supervise from.

Doug had control only of his brakes and relied on them, with alert chockmen and good chocks as his only backup. The nose steering castored and was being controlled by a tiller bar. The only other thing he could have done if the brakes failed was drop his tail hook, which probably would not have helped stop the A-4 tipping backwards even if the hook caught in the net.

Moving an aircraft sometimes required three or four attempts to clear the hump between the deck and elevator. This was accepted as normal. Edmister said that manually pushing aircraft was also normal even though there were tractors to hand. There were probably too many people around. Some sailors insist that only authorized men should be able to get close to a loading exercise, but on this afternoon a bomb cart was being moved, an airman was delivering a spare part and a chow line was forming, all close to the moving A-4.

The Navy's Bureau of Aeronautics specified a minimum tip-back angle of 15 degrees for tricycle-geared aircraft, beyond which it would fall on its tail, or, if the tail overhung the deck edge, would begin to flip over backwards. Every degree of ship's list in the direction of the tail would reduce the tip-back angle and increase this possibility, particularly with an A-4. Moving one backwards towards a list without an anchoring tractor was a highly risky business.

Conclusion

In the author's view, a combination of a slight list to port, the pilot's inability to fully reach the toe brakes and worn out chocks led to a plane, a bomb and a pilot being propelled backwards towards the edge of the deck. A dozen or so men were each pushing about a ton of mass each. Once it got moving slightly downhill there was no stopping it with some flimsy chocks. The final safety net was in fact a safety net, but one meant to catch people, not 20,000-pound aircraft.

This was not the first or last such accident, although the author hasn't found any that exactly match it, with or without a bomb. A similar one occurred in February 1962 on *Coral Sea,* when handlers were moving an RF-8 onto an elevator, presumably with a tractor, and the tow bar came undone while it was still on the hangar deck. Although men threw chocks at the wheels, it ran backwards off the edge and into the sea. Thankfully there was nobody aboard on this occasion.

Accidents occur on aircraft carriers, as we have seen. Many are due to human error. Most are minor, but some have serious consequences.

The so-called "Swiss cheese" theory posits that accidents are often caused by several omissions or factors that line up in sequence like holes in slices of cheese. Rearrange the slices and there is no pathway, but line them up the right way and things can fall through.

Pushing a heavy aircraft by hand across a tilting platform hanging over the ocean would raise alarm bells in modern day civilian life. "What could possibly go wrong?" is a joke often used when it should be obvious that too many holes in the cheese are lining up.

On December 5, 1965 the holes in the cheese seem to have been a distracted pilot in a seat positioned too far back, worn deck and chock surfaces, a handling crew that may have lost focus, and a slight port list. Maybe weak brakes, new boot soles, a dropped helmet or checklist…. The last hole was an inadequate safety rail.

No one of these factors by itself would or should have caused this accident, but together they did.

Fallout

At the time the accident was not kept entirely secret and some details were shared with those with a need to know. The next carrier heading for WestPac after *Tico* was *Ranger*, which arrived in Hawaii in early December for ORI. The pre-combat ritual for Air Wing Nineteen included a briefing from Navy Fleet Intelligence Center Pacific (FICPAC) for all the special weapons loading officers and designated nuclear delivery pilots from the carrier's four attack squadrons, during which they were told about the *Tico* accident. VA-146 A-4 pilot Hugh Magee, who had been one of Doug Webster's instructors at Lemoore, said, "The incident made our constant nucwep loading drills during the ORI very tense and nervous evolutions." The accident didn't cause the nuclear training to stop. Magee said, "We continued to have loading drills throughout that cruise and the 1967 cruise on *Constellation.* They made life rather intolerable on the air wing, as we were at flight quarters

14 hours a day flying strikes, and 'off time' often entailed underway replenishments and loading drills … Ugh!"

Loading exercises simply continued. *Ticonderoga's* post-cruise report says that loading drills were conducted on all air wing types and that "the most recent TraEx Bravo demonstrated a continuing capability to generate and load weapons in well under the programed time-frame" so there must have been another conducted (but not in the log) after December 5 unless that drill was somehow regarded as successful. William Lane said in 1989 that there were no further drills on that cruise. Elsewhere they carried on. *Kitty Hawk* conducted a weapons loading TraEx out of Yokosuka in January 1966 according to an official history. In his memoir *Rampant Raider*, A-4 pilot Stephen Gray says that in March 1967, Air Wing Twenty-One conducted nuclear loading exercises en route between Sasebo and Hong Kong and again between Yankee Station and Subic Bay in mid-June.

Crewcut was the codeword associated with *Ticonderoga* in 1965, but the author has found a number of others for loading drills on carriers. "Buckeye" was used in 1963 on both *Hancock* and *Oriskany* and "Orange Crush" on *Oriskany* at other times. *Bon Homme Richard* used "Three Queens" in 1968. *Constellation* used "Blue Bells" into the 1970s (with "Camelot" when a weapon was on the flight deck) and *Forrestal* used "Red Diamond" in the late 1980s. "Goldilocks" was *Coral Sea's* codeword at one time and "Gun Smoke" was *Kitty Hawk's*. A "Gremlin nuclear loading drill" took place on *Shangri-La* on March 24, 1970. Five days earlier the carrier had visited Rio de Janeiro.

The code for special weapons themselves across several ships was "chopsticks." A PA announcement of "chopsticks aboard" told those in the know that nuclear weapons had been onloaded.

By 1981, a rework facility had been set up at Subic Bay to refurbish the training shapes used in loading exercises by carriers operating in WestPac. These BDU dummy bombs were filled with concrete but had working arming circuits, timers and velocity sensors. If nothing else, it shows such devices were being well used in WestPac by this time, hopefully instead of the real thing.

By April 1967, at least one pilot had become disillusioned with the war based on what he saw on *Tico*. Under the headline "Pilot Says Bombs Dumped in Viet Seas," Alex Waier, a VA-52 Skyraider pilot on the 1965–66 and 1966–67 cruises but now an analyst for Dow Chemical in Michigan, told his local newspaper that competition between carriers for the highest sortie rates meant that pilots were risking their lives against cheap or worthless targets and often got sent out in dangerously foul weather on "meaningless missions." On one of these Waier's (unnamed) roommate was shot down. The thing that annoyed pilots the most was the premium on inter-carrier competition. "It was common knowledge all the time I was aboard. One time our squadron commander got us all in the wardroom and told us point-blank that we were out to beat the record of the *Enterprise*," said Waier.

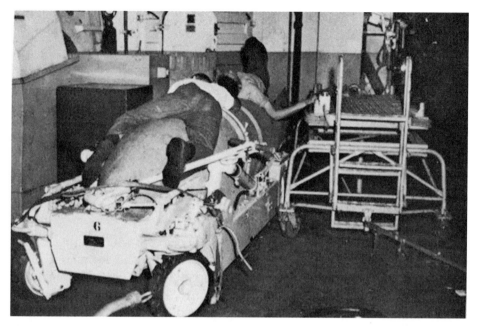

This photo of men sleeping on a Mk 7 bomb was printed in the 1960-61 USS *Hancock* cruisebook. Legend has it that most copies were recalled and the photo cut out. (*Hancock* cruisebook)

There were few profitable targets to hit in North Vietnam outside Hanoi and Haiphong. "We would zip up and down the coast and unload or dump [bombs] in the water. That way, the carrier would get credit for a sortie," he said. "About a third of our ordnance was dumped in the water, and that's a conservative estimate."

Waier echoed what Doug Webster had written in his diary about bombing a "meaningless little country bridge." He said, "A lot of pilots object to risking their necks to drop a 2000-dollar bomb on a little bridge they put back together during the night." There were times pilots would bomb the same railroad car 15 times during the month. Each time, the bomb assessment was "target destroyed.'" Waier said that "cratering" a road was counted as a successful mission. "This was even encouraged by the senior officers on the ship. They didn't like to hear you didn't drop them on anything."

"Junior officers don't get to talk to reporters," Waier said. "We had newsmen onboard, but we were told not to tell newspapermen anything. If a reporter wanted to talk to a pilot, he was steered to the squadron executive officer, and maybe his wingman." Waier said he went to Vietnam as a hawk, but that "no pilot really thinks we are in Vietnam to save democracy for the South Vietnamese. Most think it's a staging area in case of war with Red China."

Admiral David Richardson, recent head of Task Force 77, disputed Waier's claims, saying that "sortie races" were not official policy and any such competition was down to "a bunch of gung-ho lads," but admitted that as much as 15,000 tons of ordnance was jettisoned by carrier-based aircraft every month by aircraft that had failed to reach their targets and could not bring it back aboard.

Despite this apparent wastage, the Navy had "lent" the Air Force more than 400,000 bombs from its inventory between January 1, 1964 and April 13, 1966, according to testimony to congressmen in May that year. Secretary of Defense McNamara denied there was a bomb shortage affecting operations, but the most recent statistics showed that about 50,000 of the 61,000 tons (82 percent) of the bombs on hand in South East Asia were dropped on Vietnam in the previous month.

By the time VA-56 was in combat again in 1967, their A-4Cs certainly were not carrying all they were capable of. John Paisley was not impressed. "We were going over Vietnam with 250-pound bombs each and I thought shoot, you might as well give me a BB gun too."

At the same time papers were reporting Waier's claims of unnecessary missions, his state's Governor, George Romney, was having his own doubts about his previous strong support for the war. Speaking before a Senate subcommittee, and echoing one of Waier's beliefs, Governor Romney said he feared Red China would be brought into the war if the United States continued to bomb near to the North Vietnam-China border. "It is tragic that we ever got involved in this conflict, but we did get involved, and today all of Southeast Asia is involved."

CHAPTER 13

Big in Japan

In the spring of 1989, William Arkin, a 32-year-old former Army intelligence officer working at the Institute of Policy Studies, and Joshua Handler, a 28-year-old campaign coordinator at Greenpeace, had been working on a study of post-war naval accidents for over a year. They had evidence that 48 nuclear weapons and 11 reactors (mostly Soviet) had been lost at sea, but lacked information on some accidents, finding only scattered details here and there. Using the Pentagon's 1981 "Narrative Summaries of Accidents involving U.S. Nuclear Weapons" report as a starting point, they saw the few lines about an A-4 and an unknown weapon being lost in the Pacific on December 5, 1965 and tried to narrow it down to a particular ship and a more precise location. "It was like being an investigative reporter," Handler later told his hometown newspaper in Illinois. "Nobody had bothered to look at the incident. Perhaps they didn't know where to look."

The pair made a Freedom of Information Act request to the National Archives for the deck logs of any carriers that were in the Pacific on that date. At the very least this would have included *Hancock, Enterprise, Oriskany, Bon Homme Richard* and *Kitty Hawk* as well as *Ticonderoga*, which were all in or transiting to or from Vietnamese waters.

Among them they found the smoking gun neatly written in blue ballpoint on the loose-leaf pages of *Ticonderoga*'s deck log for December 1965. The relevant entry read:

> 1450 While being rolled from No.2 Hangar Bay to No.2 Elevator, A4E aircraft BuNo. 151022 of VA-56, with pilot LTJG D. M. Webster USN, 666086 aboard, rolled off the elevator and sank in 2700 fathoms of water at 27°– 35.2'N, 131°–19.3'E.

In advance of publication of their report, Arkin and Handler gave *Newsweek* details of their findings, which appeared in the May 15 edition (published on the 8th) under the headline "Classified Top Secret: H-Bomb Overboard" which wrongly said that Webster was "strapped into the cockpit for a spell on duty in the Navy's 'quick reaction alert' (QRA) force" but correctly predicted that the news was likely to cause a "storm of anger" in Japan.

USS _TICONDEROGA (CVA·14)_ ZONE DESCRIPTION _-9 (I)_ DATE _SUNDAY 5 DECEMBER_, 19 _65_

AT/PASSAGE FROM _SPECIAL OPERATIONS AREA_ TO _YOKOSUKA, JAPAN_

POSITION ZONE TIME 0800	POSITION ZONE TIME 1200	POSITION ZONE TIME 2000	LEGEND 1.-CELESTIAL 2.-ELECTRONIC 3.-VISUAL 4.-D. R.
L 26°-06'N BY 1-4 λ 129°-37'E BY 1-4	L 27°-00'N BY 1-2-4 λ 130°-35.2'E BY 1-2-4	L 28°-12.5'N BY 2-4 λ 132°-02.5E BY 2-4	

REMARKS

00-04 STEAMING IN COMPANY WITH THE USS FECHTELER (DD-870), USS GRIDLEY (DLG·21), USS PRESTON (DD·795), AND USS TURNER JOY (DD·951) ENROUTE FROM SPECIAL OPERATIONS AREA TO YOKOSUKA, JAPAN IN ACCORDANCE WITH COMSEVENTHFLT EMPLOYMENT SCHEDULE, SECOND QUARTER, 1966. BASE COURSE IS 060°T, SPEED 20 KTS. BOILERS #1, #2, #7, AND #8 AND GENERATORS #1, #2, AND #4 ARE ON THE MAIN STEAM LINE FOR STEAMING PURPOSES. OTC IS THE COMMANDING OFFICER OF THIS VESSEL. SOPA IS COMCARDIV 9 EMBARKED IN THIS VESSEL. THIS SHIP IS IN STATION 0 IN A FORMATION 40. THE DESTROYERS ARE IN AN IIC4-4 CIRCULAR SCREEN, SCREEN AXIS 000. STATION #1 IS USS PRESTON, STATION #2 IS USS FECHTELER, STATION #3 IS USS TURNER JOY, AND STATION #4 IS USS GRIDLEY. THE SCREEN COMMANDER IS COMDESRON 19 EMBARKED IN TURNER JOY. MATERIAL CONDITION YOKE, MODIFIED, IS SET THROUGHOUT THE SHIP. 0059 C/C TO 040°T. 0104 C/C TO 039°T. 0118 C/C TO 049°T. 0251 C/C TO 039°T. 0322 C/c TO 049°T.

C. A. Dyer
LTJG USNR

04-08 STEAMING AS BEFORE. 0532 EXERCISED THE WATCH AT STEERING CASUALTY DRILLS. 0620 SECURED FROM STEERING CASUALTY DRILLS. 0641 RECEIVED ACCIDENT REPORT ON BORRELLI, G.F., 591-21-17, SA, USN, PATIENT STATES HE CUT HIS NOSE ON A SWAB WRINGER. DIAGNOSIS: LACERATION NOSE. PROGNOSIS: CLEANSED, SUTURED, DRESSING AND GIVEN TETANUS SHOT. DISABILITY: NONE. 0730 MUSTERED THE CREW ON STATION.

LT USN

08-12 STEAMING AS BEFORE. 1040 RECEIVED DAILY DRAFT REPORT. FWD 29'3", AFT 29'11", MEAN 29'1". 1106 CONDUCTED STEERING CASUALTY DRILL. 1123 RECEIVED DAILY MUSTER REPORT. NO NEW ABSENTEES.

J.E. Robon
LTJG USN

12-16 STEAMING AS BEFORE. 1143 CONDUCTED STEERING CASUALTY DRILL. 1300 SET CREWCUT READINESS. 1335 ELECTRICAL FIRE IN COMPARTMENT B-0205-13E. 1341 FIRE IS OUT. 1358 MANNED CREWCUT STATIONS. 1450 WHILE BEING ROLLED FROM NO.2 HANGAR BAY TO NO.2 ELEVATOR, A4E AIRCRAFT BUNo.151022 OF VA-56, WITH PILOT LTJG D.M. WEBSTER USN, 668086 ABOARD, ROLLED OFF THE ELEVATOR AND SANK IN 2700 FATHOMS OF WATER AT 27°-35.2'N, 131°-19.3'E.

J.S. McCabe
LTJG USN

16-18 STEAMING AS BEFORE. 1543 RECOVED THIS VESSEL'S LIFEBOAT

APPROVED: EXAMINED:

The actual deck log entry that revealed the secret of the _Ticonderoga_ accident. The deck logs are now in the National Archives. (Author)

At the May 1989 press conference, William Arkin and Joshua Handler revealed that the Broken Arrow was not "500 miles from land." Arkin holds up a map showing the true location. (Shutterstock)

The day *Newsweek* hit the newsstands, Arkin and Handler held a press conference in Washington. "For 24 years, the U.S. Navy has covered up the most politically sensitive accident that has ever taken place," Arkin told reporters, holding up a map showing the location of the accident. "The Navy kept the true details of this accident a secret not only because it demonstrates their disregard for the treaty stipulations of foreign governments but because of the questions it raises about nuclear weapons aboard ships in Vietnam." He added, "There is no doubt in my mind that U.S. ships still transit Japan with nuclear weapons aboard."

Arkin said there was no danger of detonation of the weapon but there was environmental risk from the "33 pounds of plutonium" in the weapon as it deteriorated. Where he came up with this precise figure is unknown, but it appeared in news stories for months, although Shannon Fagan of Greenpeace gave the press a revised figure of 5.5 pounds the day after the press conference.

"These things are dropping into the drink at a regular and alarming rate. Something terrible is going to happen. If not this one, then the next time," Josh Handler said in a follow-up interview.

The following day Daniel Howard, Assistant Secretary Department of Defense for Public Affairs and a former Marine, stood before the Pentagon press corps for a regular briefing. The extraordinary performance deserves footnotes. Howard started by discussing a fire on the USS *White Plains* in the South China Sea which had killed six sailors, the growing crisis in Panama and issues about the B-2 bomber program before a reporter asked, "Did the United States lose an airplane carrying a nuclear weapon near a southern Japanese island in 1965 ... as reported?"

Howard's reply was a succinct "Yup!"

"Do you have any further details of the incident?"

Howard held up a copy of the Narrative Summaries, and said, "First of all I'd like to tell you that this report has been a matter of public record since 1981. It *is* current because there have been no nuclear accidents to report *since* 1981. There are copies of this available back in D. D. I. [Directorate for Defense Information], it was reported *widely* in its time back in 1981 including this particular incident. We had another round of it in 1985[1] again including the incident with the A-4E, so it's difficult to see what the news is in this." Reaching for a photocopy of the Periscope column from the previous week's *Newsweek* magazine, he read: "'Periscope: Navy new cover up.' It says Greenpeace is going to put out their report due next month." He read more: "...estimates that there are 1,200 major naval accidents, mostly American or Soviet which have occurred at sea since 1945 ... many involve nuclear weapons, power plants blah, blah, blah. It also says among the incidents the report will detail is a major radiation accident aboard a U.S. nuclear sub in the Pacific in 1973. We've been back through every record we can find and there was no such nuclear accident."[2]

"I also note that the Navy, which hasn't seen the report yet, had no comment on it. Well, the Navy still hasn't seen the report because Greenpeace hasn't made that report available to anyone. What they are doing is flogging their report by selective leaks to various news organizations. That leak last week was wrong. There's nothing there." Holding up the Narrative Summaries again, he continued. "This leak, this week, also in *Newsweek*," he read the headline from a printout, "'Classified Top Secret: H-bomb overboard' was declassified in this report eight years ago. I commend this to your study," Howard said, smiling. "It appears to me that all Greenpeace has done is used this report as a shopping list and has gone in and requested a lot

---

1 Possibly a reference to the documents extracted by the Quakers after a long lawsuit in 1985.

2 This was an April 1973 reactor leak on the USS *Guardfish* that saw five sailors sprayed with radioactive coolant, also discovered in a search of deck logs.

Pentagon spokesman Dan Howard holds up the 1981 Narrative Summaries document, claiming that the Greenpeace revelations were "old news." (C-Span)

of documents under FOIA. Those documents will add detail but there is no new news per se that will come out of those FOIA documents."[3]

Smiling again, he continued. "I assume that this—what appears to me as an uninitiated observer is a PR campaign to flog their report—will have other similar incidents. With regard to the 1965 incident—a Navy A-4E loaded with one nuclear weapon rolled off an elevator on the USS *Ticonderoga* and fell into the sea in more than 16,000 feet of water on December 5, 1965—a Department of Defense/Department of Energy summary of the accident released in 1981 stated that the accident occurred 500 miles from land. The later follow up from the State Department[4] stated it was 500 miles from the Asian mainland. The actual site is in international waters about 200 miles northeast of Okinawa and about 80 miles east of the nearest point of land in the Ryukyu island chain. The aircraft with its weapon and pilot sank immediately and was not recovered."

Howard looked up from the lectern. "There is no cover-up here. The incident was reported through the proper channels, was investigated and the information used to further improve the safety and security of nuclear weapons.[5] There are a whole set of procedures as I think those of you who cover this building on a regular basis know. There are detailed … an exhaustive set of procedures for reporting any

---

3 He was wrong.

4 Never made public to the author's knowledge.

5 Hardly.

kind of incident involving nuclear weapons, nuclear materials. They were used in this case. The weapons themselves, in this case, the belief was then and still is that the weapon poses no threat to the environment. It's designed to be inert. During *storage, handling* and *transport...*"[6] Howard emphasized each word then trailed off and began shuffling the papers on his lectern.

A reporter took this as his chance and asked, "What was the A-4 doing with a nuclear weapon on board sitting on the elevator on a carrier? Were they planning to use it?" Howard drank from a cup of water and swallowed slowly. "It's not a normal place for it," the questioner continued.

Howard locked on to this, asking the reporter directly, "According to what authority?" Then he said to the room: "We have nuclear-capable, dual-capable aircraft serving with our Air Force and we have them serving in the Navy ... and they are deployed. This is not only common knowledge, we have acknowledged this publicly. It has nothing to do with our neither confirm nor deny policy. We do have naval aircraft, which for many years have had the ability to carry nuclear weapons. You train with those weapons you deploy with those weapons and I think that you'll recall that for a great many years we had a very substantial part of SAC in the air at all times, armed with those weapons. So, I don't think there was anything out of the ordinary about the aircraft having been loaded up with a..."

A reporter interjected, "Was the carrier en route to Japan or Japanese territories, and wouldn't that have violated Japanese law?"

Howard listened, took another drink and lied. "The carrier was en route to Vietnam ... off the coast of Vietnam, at the time."[7]

"Just one follow up and not to belabor the point. I know the Air Force does fly with nuclear weapons but does the Navy normally launch off the carrier deck an aircraft with a nuclear weapon on board unless it intends to use it?"

"I'm not going to speak to that particular issue," Howard said, shaking his head.

"The State Department follow-up said it was 500 miles from the Asian mainland ... could you double check that last answer and make sure it was en route to Vietnam and not Japan as publicly reported—leaving Vietnam and heading for Japan on R&R?"

"I'll go back and take a look at that for you. I'd be happy to," Howard replied in a tone of voice that suggested that he would be happier at the bottom of the Pacific with the bomb.

A reporter named Charlie pressed Howard. "You say there was no cover-up here. And yet that report says it was 500 miles from land ... I mean if you lose one in Manila Harbor are you going to say it was 3,000 miles from San Francisco? It

---

6 But when left on the ocean floor forever?

7 No.

certainly was *misleading* to say it was 500 miles from land, when it was in fact 80 miles from…"

"The second report says it was 500 miles from the Asian mainland," Howard said, correcting him on the paperwork. "Charlie—the report was not complete. That I will acknowledge. But … main point is this. It was … 200 miles from Okinawa. It was 80 miles from the nearest point of land, a very small island in that chain.[8] It was *way* out to sea in international waters. And the weapon went down in 16,000 feet of water and there was no danger to … anyone … other than the unfortunate pilot of the aircraft … in this incident." He added emphatically, "There was not then, there is not now…"

Another reporter chimed in, "Has the Navy ever lost another nuclear weapon?"

Howard picked up the papers again. "Let me commend you this report. That's all here. Every single one of the incidents which we've had a nuclear accident involving the loss of a weapon is here.

"The aircraft carrier was on its way to Vietnam for operational purposes, correct?"

Howard gave out an enormous sigh and leaned on the podium. "My recollection is that, I could stand corrected on it, but we will check and let you know."

"Do you know if was there any attempt to recover or observe the bomb?"

Howard responded with incredulity. "Sixteen thousand feet of water? I don't think we had the capability then. I'm not sure we have capability now to recover anything from that depth." With that he took another sip of water.

"And you say we currently still train with nuclear weapons on aircraft carriers?"

"I said I think that has been common knowledge for a great many years." He gave out another sigh. "The answer is—of course."

He turned to another reporter. "Yes?"

"Are you saying this was first made public in '81?"

"That is correct."

"Why wasn't it made public any earlier than that?"

"We did a summary, we did a compendium of all of the incidents and accidents which was published in 1981. I was not the spokesman for the Department of Defense in 1965." He added with a smile, "I can't go back that far with you but I am telling you that this is very old news. And I can tell you that we've had no incidents since this time, since the time this report was published."

Another reporter piped up, "Change the subject?"

A colleague interjected, "No."

Howard turned to the first man and said, "I didn't pay you enough," evoking laughter in the room. Looking back at the persistent reporter with a smile he said, "I'm surprised nobody is interested in Panama."

---

8 The island's population is 7,600 today and it is only 15 nautical miles further to Amami Ōshima with a population of 73,000.

<u>December 5, 1965 / A-4 / At Sea, Pacific</u>

An A-4 aircraft loaded with one nuclear weapon rolled off the elevator
of a U.S. aircraft carrier and fell into the sea. The pilot, aircraft, and
weapon were lost. The incident occurred more than 500 miles from land.

What the 1981 list actually had to say about the *Tico* accident. (DoD)

Several reporters exclaimed together, "We're getting there! We're warming you up!"

Howard replied, "That's what I thought." He drank some more water.

"Setting aside the answer that you are going to get for us on whether the ship was either bound *to* or bound *from* Vietnam, the evidence is fairly clear, Dan, that this particular carrier quite normally made runs up from the Vietnam coast to Japan for R&R."

"Uh-huh."

The reporter continued, "Let's assume for a second that...." But Howard cut him off. "You can make all sorts of assumptions I'm not going to take any further with."

The reporter persisted. "The nuclear weapon, which we've acknowledged ... it's rather unlikely that this entire carrier was carrying only one nuclear weapon, which she lost—so would you confirm or deny...."

"No."

"...that this vessel ever went into Japanese waters..."

"No," he said, shaking his head.

"...carrying a nuclear weapon?"

"Listen, I spent nine years in Japan, I have dealt with this issue, you're not going to get me wrapped around that axle." He read flatly from another sheet of paper: "We are aware of the special sentiments of the Japanese people with regard to nuclear weapons, and we have faithfully honored our obligations under the U.S.–Japanese Treaty of mutual security and its related arrangements, and we will continue to do so." He paused. "That is all we have ever said on this issue—that's all we will ever say on this issue."

A new voice is heard. "Will you say you offload nukes if they are there before you enter Japanese waters?"

"I can repeat this statement for you again, if you'd like, George."

Another reporter tried to ask something about Panama to which Howard lifted his eyes hopefully, only to be dashed. "Does that statement mean..." asked another voice to the accompaniment of general laughter from everyone except from Howard and the reporter, who persisted; "...that the Japanese people don't want nuclear weapons around and you don't carry them in there...."

Howard looked at his paper and read slowly and deliberately. "We are aware of the special sentiments of the Japanese people with regard to nuclear weapons, and we have faithfully honored our obligations under the U.S.–Japanese Treaty of mutual security and its related arrangements."

"Can you translate 'wrapped around that axle' into Japanese?" asked another reporter. Howard just sighed again and smiled.

The questions continued. "The location of the bomb, that it was 80 miles at the closest approach to the Ryukyus, was that in the '81 report?"

Howard shook his head, "No it was not, it was not, it was in the subsequent… it was not, it was right now." He looked down and pointed briefly at his papers, as it appeared to dawn on him that he had been caught in acknowledging that there was "new news" in the Greenpeace paper, but the reporters talked over each other and none called him out on it.

Charlie piped up, "What are the obligations? What are the obligations under the treaty? You say, faithfully … what are they?"

"Charlie. I'm not going to take this any further. I will stand here and read that statement to you all day if you feel like it. That is all I'm going to say on the matter."[9]

Howard returned to the papers. "The 1981 report. It's basically two–three 'graphs. It was later corrected … the 500 miles from land was corrected to 500 miles from the Asian mainland but no more details were given. Now I assume what Greenpeace has done has gone through the documents it has gotten through the Freedom of Information Act and pinpointed the location."

"Is there anything wrong with that?" came the question.

"There's nothing wrong with that. Whether it's news or not is another matter."

Finally Howard got to change the subject to Panama. "Any troops down there?" someone asked.

"I can't make predictions about any future military activities," he replied. Two days later he would announce the deployment of nearly 2,000 soldiers and Marines to Panama. Dan Howard later served as Under Secretary of the Navy and acting Secretary of the Navy before his retirement in 1992.

Lost Bomb, Lost Credibility

The reports that followed the Defense Department's press conference in American newspapers didn't follow up the question about which direction *Ticonderoga* was sailing, but highlighted the Pentagon's lack of concern and candor. An *Anchorage Daily News* editorial headed "A bomb forgotten in the briny deep" summed up the Pentagon's attitude. "You'd think all that happened was a marble fell out of a sailor's pocket. The Navy apparently doesn't see it as any big deal. When it occurred, the Navy didn't tell anybody, not even people living in the area, and then kept it a secret

---

9 By threatening to read his script yet again, Howard ducks having to discuss the prohibition on introducing nuclear weapons into Japan.

until researchers found evidence of it in the National Archives." The *Boston Globe* editorial "More Lies, More Nuclear Litter" praised the "Greenpeace nuke-sniffers" for "backtracking upon the spoor" of the lost bomb and reprimanded the government for playing "catch-me-if-you-can" with matters nuclear. The *Los Angeles Times'* article "Lost Bomb, Lost Credibility" chided, "The fact remains that as long as sixteen years after the accident the Navy still was trying to mislead Congress and the public about what took place. It lied—a gentler word would be inappropriate—about the proximity of the accident to land."

Margaret Webster was in the Cancer Society's Cleveland office when she saw a man reading a paper with a story about the lost bomb. Susan McKee's boyfriend in Pennsylvania showed her the same story and she realized it was about her favorite cousin. It was only later that afternoon when she got home and the phone rang off the hook that Margaret learned the newspaper story was about her son. Friends wanted to tell her and soon they were joined by newsmen who wanted her opinion, which on learning for the first time that a nuclear bomb was attached to his plane ("a shock, an absolute surprise") was, "I just feel bad that he didn't get to deliver it. He gave his life for God's sake, he should have at least got to deliver the bomb." She understood why the government can't reveal everything it does during wartime, lest surprise be lost. "Doug believed that too," she said. "He believed in what he was doing and he didn't understand the protesters."

Former airman Gary Loudenslager was reading the paper when his wife in another room heard him say "Holy crap, they published it!" He then went on to tell her a little about the accident, the first time he had never told anyone about it. He described it as a very stressful and sad time aboard the *Ticonderoga*. Other former sailors told their local papers. William Smith (who had since taken his stepfather's surname Lane) who thought the pilot's name was Daniel Webster, told the *San Diego Union* that the runaway A-4 could not be stopped. "It was like trying to stop a trolley car." He recalled looking over the edge and seeing what he thought to be "the bomb bobbing around out there. There was smoke coming out of it. Then it disappeared." What Lane saw was almost certainly the broken end of a drop tank, but the San Diego *Evening Tribune's* article was headlined "He stared in awe as smoking H-bomb sank." Former ordnanceman Phillip Weldon, now in the army in Germany, told *Stars & Stripes* how the pilot gave the plane handlers a look as if to say "there are no brakes" or "I can't reach them" before the jet flipped into the water.

Reaction in Japan

If the reaction in the United States was one of mild annoyance at government dishonesty, in Japan the story went, well, nuclear. The bomb story was first reported on the noon radio news in Tokyo on May 8, 1989. The source was the *Newsweek* report rather than the Washington press conference, but the continuing media coverage in the United States fed the Japanese press, which in turn kept the story running in America.

The Pentagon may have thought there was no "new news" in the Greenpeace/ IPS report, but the lost bomb was on the front pages of all the major Japanese newspapers and led the TV news that night. One station created an animation of the accident. The *Mainichi Shimbun* headline read "US Navy Lost H-Bomb Off Okinawa in 1965." The *Asahi Shimbun* editorial called it an "H-bomb nightmare" and demanded clarity on radioactive contamination. A Foreign Ministry official said the United States had not brought the 1981 report to their attention at the time. It was clear from government statements that this was the first time Japan had been aware of the incident, let alone the few vague lines in an old report mentioning a bomb lost on a vast ocean.

The Japanese government reaction was initially to deny any responsibility "Since the incident occurred in the open seas, it really has nothing to do with the Japanese government," said a spokesman for the Foreign Ministry on May 9. "And we have no plans to raise the issue with the American government."

"This happened in international waters so we have no right to make a loud demand," said a senior Foreign Ministry official who declined to be named. "We are just asking the United States to give us an explanation."

Environmental groups and peace activists had a different view. Author and academic Tetsuo Maeda, a prominent critic of Japan's military and its government's nuclear policies said, "This is an issue that should be discussed. An accident like this means a lot to us Japanese and should not be ignored, even though the foreign minister would like to ignore it." He believed the 1981 report was purposely vague because the accident occurred outside of the United States but that it was a matter of human decency that people living near a nuclear accident were informed about it. "There may be many nuclear time bombs under the sea, for all we know," Maeda added. Hiroaki Fukuchi of the Okinawa branch of the Japan Congress Against Atomic and Hydrogen Bombs (*Gensuikyo*) said, "We are worried that the bomb will generate radioactive pollution in the sea. It might already have taken place."

The official Japanese desire to deny knowledge or interest in the bomb was a misjudgment on the part of the Liberal Democratic Party government. They should not have been taken by surprise by the report. A political-military officer at the U.S. embassy privately informed the Ministry of Foreign Affairs security division's Deputy Director Mr. Sugiyama that Greenpeace were about to release the story and, thanking them for the report, he told them he already knew about it from Japan's Washington embassy. Sugiyama's sources seem to have gone only so far, however, as he then asked if the United States could provide some more background to the incident, such as an indication of where it had taken place. All they could do was provide him with the texts of the approved public announcement and the 1981 release.

Two days before the *Newsweek* story was published, the Tokyo embassy was notified by the State Department to expect Greenpeace to announce the accident in front of the media. Michael H. Armacost had only been appointed ambassador to Japan in February and took up his post on May 8, with spectacularly unlucky timing.

Although they had been forewarned, the U.S. embassy was also wrong-footed. Pressed by the Ministry of Foreign Affairs (MOFA) for confirmation that the carrier was *Ticonderoga*, they could only respond that that was what the press was saying. Until they received confirmation from Washington, which they had by the 11th, but possibly not much before, all they could do, like the hapless Dan Howard at the Pentagon, was repeat the mantra that they were aware of the special sentiments of the Japanese people concerning nuclear weapons.

MOFA persisted in asking for clarification as the press storm continued. Was the "80 miles" distance from land in the initial Pentagon release statute miles or nautical miles? Did the United States know the precise location of the accident? Facing repeated press questioning about *Ticonderoga's* next port of call, MOFA themselves could only respond with their own mantra: since there were no consultations called for by the United States, there was no introduction of nuclear weapons.

A Foreign Ministry official told reporters on the 10th, "We are concerned about reports that the incident occurred much closer to Japanese land than we were first told, and we are trying to determine if the ship was headed for the Japanese mainland (with nuclear weapons aboard)."

Prime Minister Noboru Takeshita of the conservative Liberal Democratic Party (LDP) had announced that he would resign later that month over an insider trading scandal. The LDP's political opponents seized on the incident to further embarrass the government, demanding the government seek more information from the Americans. By Wednesday, the Foreign Minister Sosuke Uno, who was to become prime minister on June 3, told the Japanese parliament (the Diet) that the government was "seriously concerned" about the bomb and that the government would press the United States for full details.

Facing pressure from all directions, the Pentagon ordered "several national laboratories" to provide an urgent report on what would have happened to the bomb after it sank into the Philippine Sea.

Diplomatic cables were flying back and forth between Washington and Tokyo. On the 12th, while a small group of protesters stood in steady rain outside the U.S. embassy in Minato-ku waving anti-American banners, ambassador Armacost summarized the week's Japanese news in a cable to Washington. The *Asahi Yukan* carried the latest "helpful" revelations, Armacost said ironically, when it repeated the claims of "eyewitness" William Lane that *Ticonderoga* was carrying "thirty to fifty" nuclear weapons when it docked in Yokosuka. The financial newspaper *Sankei Shimbun* quoted an unnamed government source who said that requests for more information on the weapon on the ocean floor were met with a reluctance to offer details for "security reasons" by the United States. The story was not going away. "We are beginning to receive what we expect will eventually become a torrent of protest mail about the incident," Armacost wrote. The embassy expected that they, and the Japanese government, will "…see quite a few more protesters and petitioners before this blows over."

Although he admitted it was difficult to find any humor in the still unfolding crisis, Armacost related a couple of stories that lightened the serious mood a little. A contact from Ampoka, MOFA's security division, said to have recently seen his fair share of battles amid difficult negotiations for the U.S.–Japanese fighter aircraft project called FSX, muttered during a conversation, "First FSX, now an H-bomb. The only thing that could be worse is an FSX with an H-bomb!"

Another Ampoka counterpart called with an important enquiry to make about the incident. "We immediately held our breath expecting to have to deal with a difficult and sensitive question," Armacost said. "Our 'important enquiry' turned out to be: 'What does the word *Ticonderoga* mean?' We are pleased to report that we were able to respond to this important enquiry on the spot and provide the date of the battle (1775 if you're interested)."

In Okinawa, there was little levity and feelings were running particularly high. Masaji Shinzato, a reporter for the *Okinawa Times*, told the Associated Press. "Shock is running through Okinawa. This [incident] seems to represent how Okinawa was used freely by the American military in those days,"

Richard M. Gibson, the political-military advisor at the Naha consulate reported that the press there was giving the consulate a harder time, with their "sensationalist" treatment of the story feeding Okinawans' anger and concern that nuclear weapons were once stored on their islands and may still be or may be brought in on U.S. ships and aircraft. Although the consul expected that the current sharp reaction would die away over time, he thought it would likely add to the long-standing distrust of the United States' presence. He worried that the press would report how a Marine Corps base on Ie Shima was once used for testing nuclear bomb delivery and that this could affect plans to operate Harrier jets from the island. The local press were already digging up photos of weapons or training dummies said to have been taken on Okinawa and writing "inflammatory" headlines such as "Will the bomb someday explode?" and "What is the U.S. hiding?" Articles emphasized that the power of the lost bomb was 50 to 100 times of those dropped on Japan in 1945 and that A-4s, along with other nuclear-capable aircraft, frequently visited the island's Kadena Air Base.

Okinawa's governor Junji Nishime's initial response to this political hot potato was that the situation was unclear and that further clarification was needed. This went down poorly. The media criticized his wishy-washy approach. He tried slightly harder the next day, demanding Tokyo provide "prompt confirmation of fact and necessary countermeasures to alleviate uneasiness of Okinawans over the danger of radioactive pollution." He was still cautious, noting that the matter was still being investigated by government authorities, and happened 24 years ago, but; "if true, it is extremely serious." That Thursday, the Base Affairs Committee of the Okinawa Prefectural Assembly unanimously voted for the bomb to be recovered. The local LDP spokesman said that his party was convinced the United States was still abiding by the three non-nuclear principles. Opposition politicians said the incident proved the principles were only a subterfuge and the government's prior consultation system was not functioning at all. Newspaper editorials said that because *Ticonderoga* was bound for Yokosuka, the incident showed up the hollowness of the principles. Local reformist elements played heavily upon public fears of an explosion or radiation leak. The Communists called for the removal of American "nuclear bases." Local citizens who spoke to consular staff expressed fear and anger, the latter directed both at the United States for causing the incident, and the Japanese government for not enforcing its principles.

On May 14, about 500 protestors marched through Tokyo. They carried a mock nuclear bomb and others held banners reading "Remove Nuclear Arms" and "Let's Repeal the U.S.–Japan Treaty."

On the 13th a source had contacted the embassy to call their attention to the Pacific edition of *Stars and Stripes*, which was reporting stories of *Tico* veterans who came forth after the story broke. *Stars and Stripes* is a unique "authorized unofficial" publication, produced within the Defense Department, but editorially independent under the First Amendment. Its worldwide reporters had tracked down one *Tico* crewman and collated wire reports of interviews with others. The Stuttgart bureau had talked to Phillip Weldon, now a librarian at an elementary school in Germany, who gave an accurate description of the accident and his opinion that brake failure could not be ruled out and that the pilot (unnamed) may have been distracted while reading a book. William Lane's memory of the "smoking bomb" and his fear that *Tico* was about to disappear off the earth was repeated from his interviews with San Diego papers, as was the quiet instruction not to mention the accident. *Stars and Stripes* also reported a Japan News Network television interview with Randy Wilson, which was the most alarming to the embassy. "[Wilson] is quoted confirming that there were nuclear weapons on board the vessel when it arrived in Yokosuka." The embassy's secret "action message" cable said. Wilson's actual words from the JNN report, which had been taped at Wilson's home near San Francisco, were: "There was no other place they could unload them. They would have to be on the ship at the time."

Ambassador Armacost expected these stories to be picked up by the Japanese press that weekend and the Japanese government would probably need to respond on Monday morning. "Please provide guidance to respond to MOFA requests by immediate message by opening of business May 15, Tokyo time," he pleaded.

In a terse reply sent on the evening of the 16th, Secretary of State James Baker cautioned Armacost to tell MOFA and other Japanese enquirers that reported crew statements were not authoritative concerning the loss of an aircraft and weapon. *Stars and Stripes* later quoted Florida newspaper interviews with former VF-53 airman Bud Dehnert in that day's edition, and again gave his mostly factual account of events, adding Dehnert's opinion that others on board knew that *Ticonderoga* was carrying nuclear weapons, but the United States never admitted it publicly.

Okinawa governor Nishime flew to Tokyo to meet with Foreign Minister Uno on the 17th to request the government fully investigate the report and take measures to guarantee the safety of the people of the prefecture. Uno had also felt the heat for downplaying the seriousness of the incident. The *Asahi Shimbun* said there was an "unexpectedly profound gap" between the people's feelings about the presence of nuclear weapons and the government's willingness to ignore that presence to maintain good relations with Washington.

The Foreign Ministry's initial assertion that because the incident occurred in the open seas, it had nothing to do with the Japanese government met the rebuttal from the *Asahi Shimbun* that "when we are told that a hydrogen bomb is left undisposed on the seabed near Japan, we cannot brush it aside as something about which someone else should have misgivings." The paper's editorial called for the bomb to be recovered.

Just before Governor Nishime left for the mainland, the annual rally to mark the anniversary of Okinawa's reversion to Japanese control turned into a massive protest against nuclear weapons. As the culmination of a week of protest marches and petitions up to ten thousand people gathered at Naha's Yogi Park, sang protest songs and listened to speeches from a variety of environmental and peace groups. Reversion Day protests had traditionally opposed what many Okinawans saw as increasing assimilation by mainland Japan, and this year they called on Tokyo to reverse a decision to end the prefecture's Memorial Day, which honored the local war dead, but the main calls were for an official explanation of the *Ticonderoga* incident. Speakers complained about the visit of nuclear submarines to the island's White Beach and of expanded military training before marching to Naha under banners calling for the closure of U.S. bases.

In 1989, there were about 35,000 Americans on Okinawan bases. The main base was the Air Force's Kadena Air Base, home to a wing of F-15s and KC-135 tankers, plus a detachment of SR-71 Blackbird spyplanes. One of these had crashed off the Philippines in April and the last pieces were retrieved on May 10.

The Naha Consul General Lawrence F. Farrar, who himself had once been a deck officer on a Pacific Fleet carrier, told Washington that the incident seemed to have revived the idea of a new "Ring around Kadena," a human chain protest previously held in 1987. The organizers had set a preliminary date of August 5, 1990, he told State, and indeed this did eventually take place, attracting 26,000 protestors.

Speaking before reporters on May 18, Foreign Ministry spokesman Taizo Watanabe made a statement that tortuously argued that the transit of nuclear weapons through

Japanese territorial waters did not amount to "introduction" of these weapons into Japan. He also refuted the remarks by former ambassador Edwin O. Reischauer about a secret agreement allowing the transit of nuclear weapons. Another ministry official added that it was true the three principles were not a law, "...but they are principles that our government has openly announced before the Diet and we have been abiding by them as a law." When asked what had happened to Tokyo's request for clarification as to which direction *Ticonderoga* was sailing, Watanabe admitted they had not received a response. The government had not been able to determine by itself the validity of media reports that it docked at Yokosuka two days later, a rather astonishing admission that there were no records of what foreign warships were visiting the country. When asked to predict what would happen if it became known that the United States did indeed bring nuclear weapons into Japan, Watanabe said, "We just trust that America could abide by this stipulation with regard to prior consultation."

While Nishime was meeting Uno in Tokyo, the American bomb designers issued their report. The four-paragraph document said: "Neither a nuclear or high-explosive detonation could have occurred at the time of the accident." It went on: 'The nuclear device involved in the accident was not designed to remain structurally intact at extreme ocean depths." The experts said, stating (it would seem without any direct knowledge) that "Structural failure occurred before it reached the ocean floor at 16,000 feet, exposing nuclear material to the hydrosphere." The high explosives contained in the bomb, which initiate a nuclear explosion, would have been corroded by seawater, assuring "that no nuclear or high-explosive detonation can ever occur in the environment now or in the future." The nuclear material itself, the experts said, would dissolve "in a relatively short time," according to tests conducted by government scientists, but because the material is so dense, it probably settled quickly on the ocean floor, and mixed with other sediment. "Therefore, there is no environmental impact," the report concluded.

The question arises as to what depth the B43 started to break up and thus when nuclear materials were exposed. At 500 feet the water pressure is about 237 pounds per square inch (psi) or 16 times surface atmospheric pressure (16 atmospheres). At 16,500 feet it is around 7,350 psi or 500 atmospheres. The bomb could have been spilling radioactive substances long before it reached the bottom.

Although the report gave no details about the amounts of explosive or nuclear material in the bomb, it was very unusual for the United States to reveal anything about nuclear weapons design or characteristics at all. The Japanese were not convinced, or at least the government felt their own people would not be satisfied without their own report. The following day, the government formed a commission to investigate the possible environmental damage caused by the bomb. Foreign Minister Uno told a parliamentary committee that the bomb posed no danger, but an investigation was necessary to allay public fears. This sounds like the results were a foregone conclusion. The same day the mayors of Yokosuka, Kure, Sasebo and Maizuru, all Japanese towns with naval bases, met with Uno to ask if the *Ticonderoga* carried nuclear weapons when it entered Japanese ports.

On May 22, the prefectural assembly announced a special session to discuss the incident and former Navy Secretary and decorated Marine veteran Jim Webb visited Nishime. "I have heard the people of Okinawa are very angry about the H-bomb incident. If I can be of any use, I would be glad to serve as an intermediary between the governor and U.S. forces," Webb said. The *Okinawa Times* quoted him as saying, "I understand the pain of Okinawans about the bases, especially the H-bomb incident. If there is anything I can do about the base issue, please tell me."

On July 7, the Japan Socialist Party promised to enshrine the non-nuclear principles into law if elected. The non-nuclear policy needed to be strengthened, Chairwoman Takako Doi said during a tour ahead of upper chamber elections. She said a "no nukes" law was necessary to enforce and verify Japan's non-nuclear policy banning the possession, production and introduction of nuclear arms onto Japanese soil.

The Three Principles

It is worth discussing why the incident proved so sensitive in Japan, as opposed to the relatively muted reaction in America. As the only country to have nuclear weapons used against them, Japan has a unique appreciation of the horrors of nuclear attack. With a large population and relatively little arable land, the Japanese depend more than any other large nation on the fruits of the sea. Any radioactive contamination of the oceans from nuclear testing, power plant accidents or waste dumping would threaten the primary food source for over a hundred and twenty million people. The American military presence was not welcomed by everyone, least of all in Okinawa, where nuclear weapons were stored and deployed, and bombing ranges were used to practice nuclear weapons delivery techniques.

There is a general feeling in Japan that the United States has rarely been open or honest about the presence of nuclear weapons in and around its territory. Japan's pacifist post-war constitution forbids the country from having armed forces, although it maintains substantial air, sea and land "Self-Defense Forces." The country renounces war and the threat or use of force as means of settling international disputes. Only recently have Japanese troops participated in international peacekeeping operations and military exercises abroad.

In 1952, the United States ended its occupation of the Japanese mainland, but kept bases on Okinawa and retained control of the Bonin and Volcano islands. On March 1, 1954, the fishing boat *Daigo Fukuryū Maru* (*Lucky Dragon 5*) was contaminated by radioactive fallout from the "Castle Bravo" hydrogen bomb test at Bikini Atoll in the Marshall Islands. Although the ship was outside the notified danger zone, the blast was twice as powerful as predicted. One crewman died and the remaining 22 suffered from radiation sickness. When asked for information and help by Japanese scientists, the United States did not respond.

In 1957, Prime Minister Nobusuke Kishi first raised the three non-nuclear principles of not possessing, producing or introducing nuclear weapons. Kishi, the grandfather of later Prime Minister Shinzō Abe, actually thought privately that Japan should acquire nuclear weapons for political leverage, but never attempted to do so.

In December 1967, Prime Minister Eisaku Satō formally introduced the three principles as the basis of Japanese nuclear policy. Although these were agreed as a Diet resolution in 1971, they were never adopted into law but have held ever since.

Initially applying to the main islands of Japan (and thus omitting Okinawa and the Volcano Islands), the three principles were: no manufacturing of nuclear weapons; no possession of nuclear weapons; and no allowing their introduction. Later Satō walked back on these straightforward ideas, saying that chaining the government to them for eternity might be asking too much. In April 1968, Foreign Minister Takeo Miki explained that the policy did not apply to foreign warships passing through Japanese waters. Such transits did not constitute "introducing" nuclear weapons to Japan, he argued.

At this time the Tokyo government was pressing Washington hard over the reversion of Okinawa and the Ryukyus to Japanese control. Tokyo hoped to achieve this by 1970, and in informal 1969 discussions, new Foreign Minister Kiichi Aichi suggested to the U.S. ambassador that there was a way to allow the non-nuclear policy to apply to Okinawa after reversion but that the territory could retain its present status regarding "freedom of use" and nuclear weapons storage until the strategic situation in the region improved. This "temporary" solution would eventually give way to applying "homeland level" policies in the Ryukyus.

While Okinawa and the Ryukyus were under American control, there were no restrictions on the stationing of nuclear weapons or the launching of combat operations from U.S. bases on the islands. Washington could see that Aichi's proposed solution would not go down well with the anti-nuclear Japanese public. Negotiations over the nuclear status of the islands were hampered by Washington's repeated refusal to acknowledge how many weapons and of what type were stored on Okinawa

From declassified documents we now know that up to 19 different types of weapon were there between 1954 and 1972, with about one thousand warheads at the peak in 1967.

While the reversion discussions were underway a secret agreement was signed, allowing nuclear weapons to be brought into Okinawa in an emergency. A secret annex to an agreement on the Bonins was signed on April 10, 1968, and this is believed to have permitted U.S. use of Chichi Jima for the same purposes. It was only acknowledged in 2015 that nuclear weapons were kept on Okinawa until reversion in 1972, something both governments had denied. The declassification was a rare exception to the neither confirm nor deny (NCND) policy. Also classified was the fact that prior to reversion the United States and Japanese governments had discussed the possible re-introduction of nuclear weapons onto Okinawa in the event of an emergency or crisis situation.

By 1969, Washington understood that Tokyo accepted the transit of nuclear weapons through Japanese waters and that this included port visits. The Japanese government would be expected to fend off rumors and allegations of the presence or otherwise of nuclear weapons aboard visiting vessels, while the United States maintained its neither confirm nor deny policy.

In a nutshell, the introduction of nuclear weapons could not take place without prior consultation. In a uniquely Japanese way, successive governments in Tokyo decided that because there had never been consultation on the issue, there can never have been nuclear weapons in Japan. At this time there were no carriers homeported in Japan, only transiting ships. Homeporting came in with the arrival of the conventionally powered carrier USS *Midway* in October 1973, following an accord signed in August 1972.

The policy in 1965 was based on the revised Treaty of Mutual Cooperation and Security with Japan, signed in 1960. The treaty required Washington to consult with the Japanese government if they planned to "introduce" nuclear weapons onto Japanese soil, or build "bases for nuclear weapons" there. The Japanese view was that to ask directly if a visiting vessel or aircraft carried nuclear weapons would be to initiate consultation, to which the United States would be forced to respond, positively or negatively, thus violating their own neither confirm nor deny policy. Applying convoluted logic to the problem, Tokyo decided that if the United States failed to fulfil its obligations under the treaty (in other words, planned to ask to introduce weapons to Japan), Japan could not instigate consultation on the issue. The government could not foresee circumstances under which the United States would not fulfil its obligations, so would never instigate consultation. Effectively only the Americans could do that, and, if they did, they would jeopardize their ability to use Japanese ports and airbases.

The Treaty permitted "transit of ports or airbases in Japan by United States vessels and aircraft, regardless of their armament." This was understood to mean that short visits of nuclear-armed aircraft, ships and submarines could take place without consultation and excluded the Ryukyu Islands, then under United States control.

Keeping weapons secret kept America's enemies guessing, but also its allies. By the 1980s other countries in the Pacific and elsewhere were catching the "Japanese allergy" and the idea of nuclear-free zones was spreading. Only tiny New Zealand challenged NCND and as a result found itself cut off from most forms of military cooperation with the United States for 30 years.

For long periods in the 1950s and 1960s the tank landing ship (LST) USS *San Joaquin County* was stationed offshore from Marine Corps Air Station Iwakuni, south of Hiroshima. It contained some number of nuclear weapons, presumably free-fall bombs for use by Marine Corps tactical aircraft at the base. As the 1981 Narrative Summaries say, "The U.S. Marine Corps does not have custody of nuclear weapons in peacetime..." In wartime, that would change, so how would they be delivered quickly to tactical aircraft? Locating them on a Navy ship a few hundred yards away would solve that problem or allow them to be quickly taken elsewhere in the unlikely event the host nation became too curious. The LST story was revealed by Daniel Ellsberg in 1981 and the Japanese government dismissed it as "old news."

During the early May 1989 stories clips of then-Rear Admiral Gene La Rocque speaking before a Congressional subcommittee resurfaced. "There is no question in my mind that all U.S. warships which routinely carry nuclear weapons do not take weapons off when they enter harbors in Japan," said La Rocque. Although the remarks hadn't caused much of a stir in Japan when first made in 1974, La Rocque, who after retirement founded the anti-nuclear Center for Defense Information, now appeared on TV saying much the same thing.

In 2000, the *Bulletin of the Atomic Scientists* revealed that nuclear weapons had also been stored on Iwo Jima, south of Tokyo in the Volcano Islands chain and Chichi Jima in the Bonins, 500 miles southeast of the Japanese mainland. These were mainly "recovery bases" where bombers could rearm after striking China or eastern Russia, or ships and subs could reload, the expectation being that the main operating bases in the Pacific would have been destroyed.

Environmental Report

On June 20, 1989, Japanese officials announced they would test for radiation contamination in the waters around the accident site. Michiaki Okubo of the Japan Science and Technology Agency (JST)'s Nuclear Safety Bureau (NSB) seemed to think the results were a foregone conclusion. Even if radioactivity were to be found, "it will be very hard to distinguish" whether it came from the lost bomb or from nuclear tests, Okubo said.

Ten days later the JST sampled fish and seaweed from the fishing grounds closest to the site of the lost bomb. The Maritime Safety Agency (MSA) also took deep-water samples, lowering collecting devices at eight points around the accident site.

A study committee was formed to evaluate the deep-water samples. It included members from the JST, the fisheries agency, MSA, meteorological agency and—notably—the Foreign Ministry.

On July 7, the JST presented an interim report. Spokesman Kimihiko Oda said there were no abnormalities in the fish or sea life samples, with the single example of a low concentration of plutonium measured in mozuku seaweed. Mozuku is a speciality of Okinawan waters, served in soup, made into a sauce or eaten as a vegetable and is said to have various health benefits including increasing longevity.

Oda said the effects on humans [of consuming mozuku with a little extra plutonium] would be so low that there would be absolutely no cause for concern.

Every year since 1968, surveys had been taken of waters around Japan to measure fallout from nuclear tests conducted by China, the USSR, the United States and France. Oda said that there were no abnormalities in the data here either. There was no particular increase in levels of plutonium compared with survey data in the past and the overall level was extremely low, the report said. Of course, since the surveys started after the bomb was lost, it would be difficult to make comparisons with the "natural" state of the sea. Since the 1940s, plutonium, which is a totally man-made element, has been found in seawater as a result of atmospheric nuclear testing.

Oda said that seawater samples taken by the MSA at a depth of 14,850 feet had still to be analyzed, but that none were taken from the seabed near the bomb loss site, which he said was at 15,840 feet, because the survey's purpose was to determine whether the accident affected Japan's people and the marine environment (a sceptic might wonder if the United States had discouraged them from going any deeper). Before the mission, the NSB's Okubo had said the bottom would not be sampled because the agency had no previous seabed samples with which to make a comparison.

The final report seems have to passed the press by when it was released at the end of July 1989, and the author has not found a copy nor any reporting of it, but it would seem it met the Nuclear Safety Bureau's low expectations and uncovered nothing the Japanese people needed to worry about. In the election for the upper house of the Diet held on July 23, 1989, the Japan Socialist Party made big gains. This was the first time that the LDP lost the majority in the House of Councillors. Prime Minister Uno resigned in August in a scandal involving a geisha. In November 1990, after twelve years in office, Okinawa governor Nishime was defeated by Masahide Ota, an anti-base politician backed by the socialists and communists.

The visit of *Ticonderoga* to Japan in 1965 with nuclear weapons aboard was not in violation of any Japanese laws or even its stated principles. What the revelation of the accident details brought about was the certainty that nuclear weapons were routinely brought into Japanese ports through the Vietnam period and almost certainly thereafter, even after the principles had been expressed. The environmental issues were somewhat reluctantly given what seems to have been a superficial investigation.

But if the Americans were this careless with a nuclear weapon, how could they be trusted to fly over homes and schools, Okinawans asked. Memories of the 1959 crash of a USAF F-100 into an elementary school, which killed 17 people and injured over 200, were still raw. Islanders were also concerned about the requisitioning of land near villages for bombing ranges.

In 2017, NHK TV researchers found that the death of Okinawan man Seikan Ishikawa in 1960 was not caused by the explosion of wartime ordnance as his family believed, but was as the result of a Mk 28 training bomb falling outside the target area on the island of Ie Shima.

In Nagasaki on September 16, 1989, there were protests against the visit of the frigate *Rodney M. Davis* which was making the first visit of an American warship to the city since 1974. The visit was a public relations disaster. Mayor Hitoshi Mitoshima had asked the Navy if the warship would be carrying nuclear weapons and when the answer was the standard neither confirm nor deny, he refused to allow the visit but could not prevent the *Davis* docking, because the port was run by the prefectural government, not the city. A delegation of 20 U.S. sailors set off to the Nagasaki Peace Park to lay a memorial wreath at the Peace Statue. Angry crowds, with scarred survivors of the 1945 bombing among them, prevented the sailors approaching the statue so they laid the wreath about a hundred feet away. Protesters then kicked it over and stamped on it.

The Japanese environmental study may have found no significant plutonium in the sea in late 1989, but who can say what they might have detected in 1965 or 1966. How much "dissolved" or "corroded" plutonium was in the water and the food chain then, without the knowledge of Japanese, Okinawan and other fishermen, is a question that cannot be answered now.

Book Closed

In December 1989, Japan closed the book on the submerged bomb. In the Diet an opposition politician asked what the government was doing to pursue more details of the lost bomb. This prompted a meeting in Washington between diplomats. Three days before New Year, U.S. newspapers carried a story headlined "Japanese Halt Inquiry Into U.S. H-Bomb Lost Off Coast in 1965," which read in part: "The U.S. Defense Department had said further queries into the accident could endanger U.S. military policy," although not giving a source for this assertion. Washington reasserted that it understood the special sentiments of the Japanese people, but could not supply any more detail about the accident. There was one quote from an unidentified Foreign Ministry official, who told Kyodo News Service, "The Japanese government understands the United States position and has no intention of making further requests of it."

On December 30, in a story titled "Tokyo Drops Issue of Lost U.S. Bomb," Steven Weisman of the *New York Times* pointed out the announcement came on the cusp of the New Year holiday period, when Japan is virtually shut down for a week. The timing explained how the normal voices from peace groups and the political left were silent on the matter, Weisman wrote. He added one telling detail, attributed to unnamed U.S. and Japanese officials: "The agreement to drop the matter came after an oral message conveyed by the United States Defense Department to senior members of the Japanese Embassy this week in Washington" agreed that further discussion about the accident might "compromise" American operations and create an "adverse effect" on American national security interests.

So, here is where the story ends, with the Pentagon having a quiet word with Japan, leaving no paper trail, and slipping an announcement out when it was least likely to be picked up.

Hydrogen bombs degrade with age. Tritium, which is radioactive, has a half-life of 12.33 years, and therefore roughly three-quarters of the tritium originally inside the lost warhead would by now have decayed to the non-radioactive helium-3. Plutonium has a half-life of 24,100 years.

CHAPTER 14

Cover-up

So why did the secret of *Tico*'s Broken Arrow take so long to come out? Champs skipper Bill Nealon recalled Captain Miller making an announcement over the public address system that none of the personnel aboard ship should write or say anything about the accident. Dale Palmer's son Dennis recalls his father saying that President Johnson himself was broadcast, telling the crew it was absolutely top secret.

Other veterans interviewed by the author do not recall a ship-wide announcement or any orders from the president about the matter. William Lane told reporters 24 years later; "The word was passed that they would appreciate it—they didn't say don't or anything else—if you didn't mention it in your letters home and just kind of kept it quiet." He added, "In those days, you more or less did everything you were told ... There was a great deal of patriotism on that ship. We were proud of the *Ticonderoga*."

The official instruction to keep quiet in the interests of national security was adhered to. If any sailor called from a payphone in Yokosuka or posted a letter home with the details of this potentially explosive (in every sense) story, no one acted on it and contacted a newsman.

Sailors who reported aboard *Tico* later in 1966 found a new Captain Miller (Wade) but were never told about the accident. When Ed Ofstad left the Navy two years later, his last three days were spent hearing how he knew nothing about this or several other events he was involved in. His discharge papers omit several classified courses he took. "I thought nothing of it at the time but questioned it years later. This is why the deck log is on loose-leaf paper ... trust me, I'm from the government...."

The enquiry report was unclassified, but went unnoticed until Masayo Duus received a copy from Nealon in the early 1990s. Her version was unredacted, unlike the one made public by the Navy Judge Advocate General's office in 2010, which erased all names except Webster's. The JAG report failed to mention the weapon at all and could have been mistaken for the findings of a routine accident board other than one reference to "loading" that evaded the censor.

Captain Miller made a shipwide inspection before *Tico* called into Yokosuka. Did he tell his men to be quiet about the accident? (Cruisebook)

The accident had been raised in Washington, however, while *Tico* was still in WestPac. On April 19, 1966, W. J. "Jack" Howard, Assistant to the Secretary of Defense (Atomic Energy) was testifying before a closed session of the Joint Committee on Atomic Energy. Howard was asked by committee Chairman Chester "Chet" Holifield to furnish a list of all accidents in which complete nuclear weapons had been lost and never recovered. Three days later he came up with just two; the 1958 Savannah accident where an Air Force F-86 collided with a B-47, which was forced to jettison a Mk 15 weapon, and the *Ticonderoga* accident. That part read in full:

> On 5 December 1965 in the western Pacific an A4 aircraft with a [redacted] weapon on board was lost over the side of the aircraft carrier TICONDEROGA in 2700 fathoms of water. The aircraft, pilot and weapon were not recovered. No public announcement of this incident was made, *nor is any intended* [author's italics]. This subject is considered sensitive because of its potential impact upon visits of the TICONDEROGA and other warships to foreign ports.

That day, *Tico* was at anchor in Subic Bay, but Howard's testimony caused no fuss there or any other port, because it was a secret until author Doug Keeney discovered it while researching a book about Strategic Air Command in the mid-2000s. In contrast, the Savannah incident, including the loss of a weapon, was announced to the press at the time, although there is still debate today whether the Mk 15 bomb in this case was complete with its nuclear capsule or not. Howard also described two further losses of weapon-less capsules. These were a July 1957 event where two bombs were jettisoned by a struggling C-124 transport into the Atlantic off New Jersey and the dumping of an unarmed Mk 7 Betty antisubmarine bomb from a ditching P5M Marlin flying boat off Whidbey Island, Washington in September 1958.

These four cases were far from being the only ones. The earliest known official nuclear weapons accident list was produced in May 1966 and covered 32 accidents involving nuclear materials up to 1964. The battered copy released to John Greenewald of The Black Vault website in 2016 after an FOIA request had handwritten notes extending the list up to 1980. Much information later released and long in the public domain was redacted. The *Ticonderoga* bomb was scrawled in as the 34th accident, reading in full:

> [DELETED DOE b (3)] lost off carrier at sea.

In Department of Energy documents, a b (3) exemption from declassification signifies the material contains Restricted Data or Formerly Restricted Data, classes of information relating to nuclear weapons. The latter covers such things as the yields of weapons, stockpile quantities and locations as well as weapons safety and storage information.

An updated 1971 Department of Energy (DoE) list, again classified until 2016, added summaries of two more pre-1968 events although one, identified only as "Buffalo, N. Y.(?)" was so redacted as to be meaningless. The 1966 Palomares and

1968 Thule B-52 crashes were new additions, as was a lesser-known August 1969 LaGrange, Georgia weapons convoy road accident. This is the first known published summary to include the *Ticonderoga* accident, although the redacted first paragraph eliminates the specifics of location or weapon:

> At Sea – [DELETED DOE b (3)] The A-4E was being pushed onto Elevator #2 by a properly constituted hangar deck handling crew with a safety director present. When the hold brakes signal was given by the director blowing his whistle, there was no apparent application of brakes.

Broken Arrows and Bent Spears

The Defense Department has a number of categories of nuclear weapons accidents/ incidents for reporting purposes. The formal message is an OPREP (Operational Report) 3 Pinnacle (highest priority) Broken Arrow. The terms evolved over a few years and the definition of individual accidents can be vague.

There has not been an official Pentagon account of serious nuclear mishaps since 1981, the last one recorded being the Damascus, Arkansas Titan missile explosion on September 19, 1980. Four days earlier a Pinnacle Broken Arrow message was issued as a B-52H bomber burned at Grand Forks, North Dakota. The fire in one wing threatened no fewer than a dozen cruise missiles on the bomber, but fortuitously strong winds kept the flames from the fuselage and the fire was subdued after a civilian firefighter got aboard the aircraft and shut off the fuel supply to a blazing engine. This incident is not on the official lists. The categories are:

> **Nucflash:** The actual or possible detonation of a nuclear weapon and consequent risk of an outbreak of nuclear war.
>
> **Broken Arrow:** A weapon that is detonated, destroyed, ruptured, burnt or lost, but not likely to risk nuclear war. This was term was in use since at least 1962, although its exact origins in the nuclear context are obscure. Broken Arrow is a city in northeastern Oklahoma, and also Jimmy Stewart's first Western drama released in 1950. In the movie a broken arrow is said to symbolize an end to fighting.
>
> **Bent Spear:** An unexpected event that leads to damage to a weapon requiring rework, or that may result in adverse national or international public reaction, or that could lead to a nuclear weapon accident.
>
> **Empty Quiver:** The seizure, theft, or loss of a U.S. nuclear weapon.
>
> **Dull Sword:** This was in use by 1962 and refers to material deficiencies that render a weapon inoperative. A Dull Sword can be as trivial as a warning lamp that illuminates or a check lamp that doesn't or a weapon failing a pressure check, but also exploding detonators and radioactive leaks.
>
> **Faded Giant:** An uncontrolled reactor criticality resulting in release of fission products to the atmosphere.
>
> **Gray Mare:** This appears to be an Army-specific term found in a few 1970s-era documents, signifying an incident equivalent to a Dull Sword. Its origin may be in the song "The Old Gray Mare, She Ain't What She Used to Be."

There is considerable overlap between some of these categories. The 1996 John Woo movie *Broken Arrow* would more accurately have been named "Empty Quiver."

Others had been keeping count, however. In June 1960, as Doug Webster was beginning his freshman year, Ohio State University's publishing house released a research report entitled "Accidental War, Some Dangers in the 1960s," by John Bedford Phelps of the university's Mershon National Security Program. It included one of the first public lists of nuclear weapons accidents, listing 50 between 1945 and 1960, including 12 serious ones. The later [1969] official Pentagon list only had 18 in total. The OSU paper was later republished by the Campaign for Nuclear Disarmament in the United Kingdom as the Mershon Report. This appears to have been the first public mention of Broken Arrow in the nuclear context outside of the military, particularly the USAF, where it was used in classified training films such as 1962's "Broken Arrow Procedures" made by the Defense Atomic Support Agency. By 1963, Phelps was using "Broken Arrow" in public talks on the topic.

The USAF's Air Material Command circulated secret "Airmunitions Letters" between 1960 and 1964, each featuring a particular Air Force mishap and focusing on the explosive ordnance disposal aspects. Issued as necessary after accident reports were completed, five letters were published in the second half of 1960 alone but only eight have been declassified while their numbering sequence suggests that at least 14 exist.

A 1968 USAF list of Broken Arrows then considered "U" (Unclassified) was later reclassified "Secret" and only released via the National Nuclear Security Administration in 2016 with many "b (3)" redactions, which removed all the location and weapons information. This list had 25 serious incidents from 1950–1966. Penciled annotations on these well-handled documents filled in some of the locations but cautioned that the list was incomplete.

In 1977 the USAF issued a secret list of 26 Broken Arrow incidents involving only its own weapons. With the help of the Center for Defense Information, reporter Stephen Talbot of PBS got the 1977 USAF list released. The story was published in newspapers on December 22, 1980 and included the information that "there have been up to ten other accidents which are too sensitive to describe because of the countries where they had occurred." In 1981 the Pentagon issued the actual report as "Narrative Summaries of Accidents and Incidents Involving U.S. Nuclear Weapons 1950–1980." It covered 32 accidents from 1950 when a B-36 jettisoned a Mk 4 bomb off British Columbia to the 1980 Damascus Incident when a Titan missile exploded in Arkansas. The *Tico* accident was number 28. The 1968 USS *Scorpion* accident was not declassified until 1993.

Accident Number 28

The Narrative Summaries included reasonable detail on various SAC bomber crashes and missile silo explosions, but the *Ticonderoga* accident was one of the shortest at 42 words. The full text read:

December 5, 1965/A-4/at sea/Pacific. An A-4 aircraft loaded with one nuclear weapon rolled off the elevator of a U.S. aircraft carrier and fell into the sea. The pilot, aircraft, and weapon were lost. The incident occurred more than 500 miles from land.

The ship was not named and the location was incredibly vague. The Pacific is a big place. "More than 500 miles from land" is a barefaced lie or perhaps an "alternative fact." Not naming the ship or the aircraft variant made it impossible to narrow down the location, which was surely the intent. Five attack carriers were in the Western Pacific at the beginning of December 1965, each with between one and four A-4 squadrons embarked. Ironically, the information provided to Doug Webster's family and the press in 1965 was closer to the truth, stating "180 miles north-east of Okinawa," and identifying the aircraft as an A-4E from *Ticonderoga*.

Navy Accidents

The major Broken Arrow incidents with USAF bombers and missiles and Navy submarines have been well documented. The crash of a B-52 or loss of a submarine is hard to conceal. This book focuses on an air-launched tactical weapon lost by a U.S. Navy aircraft. It was the only loss of a complete Navy bomb, but there are numerous other cases of bombs without nuclear components being destroyed and live weapons being damaged in Navy hands.

The U.S. Navy does not like to admit accidents with nuclear weapons or training shapes. "I have seen firsthand a live nuclear weapon caught in a fuel fire. I have seen a nuclear weapon crushed in a hoist, in an elevator that carries nuclear weapons to the flight deck," said retired Rear Admiral Eugene Carroll in an interview shortly after the details of the *Tico* accident were revealed. "The military does not announce every time they have a dicey accident. They do so when the knowledge becomes public." Carroll had commanded a task force including the cruiser *Belknap* when it collided with the carrier *Kennedy* in 1975 and sent a Broken Arrow message warning of the high probability that the cruiser's nuclear weapons were involved in explosions and fire.

There is one incident that is not in available records but was noted by famed British test pilot Eric "Winkle" Brown, who was on exchange duty at NAS Patuxent River from August 1951: "Just after I arrived our flight had a big panic, which spread like a forest fire, when a small A-bomb fell off one of our aircraft during routine tests near the airfield. It was being carried on one wing to see how drag affected performance. Within hours of its falling the National Guard had sealed off an area of seventy-five square miles." A farmer discovered what he called a "piece of junk" in one of his fields, heaved it onto a trailer and was driving over rutted roads to dump it when he ran into a search party.

This was probably an unarmed operational suitability test (OST) weapon, complete except for its nuclear components. There were in fact numerous accidents involving these. On June 30, 1966, an A-4C operating from *Franklin D. Roosevelt* was conducting a practice strike on a simulated airfield target on Vieques, an island a few miles off the east of Puerto Rico. The OST weapon was not supposed to leave the aircraft but somehow it did, falling in shallow waters. A search was launched involving seven minesweepers, a landing ship and a salvage ship. A ten-square-mile area was scanned, but the bomb was not found until August 20, at a depth of 120 feet, 1,500 yards offshore, two miles northeast of Punta Este, the eastern tip of the island. The search was hampered by the large amount of metal debris lying on the seabed, the legacy of years of practice bombing and gunnery by Navy ships and aircraft. The OST bomb was badly damaged, with only the center section intact and fragments of the rest scattered in a hundred-yard radius. It took two and a half days to gather the major components and transport them back to the Naval Station at Roosevelt Roads on Puerto Rico's mainland. They were later returned to Sandia for disassembly. As with the *Ticonderoga* incident, no public announcement of the incident was made, because of "fear of attempts of recovery by unauthorized or hostile parties."

This was by no means the only lost OST. A Mk 28 OST had been lost on September 18, 1959, off Kaʻena Point lighthouse on Hawaii when it was inadvertently released by a Navy FJ-4B Fury. The fighter-bomber dropped its external fuel tanks and the OST went with them. It fell into 3,600 feet of water "in safe condition" and was never recovered. Another Mk 28 OST was jettisoned in "an approved dump area" in either December 1960 or January 1961 when the carrying aircraft suffered a nose gear failure and could not land with the bomb aboard. This was preferable to a belly landing as OST weapons contained the same high explosive contents of an operational weapon.

An OST of unknown type was jettisoned on July 26, 1955, from a Navy fighter suffering engine trouble 40 miles from Roswell, New Mexico, but was later retrieved. On the night of June 19, 1957, a Mark 39 Mod 0 training weapon was jettisoned near Jacksonville, Florida by an A3D-1. The Skywarrior launched from *Roosevelt* but could not lower its left landing gear. After three attempts to land at NAS Jacksonville, the three crewmen bailed out and the bomber crashed at sea two miles east of Mayport. It would appear the bomb was never recovered.

On the evening of March 20, 1963, two A-4Cs of VA-172 collided at 9,000 feet over the Mediterranean. A Mk 108 OST (a training version of the Mk 101 "Lulu" depth bomb) was onboard Gary Wheatley's Skyhawk when it crashed 10,000 yards from *Roosevelt*, which was en route from Taranto, Italy to Athens, Greece. Both Wheatley and Paul Meinhardt ejected from their A-4s and were rescued within ten minutes. A salvage operation was mounted and recovery of the OST required the weapon to be disassembled to facilitate its removal. Wheatley later became the captain of USS *John F. Kennedy* and retired as a Rear Admiral.

The Navy came very close to losing another live weapon at sea in late 1959 or early 1960 from an unknown ship and location, although one vessel was likely a carrier. The report stated: "A War Reserve Mk 12 weapon was beeing transferred from ship to ship in rough seas. The weapon was suspended from a hawser by a hook without a keeper. The hawser suddenly developed slack and the weapon was lowered into the water. Upon contact with the water, the weapon became detached from the hook and floated in rough seas until recovered. Approximately one pint of water was found in the weapon case. No appreciable damage was incurred."

It is hard to believe that after this alarming scene this bomb was simply dried out and returned to stockpile, but if so that would have avoided returning it to AEC control and declaring a serious event. Before Dull Sword entered the Navy lexicon in February 1974, such incidents were lumped together as "URs" or Unsatisfactory Reports.

The Defense Atomic Support Agency (DASA) catalogued Unsatisfactory Reports and incidents for all services. The available documents covering 1958 to 1967 list hundreds of URs. In the last quarter of 1965 there were 60, including the *Ticonderoga* bomb.

The Naval Weapons Evaluation Facility recorded accidents through the 1970s on a report called NWEF 1070. Ian Lind of Quaker organization the American Friends Service Committee sued for release of these reports, and after six years of legal battles documents revealing 630 accidents and incidents from 1965 to 1977—all involving Navy weapons—were made public in 1986. These were heavily and crudely redacted and mainly statistical in nature, although they revealed that only one event, the 1965 *Ticonderoga* accident, involved the complete loss of a live weapon, at least in this timeframe (although this would seem to have disregarded the loss of the submarine *Scorpion* and two Mk 45 ASTOR torpedoes in May 1968.) NWEF 1070 reports for 1981 through 1983 were subsequently released under FOIA and give narrative details (but not locations) for 86 incidents in these three years. A 1985 Government Accountability Office report based on Navy data says there were 583 incidents in 1965–1983, 65 of them involving nuclear weapons aboard ships in port.

The NWEF reports seem to have stopped in the early 1980s. Available "nuclear surety" reports prepared for the president for the years 1985, 1987–89 and 2000 claim there were no significant incidents in those years. The report for 1986 has the relevant paragraphs redacted.

The preamble to the 1981 Narrative Summaries boldly claims that the U.S. Marine Corps does not have custody of nuclear weapons in peacetime and that the U.S. Army has never experienced an event serious enough to warrant inclusion in a list of accidents involving nuclear weapons. The author has not uncovered any USMC incidents, but just because there were never any Army accidents listed doesn't mean they never happened. This book is primarily concerned with the U.S. Navy's custody of nuclear weapons, but for the record: on June 22, 1959 an Army Nike SAM was accidentally launched at Naha, Okinawa, killing two soldiers before it crashed on a beach. It is believed to have been a nuclear-tipped variant; on October 29, 1969, a W50 warhead

A 1969 safety poster emphasizes deliberate actions over haste in nuclear weapons handling. The red turtleneck signifies a gunner's mate or weapons technician. (NARA)

from a Pershing I missile was ejected during maintenance at Böttingen, West Germany, falling onto a sidewalk; on February 22, 1970 there was an almost identical accident at the same site; on November 28, 1977, a CH-47 helicopter reportedly suffered an engine fire and crash-landed shortly after take-off in West Germany. An unknown number of nuclear weapons onboard (probably artillery shells) were recovered to safety.

There are also known events of fires involving the Army's atomic demolition munitions, otherwise known as "nuclear landmines." While these Army incidents were later downgraded as Bent Spears, they were initially reported as Broken Arrows. With the many thousands of Army nuclear weapons employed from 1952 to 1991, from the 0.1-kt Davy Crockett "atomic rifle" and 155mm artillery shells to the 80-kiloton Pershing II missile it is hard to believe that they never dropped, damaged, burned, launched or lost more weapons than the above, none of which were admitted to in the official accident lists.

The preamble to the Narrative Summaries says that nuclear weapons are *never carried on training flights* (emphasis in original report) but that accidents have occurred during logistical and alert flights. This is contradicted by an official DoE description of a Training Exercise Alpha supplied as a response to an FOIA request by the author: "The Alpha exercises involved loading the weapons on the aircraft and an actual launch of the loaded aircraft with recovery at a Naval Air Station ashore."

For whatever reasons, live nuclear weapons were flown from carriers, as evidenced by the DASA incident reports for 1958–67. A B43 Y1 war reserve weapon under an A-4E was damaged in January 1965 on launch from a carrier's waist cat when it was struck by the catapult bridle. The flight was part of an operational readiness maneuver. On inspection ashore by the pilot and base personnel the weapon had no obvious damage, but closer inspection when the drill was over showed structural damage to the bottom of the forward fuze section including pulled rivets and a distorted stiffener ring. A similar bridle slap incident tore a fin from a B43 in August 1966, and going further back, a Mark 7 Mod 5 was dented and gashed by a bridle sometime in the second quarter of 1961. The warhead was not damaged, but the proximity of the impact to the high explosive sphere saw the weapon removed from inventory and sent back to the AEC. In December 1959, the casing of a Mk 7 was found to contain fuel that had leaked from the A4D-2 Skyhawk carrying it on an operational readiness maneuver. The loading crew had forgotten to cap the fuel transfer valve when they removed a centerline fuel tank sixteen hours earlier, and five gallons of JP-5 had leaked in, saturating parts of the electrical system and sloshing around under the explosive sphere. It was wisely decided not to carry out a systems check in situ and the bomb was returned to the AEC.

Incidents where a weapon was damaged enough to withdraw it for overhaul or dismantling were designated Bent Spears, Dull Swords or Unsatisfactory Reports. There were dozens of these in the 1958–1967 period, many of them involving shipboard bombs. These are some highlights:

[December 1959 through February 1960] Ten dummy bombs were stored in the same ship's hold as were a number of live Mk 7s in shipping containers. Rough seas caused seven of the 2,000-pound bombs to break free and roll about the hold, colliding with and damaging two Mk 7 containers. As a result of this incident, procedures were changed so that nuclear weapons would no longer be stored with any other material, and weapons storage spaces would be inspected hourly. On a carrier, heavy seas caused a forklift to break loose from its tie downs and collide with a Mk 28, damaging components in the tail.

[June–August 1960] A mechanical failure with the interlocks on a carrier's elevator saw a Mk 27 bomb dropped on the deck, damaging both the nose and tail. A broken fire main flooded a carrier's magazine, damaging at least six Mk 28s with saltwater. All were rejected for war reserve use, the AEC reckoning that several failures would occur if they were used even if they were rinsed and dried first.

[February 28, 1962] A Mk 28 was dipped in the sea when a transfer line between two ships went slack.

[October 13, 1962—the day before U-2 photos triggered the Cuban Missile Crisis] A Boar ASW rocket was caught between the elevator and the deck edge when the elevator raised because the bomb truck shifted.

[Feb 8, 1963] A Mk 7 training weapon was jettisoned when an A-4C settled towards the sea after catapult launch.

[October 31, 1964] A ship's sprinklers flooded a magazine and soaked Mk 28s and Mk 43s, which were dried and returned to service.

[July 7, 1966] A deteriorated fire main on a carrier sprayed salt water on three Mk 28s for 15–20 minutes. After drying they were returned to service.

Between October and December 1965, there were four reported incidents of B43s leaking pressure, attributed to failing sealant compounds (although it is unclear how many were Navy bombs and if any, how many at sea). On December 2, a B57 was dropped from a hoist (again, further details unknown) and dented. Some of these could be candidates for the weapon Jim Weber saw on *Ticonderoga*.

In the 1980s there were other incidents with B43s, some of them quite mysterious:

[April 28, 1983] During onloading operations, personnel noticed a yellowish liquid leaking from the nose section of a Mark 43 [redacted] bomb. Loading operations were halted and a thorough inspection was conducted of all weapons being loaded. Another weapon was found to have leaked the same yellowish liquid. No subsequent reports were received and it is not known if the nature of or cause associated with the yellowish liquid was determined. There was no evidence of permanent damage to the weapons. The affected bombs were washed down, dried and returned to the issuing activity. All other Mk 43 bombs were inspected by the issuing activity but no additional bombs were found to contain the yellowish liquid.

[March 21, 1983] During routine maintenance of a B43, a tritium monitor alarm sounded, indicating contamination of the magazine on the Atlantic Fleet carrier. The compartment was evacuated and a Broken Arrow message was transmitted. After operating the emergency blowout system, an explosive ordnance disposal team in protective clothing reentered the compartment with a second handheld monitor, which also read positive. The procedure was repeated a third time with the same results. Finally swabs were taken around the bomb and proved negative. The weapon was isolated until the carrier reached port. It was eventually concluded, as unlikely as it may seem, that both radiation monitors were defective. The incident was downgraded to a Bent Spear and replacement monitors ordered.

It was found that over time, B43s and other bombs lost their destructive power. In 1962, a B43 was pulled from the stockpile and expended in a test and found to only generate half the expected nuclear yield. The same problem was then found with B28 bombs and W59 (Minuteman ICBM) warheads. In particular, tritium reservoirs were subject to degradation over time from hydrogen embrittlement, helium embrittlement and radiation induced effects such as loss of permeability. A tritium release had consequences for weapon reliability (it might not go off), personnel safety (it might kill your own folks) and political/environmental ramifications (it might be noticed). Reservoirs were delicate things; they had to be inspected and cleaned with specific chemicals and rinsed with high purity water then vacuum baked to prevent corrosion and the build-up of oxide film. The science of all this was not fully understood, as a contemporary report states: "We have no reason to assume we have found all the tritium surprises" and "It is not possible to extrapolate, with adequate confidence, tritium effects on components."

There is anecdotal evidence of a fully assembled B28 having its nose crushed by an elevator on *Midway* around October 1990, generating a Bent Spear report. This is possibly one of the last involving a shipboard Navy bomb. Only a few months later, President George H. W. Bush declared that nuclear weapons would be removed from surface ships, but W Divisions deployed on carriers up to 1993 and the (nuclear) Weapons Technician rate was not abolished until April 1996. The B43 was retired in 1991 and the last B57 was scrapped in 1995, but as late as 2012, tens of thousands of components for these obsolete weapons were stored at the Pantex plant in Amarillo. A lack of funding prevented a proper assessment of the need to retain some parts for use in active stockpile weapons.

After his retirement, Rear Admiral Eugene Carroll joined the Center for Defense Information, which lobbied against Pentagon waste and secrecy. He said in 1989 that accidents like the *Belknap* collision showed the dangers of equipping Navy vessels with nuclear weapons. "It is the dumbest place in the world to use nuclear weapons," he said. "I started writing in 1958 that we should remove nuclear weapons from warships."

Cultural Impact

After Japan closed the book on the incident in late 1989, the *Ticonderoga* story faded from view, at least in the USA. In Japan, however, it was the subject of several fictional and factual treatments.

In 1990, Japanese publishers Iwasaki Shoten produced an illustrated children's book called *Ticonderonga No Iru Umi* (The Sea of Ticonderonga)—the misspelling

In Japan Masayo Duus wrote *The Death of a Top Gun* about the *Ticonderoga* accident, and a children's book and an *anime* film were loosely based on the story. (via author)

is believed to be intentional. In the tale, an Okinawan boy wonders why the fishing is bad and people in his village are becoming ill. A talking whale takes him to the bottom of the ocean where the cause is revealed to be the lost bomb. A final chapter describes the real-life story of the incident. An *anime* version was produced in 1991, directed by Yuji Nichimaki.

In 1994, author Masayo Duus completed a book *Toppu gan no shi* (*The Death of a Top Gun: The Story Behind the Ticonderoga Nuclear Incident*), but being published in Japanese it attracted little notice elsewhere, except by an upstart news channel founded in 1996 by a man from Warren, Ohio called Roger Ailes. They had it translated and tracked down a number of those Duus interviewed.

On the evening of May 7, 1998, Fox News Channel aired a special called "Washington Classified: Too Many Secrets." The first part of the hour-long show dealt with what would later be called the Black Hawk Down incident in Mogadishu before it moved on to the *Ticonderoga* accident. Several ex-*Tico* crewmen were flown to New York and interviewed on the museum ship *Intrepid*, a close sister to *Tico*. These included William Lane and Rick Bailey (described as a "member of the fuze crew," whatever that was). The program included a computer animation that had the basics of the accident right, but was poor on details, no doubt in part because of the lack of official information, which ironically was the point of the show. The animated A-4 shown plunging into the sea had VA-144's lightning bolt on the spine, national insignia on both wings and the side number "470." It had no underwing fuel tanks or bomb and there were no sailors present, making it look like Doug Webster somehow reversed the A-4 out of the hangar bay and off the elevator by himself. The narration constantly referred to a "500-pound nuclear weapon," which was not only wrong on its weight by a factor of four, but spectacularly missed the point. In terms of explosive power, it was a one million-ton weapon. Lane recalled how he thought the bomb might detonate. He said that his life flashed before his eyes. He could see the big headline, "Ship Disappears in Cloud of Vapor."

A map shown on screen located the accident at a position 27-degrees north, 131-degrees east, which is about right, but depicted Okinawa as just offshore of Kyushu on the Japanese mainland. Despite the various detail errors, the show was generally accurate. A reporter interviewed Margaret Webster, feisty at eighty-five, and described how a taxi driver brought her the news of her son's death. Margaret had not opened Doug's diary for 20 years as it brought back a lot of painful memories. "No one from the military reached out to me in any way," she said, except for a letter from Commander Nealon, which implied the accident was Doug's fault because he wrote that the deck crew was not responsible. Bill Nealon, bespectacled, gray-bearded and retired in Colorado, responded that, "To assess blame directly on Doug or for her to feel that the only thing left because nobody else was assigned a level of error or blame that then it must have been Doug's error … I can understand how she could feel that way. It certainly wasn't meant to be." Margaret said it was as though Doug had never lived or never died, with the Navy refusing to acknowledge the accident.

The Hannity and Colmes show that followed included a discussion with guests retired colonel and author David Hackworth and Joshua Handler, now at Princeton University. Handler said that it was news to him that the Broken Arrow report had gone all the way up to the president and that there were actually concerns that the bomb could have exploded and vaporized the ship. When asked why a hydrogen bomb would be near Vietnam in 1965, Hackworth said it was the old Boy Scout motto "Be prepared," in case the Chinese or Soviets entered the war. He hoped that with the Cold War now over, many of the "miles and miles" of classified documents stored in government archives would be released to the public. Host Sean Hannity said it did not bother him that the Navy broke the treaty with Japan as it was important not to reveal your hand when you were at war and in a potential war situation with Russia and China. Handler said that nuclear weapons floating around on Navy ships were susceptible to accidents and inadvertent use. Hackworth said that in a crisis you cannot call via Western Union to "send up six nuke weapons, we need them right now."

Co-host Alan Colmes brought the discussion around to Doug Webster, whose name would never be on the Wall, and whose family could have had more and better information from the government. Handler thought that aspect was one of the better parts of the show, the human tragedy that was part of the overweening secrecy, which meant the family had to wait 30 years for the truth.

Dennis Palmer remembers that over the years his father Dale received several phone calls from a woman who wanted to know what the real story was but that he would never want to talk to her. He recalls a TV program about lost bombs that included other Broken Arrows before it came to Doug's accident and his mother's wish for him to be on the Wall. This can't be squared exactly with the Fox special or any other known program, but Dennis Palmer is sure it was aired in 1997. When the program came out he called home at that time to talk to his mom and to tell his dad that this was on TV and she said he was watching it. She said he didn't want to talk and was really upset. Dale later told his father he really should call this woman and tell her what really happened but doesn't think he ever did.

A couple of weeks after the Fox News show was aired, Margaret Webster wrote to her local paper, giving away its originator:

Facts of soldier's (*sic*) death aired by boyhood pal

Dear editor:

I would like to let the many friends of Roger Ailes know that he was responsible for the special on TV, "Washington secrets," which aired on May 7 on the Fox News Channel, that told of LTJG Douglas M. Webster's death. Ailes is chairman of Fox News.

He did not want it known that it was through his efforts Webster's story was told. Doug and Roger were friends through elementary and high school.

Roger felt strongly that the facts should be known and arranged to have the story told.

I am most grateful for his effort and I am now able to put my son, Doug, to rest.

MARGARET L. WEBSTER

Warren.

CHAPTER 15

Fade Away and Radiate

Not every sailor left *Ticonderoga* behind the day they walked down the gangplank the last time. In 1994, an unnamed veteran claimed recognition from the Navy that his post-traumatic stress disorder (PTSD) was caused by his service on *Ticonderoga* in 1965–66. A Veteran's Affairs (V. A.) appeal board heard that he had suffered bullying by both black and white sailors because he was of Iranian descent and fitted in with neither group. He had been beaten and robbed on several occasions and was threatened with being thrown overboard. The sailor's sea service ended with his sea bag being thrown in San Diego harbor as *Tico* returned home. He struggled in civilian life and by 1993 was having nightmares of plane crashes and bombs, telling a social worker that black and Hispanic gangs sabotaged planes and one time in particular they pushed a plane with a pilot in it off the elevator and into the ocean.

Later he told a V. A. psychiatrist that "white racist guys" sabotaged planes by putting holes in fuel tanks and that many pilots had died as a result. The captain ordered a Marine guard placed on the planes at night, he said. Apart from a passing mention of there being "atomic bombs" on the carrier, the nuclear weapons accident was apparently not a factor in his case. The ex-airman had a number of other psychiatric issues and although there is no evidence of losses from fuel leaks or his other claims about the killing of an officer by a "murder for hire ring," the airman's PTSD claim was granted, and further upheld in a 1999 appeal.

Other sailors say they have nightmares or trauma from their experiences, including the Broken Arrow. "You know I was affected so bad [after witnessing the accident]," says Dave Lesley. "I was in the Navy for years and then I came out. I retired to the Highway Patrol, so I had a drama in the Navy and the drama in the Highway Patrol for twenty years, it got to me so bad that I actually went to a therapist with PTSD about that aircraft rolling off the side."

Did They Search for the Bomb?

So, what happened to the B43 after it sank into the South China Sea? "The aircraft and weapon sank in water 2,700 fathoms deep and were not recovered," DASA wrote in its Technical Letter publication in 1966. Is it still there? Was there any later attempt to recover it? An undated document released by the National Nuclear Safety Administration described the accident in more detail than the 1981 Narrative Summaries and other official lists, but part or all of sections headed "Commander's Summary", "Recovery Actions" and "Management Summary" were deleted. The author's request for this information to be released was denied by the NNSA because the deleted portions "contain information about weapon locations that have been classified as FRD (Formerly Restricted Data). Disclosure of the exempt data could jeopardize the common defense and security of the nation." One could interpret this in different ways, but it is not unreasonable to infer from the NNSA's response that the weapon was not recovered at the time or subsequently.

In 1966, the U.S. Naval Radiological Defense Laboratory conducted a study of the dissolution of plutonium metal in seawater, which established the rate and extent of its reaction to the sea and determined methods for accurately measuring it in solution. Applications of this work were said to include finding the location of nuclear weapons or SNAP units (small reactors used to power spacecraft) "...that have inadvertently been placed in the ocean in such a way to expose plutonium metal to seawater" and determining the rate of uptake of plutonium from such accidents in the marine food chain. The date of this study may be coincidental or maybe not.

The assumptions made in 1965 and 1989 were that the B43 would be crushed and its nuclear material broken up as it descended to the ocean floor 2,700 fathoms below. The water pressure at that depth is about 490 times that at the surface, or 7,200 pounds per square inch, so this is not an unreasonable belief, but a study of similar recoveries and discoveries suggests otherwise.

In the case of the 1966 Vieques OST weapon loss, it took 51 days for nine ships to find a B43-sized object in shallow waters controlled by the U.S. Navy. In August 1974, the recovery ship *Glomar Explorer* built by Howard Hughes for the CIA retrieved some components and crew remains from the Soviet submarine *K-129* which sank off Hawaii in 1968. The depth of the sub's wreckage was equivalent to Webster's Skyhawk. Many details remain classified, but it seems that while the main goal of the project, to recover the sub's three SS-N-4 "Sark" ballistic missiles was not met, two or more nuclear-tipped torpedoes may have been brought ashore for analysis. Presumably they had not been crushed at that depth.

After the partial success of Project "Azorian," as the overall *K-129* recovery mission was known, the colossally expensive *Glomar Explorer* was mothballed for many years and is not known to have conducted any other missions for the U.S. government. That does not mean that the ship never did or never searched for the *Ticonderoga* bomb, although it had been submerged for nearly nine years by the time the *Explorer* was completed.

The Broken Arrow in 1966 when a B-52 collided with a KC-135 tanker over Palomares, Spain, scattering B28 bombs over land and sea, prompted the most

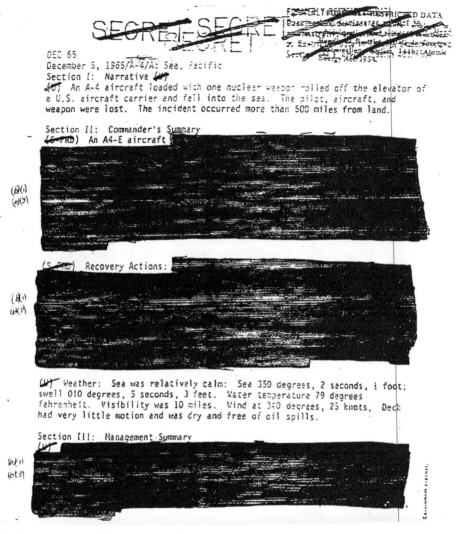

OEC 65
December 5, 1965/A-4/At Sea, Pacific
Section I: Narrative
(U) An A-4 aircraft loaded with one nuclear weapon rolled off the elevator of a U.S. aircraft carrier and fell into the sea. The pilot, aircraft, and weapon were lost. The incident occurred more than 500 miles from land.

Section II: Commander's Summary
(S-FRD) An A4-E aircraft

(S-FRD) Recovery Actions:

(U) Weather: Sea was relatively calm: Sea 350 degrees, 2 seconds, 1 foot; swell 010 degrees, 5 seconds, 3 feet. Water temperature 79 degrees fahrenheit. Visibility was 10 miles. Wind at 340 degrees, 25 knots. Deck had very little motion and was dry and free of oil spills.

Section III: Management Summary
(U)

The longer version of the summary of the accident was released with heavy redactions. A version declassified in 2014 still has many portions redacted, including the management summary. Was anybody punished for the *Tico* accident? (DTRA)

extensive underwater search to that date. The submarine *Alvin*, owned by the Navy but operated by the Woods Hole Oceanographic Institute, eventually found the fourth B28 at a depth of 2,500 feet. The Navy's unmanned CURV (Cable-controlled Undersea Recovery Vehicle) actually recovered the bomb after 57 days. It was dented, but not crushed or split by its fall or the pressures at that depth.

Having found one bomb, it is not unreasonable to assume *Alvin* was used to search for another, but *Alvin* and sister craft *Turtle* and *Sea Cliff* originally had a maximum dive depth of 6,500 feet, although they were later modified to reach greater depths. CURV had a depth limit of 10,000 feet. Woods Hole's *Jason Jr.* discovered the *Titanic* at over 12,000 feet in 1986, and *Jason* (launched 1988) has a depth limit of around 21,000 feet. So it is entirely possible for modern remotely operated vehicles to search and recover items at the depth of the *Ticonderoga* bomb.

In March and April 2018, billionaire Paul Allen's research vessel *Petrel* discovered several wartime wrecks, most notably the carrier *Lexington*, which was sunk at the battle of the Coral Sea, and also the *Helena* (Robert Miller's old ship), sunk in the Solomon Sea. A number of the carrier's Wildcats, Dauntlesses and Devastators were found in remarkable shape, apparently suffering most damage from the explosions that wrecked the carrier rather than the effects of the 9,800-foot depth, all with painted markings visible and some with Perspex canopies intact. A dud torpedo was photographed on the sea floor, separated into three parts but not burst or crushed. Like the torpedo, the B43 warhead section is steel, and with almost no oxygen at such depths, will corrode very, very slowly. There is every possibility that the *Tico* bomb is intact, "Y1" still readable on its sides, on or near the wreck of Champ 472 on the floor of the Kita-Daito basin.

At time of writing, Allen's team was assisting the Navy in recovering the wreck of a Navy C-2 Greyhound transport, which crashed into the Philippine Sea in November 2017. It sank to a depth of around 18,200 feet and weighs at least 36,000 pounds.

The NNSA's copy of the *Tico* accident summary says: "The condition of the weapon is unknown, but because of the nature of the training exercise, it is highly improbable that the weapon armed. It *may or may not* have left the aircraft, and *may or may not* have broken up upon sinking to the ocean floor." (Author's italics).

The Wall

When Susan McKee read the May 1989 stories about Doug, it brought back painful memories for her and her sisters Nancy and Barbara, but maybe explained why there had been so little information. They had always wondered why their cousin's name was not on the Wall. Susan McKee called the Defense Department, but the response was less than encouraging. "Essentially it was: 'Well, if his name deserved to be on it, it would have been,'" she said. At that time one of the specific criteria for listing on the Wall was that the serviceperson "…died while participating in, or providing direct support to a combat mission immediately en route to or returning from a target within the defined combat zone." This would seem to exclude Doug.

Barbara McKee wrote to her congressman, Representative Peter H. Kostmayer. "In 1965, [Doug's] loss was attributed to a mishap during a training mission and at this time the family had hoped that he could be remembered as a Vietnam casualty … NO! When asked of the Department of Defense, 'Can we now have his name added to the Vietnam memorial?' the answer was NO! Reason? Because he was not in

Vietnam, this is nothing to do with Vietnam ... Excuse me." She enclosed newspaper clippings that stated clearly that the *Ticonderoga* was bound from Vietnam. "Were they there for a casual lunch then cruise to Japan for early afternoon cocktails?" She also questioned whether the weight of the bomb on the Skyhawk, many times more powerful than that dropped on Hiroshima, was what caused it to fall off the carrier. The news media or their sources seemed to have forgotten the pilot who "lies in a deep grave at the bottom of the sea."

The McKees had lost touch with Margaret but reconnected after the revelations. What she told them and the news stories they read only reinforced their belief that Doug was returning from a combat mission at the time of his death. They wrote to the Navy Casualty Assistance Office: "The fact that he was in a plane carrying a hydrogen bomb may have something to do with the Navy's reticence in revealing the combat status of his mission, therefore inadvertently concealing his eligibility for the memorial."

Cindy Sublett of the Casualty Assistance Branch wrote to clarify that despite the 1985 expansion of the eligibility criteria, Doug was outside the defined combat zone and not on a combat mission at the time of his death so his name could not be added to the memorial, which honored all those who served in the Vietnam War. Sublett concluded her reply: "That a serviceman's death might not have occurred under circumstances that permitted the inclusion of his name on the memorial in no way diminishes the value or honor of his service to his country."

The McKees wrote letters to Senator John Heinz, which were forwarded on to others including Ohio's John Glenn and the Secretary of the Navy. A friendly lawyer and former Pennsylvania representative added his plea for Doug's inclusion on the Wall, but all to no avail.

In 1998 Margaret Webster told Fox News, "I think they could erase a great deal of my hurt by putting Doug's name on the Wall where it belongs."

Mike Rawl appealed in 2005 for Doug's non-inclusion to be reconsidered. Confusion about the direction of *Ticonderoga* on the day did not help his cause. "The USS *Ticonderoga*, while not at that particular time in combat zone waters, was on its way to various combat zone destinations," wrote Rawl in a letter to T. E. Decent at Navy Personnel Command. "Thus, the criteria stipulated in the 1998 Memorandum regarding criteria for inscription was met in Doug's unfortunate death." (The author cannot find any further references to a 1998 memorandum.)

This appeal too was unsuccessful, but Rawl tried other means to get Doug remembered. He nominated Doug's name to be included at an annual service at the Wall called In Memory Day, which recognizes people who died because of the Vietnam War but were not killed in combat. On a spring day in 2006, Rawl read out his stepbrother's name in front of the Wall and his name was inscribed in a memorial book.

The same year the Lieutenant (Junior Grade) Douglas M. Webster Memorial Fund was established in Warren with start-up funds supplied by Mike Rawl and

The Vietnam Veterans Memorial in Washington, D. C. is currently inscribed with 58,318 names, but not Doug Webster's. (Author)

Roger Ailes. Administered by the Community Foundation of the Mahoning Valley, the fund is mainly used to help kids from low-income families join the YMCA and to get some of the opportunities it gave young Doug.

In 2015 a new podium was dedicated at the Trumbull County Veterans' Memorial in Warren. Roger Ailes paid for it and he and his family unveiled a plaque that noted it was in honor and memory of all veterans, but also included a special tribute to Douglas Webster. Ailes had already contributed to the memorial itself, which was opened in 2008 on Courthouse Square. At that time he said he was moved to donate by the memory of his friend Doug, who was "like a brother" to him. The podium dedication was probably the last time he saw Warren, which he visited rarely.

The Vietnam Veterans Memorial, usually known as the Vietnam Memorial Wall, or just the Wall, was dedicated on the National Mall in Washington, D. C. on November 13, 1982. At that time it listed 57,939 names based on Pentagon casualty lists and it was not expected that many or any would be added. This was not to be the case and today the Wall is inscribed with 58,195 names.

In September 1985, following pressure from Oklahoma's senators, the Pentagon expanded the definition of a combat casualty to include accidents that happened during flights to or from air combat missions with targets in the war zone, which included North and South Vietnam, Laos and Cambodia and coastal waters. This opened up the possibility of inclusion on the Wall of many more names.

Dick Hastings died following an accident aboard *Tico* caused by an aircraft returning from a combat mission and was buried in 1966 at Ft Rosecrans National Cemetery overlooking San Diego Harbor, but his name was not on the Vietnam Wall. Through efforts of many people, his name was added to the wall in May 1986, as was that of Charles O. Dixon Jr, who died on *Tico*'s flight deck in a non-combat accident in January 1966. Joe Lee Williams of VA-56, who died in a 1964 flight deck accident, was added in May 2004.

Against and For

Douglas Webster is memorialized in a number of places and ways. His name is on headstones, plaques, funds and awards. Does he deserve to be on the Wall? Based on the Pentagon's stated criteria—no. His death occurred during a training exercise far from the war zone. Doug was a more a victim of the Cold War than Vietnam and if one day there is a Cold War memorial in Washington or elsewhere, Douglas Webster should be remembered alongside the reconnaissance crews shot down over the USSR, China and Cuba, the submariners on eternal patrol and the victims of other Broken Arrows in the USA, Europe, Africa and the Pacific.

On the other hand, there is precedent for a death in Doug's circumstances to qualify for addition. On September 6, 1964, VA-56 pilot Donald Vol Hester died when his A-4E crashed in the Philippine Sea. Hester was from the same squadron, flying the same type of aircraft off the same carrier as Douglas Webster. He died in a non-combat accident while en route to Japan following a line period in Vietnam. The location of Hester's accident was 217 miles to the northeast of Webster's and thus further from the war zone. Hester's name was added to the Wall in 1986. The only material difference between the two deaths was that Webster's aircraft carried a thermonuclear weapon.

At the time of Hester's addition, the location and details of Webster's death were secret. Hester's family and friends successfully lobbied for his inclusion, while Webster's relatives were denied it a few years later even when the veil of secrecy had lifted. If it is deemed appropriate within the Pentagon's revised rules that Donald Vol Hester should be commemorated on the Wall, then the same honor should be accorded to the memory of Douglas Morey Webster.

As of 2018 the Pentagon had not accepted that 74 sailors who died when the destroyer *Frank L. Evans* collided with the Australian aircraft carrier HMAS *Melbourne* in 1969 should be added to the memorial. The location of the accident in the South China Sea is regarded as outside the combat zone although the *Evans* was on a break between operations in Vietnamese waters when it occurred. An act of Congress would be needed to include them, something which is being lobbied for, and if these names were to be added, then Doug's should be with them.

Doug Webster's memorial headstone in Arlington National Cemetery. The original was installed in early 1966 with a misspelled inscription. (Author)

Arlington National Cemetery has a section of headstones marking servicemen and women whose grave is unknown or at sea. A headstone for Doug was added on July 11, 1966 on a hill in Section MG overlooking Washington, D. C., not far from the Tomb of the Unknown Soldier.

Doug's father once made the long drive up from Florida to visit it. He found that the middle name was misspelt, which hurt Morey, because it was his. Margaret heard this story, but never visited herself. The grave was rebuilt with the correct name, but has no Christian cross above the name, unlike those around it. Morey Webster suffered a sudden stroke in Pinellas, Florida in September 1980, two days before his 69th birthday, and died instantly. His grave features the symbol of the Masons.

What Happened Next?

The USS *Ticonderoga* made two more WestPac cruises as an attack carrier and lost at least 13 more men in combat and accidents. In 1969–70 *Tico* was converted to an anti-submarine carrier and redesignated CVS-14, flying S-2 Trackers and helicopters. Although it lost its attack role, it retained storage for B57 nuclear depth bombs. The 1944-vintage ship, built for piston-engined warplanes, ended its career retrieving spacecraft, acting as the recovery ship for the Apollo 16 and 17 moon landings and Skylab. On September 1, 1973, the Big T was decommissioned once and for all and auctioned for scrap. It was rumored that the Gillette razor company was the winning bidder.

In April 1974, Robert C. Miller of the UPI press agency wrote:

> The 30-year-old U.S. Navy aircraft carrier USS *Ticonderoga* exits from front-page glory April 9 to the oblivion of a tidal mudflat. There will be no official ceremony, no obituary, when she is towed out past San Diego's point Loma, but word will get around just as it always does when a friend dies. There will be a typically Navy wake in scores of bars from Missoula to Memphis as once—brawny armed ex-white-hats with faded tattoos hoist beers for the "*Tico* ... the best (hiccup) ship in the Navy." Scotch will be sipped by a few old men still honored with the title of "Captain" or "Admiral" and there will be a few tears shed, mostly feminine, not for *Ticonderoga*, but for the men whose pictures still grace the mantle and whose "We regret to inform you…" death notices were postmarked USS *TICONDEROGA*, CVA-14

Ticonderoga was scrapped at Tacoma, Washington in 1975. Some parts are preserved at Ticonderoga, New York and others, including the ship's bell, in San Diego.

The lead ship of the CG-47 guided missile cruiser class was named *Ticonderoga* and commissioned in 1983. Decommissioned in 2004, there are proposals to turn it into a museum and some hope that a future ship will carry the illustrious name.

For the Champs' next cruise, on *Enterprise*, they were downgraded to the less-capable A-4C and lost two pilots in combat including skipper Pete Sherman. In 1969 they transitioned to the A-7 Corsair II and from 1973 were based in Japan, assigned to Air Wing Five on *Midway* and homeported in Yokosuka. The Champs were disestablished in 1986 after 28 years' service.

On 1 September, 1973, *Ticonderoga* was decommissioned for the last time at San Diego. She was scrapped at Tacoma, Washington in 1975. (NARA)

Captain Robert N. Miller next served as chief of staff of Carrier Division Six in the Mediterranean, notably during the 1967 Lebanon crisis. He was appointed Director of Command and Staff School at the Naval War College and finally CO of NAS Monterey before retiring to Paso Robles, California in 1972. He died in 1995. Bill Nealon went on to command NAS Lakehurst, New Jersey. He retired with 33 years' service. Carl Ray Smith commanded the training wing at NAS Meridian, Mississippi prior to retiring to Memphis.

John Paisley went on to become the titular head of VF-43, an extension of the Topgun school—"I can't use commanding officer," he said, "because there's no way these guys could be commanded." He died in 2018. Jack Holland made five cruises to Vietnam and was also the CO of VF-43, retiring in 1978. On return from captivity, Render Crayton remained in the Navy, mostly in shore jobs, culminating with command of NAS Rota, Spain. He retired as a captain in 1984. He re-visited Vietnam in 1998 with a group of ex-POWs. Austin Chapman became the CO of VA-83 in 1980 but didn't join the airlines on retirement. "When I ended my flying career I never looked back. I'd flown fighters my whole career and didn't want to fly anything else." He returned to Tryon, North Carolina and has served as the town's

The three Apollo 17 astronauts return to earth. Eugene A. Cernan, Ronald E. Evans and Harrison H. Schmitt. Command Module pilot Evans (center) had made many landings on *Tico* as an F-8 pilot in 1965–66. (NASA)

mayor. Eddie Phelps commanded reserve squadron VA-204 and survived an A-7 ejection in 1981. Bob Sturgeon flew over 200 missions in Vietnam with VA-56. Job Belcher retired from the Navy after 28 years' service with the rank of commander. He died in Virginia Beach in January 2016. Jim Halverson flew for Northwest Airlines and was active in the Air Line Pilots Association. Van Hough had a long career as a pilot with United Airlines. Bob Simmons flew with TWA from 1968 to 1996 while also serving as a commander in the Naval Reserve. He died in Tucson in October 2011.

Dale Palmer left the Navy in 1966 to fly for Northwest Airlines, which he did until 1982, continuing with the airline for several years beyond that. He died in 2005. Ed Pfeiffer flew a further cruise with VA-56 then worked in the family engineering business. He also died in 2005. Jim Delesie took up law, being admitted to the Florida bar in 1972 and specializing in workers compensation. Jack Kaufman later became a college professor. Jay Shower continued flying Navy aircraft until

1982, being qualified in over 20 different types. He then delivered civilian aircraft all round the world. He died in 2018. Jim Maslowski, who joined the Navy as an enlisted man and the Champs as an ensign towards the end of the 65–66 cruise went on to fly with the "Blue Angels," became the CO of *Kitty Hawk*, and retired as a Rear Admiral in 2001.

VF-51 pilot Ron Evans piloted the Command Module of Apollo 17 in December 1972, becoming the last man to date to orbit the Moon alone. The recovery ship for the splashdown was *Ticonderoga*. He died of a heart attack in 1990, aged 56.

The remains of VA-52's John Mape were recovered by a joint United States/Vietnamese team and returned to the family in March 1999. A memorial park in Dublin, California had been named for him in 1967. John McCormick's remains were repatriated in 1988. No trace of Doug Webster's friend John Worcester has ever been found.

"Smoky Joe" Logsdon, whose name featured repeatedly in the 1965–66 deck log for various scrapes signed on for another tour of duty on *Tico*. He later became active in numerous veterans' groups and looked back fondly on his Navy career.

Marcia Webster continued her academic career, earning a PhD and teaching English literature. In 1970 she married a nuclear physicist and moved with his work to England where their first son was born. She retired as a professor at the age of 75 after teaching at a New York college for 27 years.

Doug's boyhood friend Roger Ailes became an influential political operative and media figure. He resigned from the chairmanship of Fox News amid scandal in 2016 and died in January 2017. Doug's stepbrother Michael Rawl says: "From the closeness of Roger and Doug, we can only surmise what they might have accomplished. If he had lived he could have perhaps done things in concert, they could have been a powerful team. I suspect that Doug would have shared a lot of Roger's feelings and beliefs. Doug was a conservative guy. Roger got to meet Richard Nixon who was a guest on his TV show and from that he launched a career managing campaigns for political figures and around that time Doug would have probably been finishing his first tour of duty…. Doug was a true leader, he was a guy who was tough, he had the power of his beliefs, he was a world-class athlete in the sport that he chose, a bright agile mind. He could have done anything. It was a loss to the country not to have him."

Margaret Webster died in Warren in 2005, aged 91. She was buried near her hometown in northeastern Iowa. Her headstone reads:

Margaret Logsdon Webster
Nov 2 1913   Feb 15 2005
Mother of
Lt (jg) Douglas M. Webster
Naval Aviator
July 26 1941   Dec 5 1965

Bibliography

Books

Alvarez, Everett and Pitch, Anthony S. *Chained Eagle* (Donald I Fine, 1989)

Brown, Eric "Winkle". *Wings on My Sleeve* (Phoenix Press, 2007)

Burgess, Richard. *A-1 Skyraider Units of the Vietnam War* (Osprey, 2009)

Bryans, Brian K. *Flying Low 1956–1980* (Self-published, 2013)

Chafets, Ze'ev. *Roger Ailes: Off Camera* (Sentinel, 2013)

Chesnau, Roger B. *Aircraft Carriers of the World, 1914 to the Present: an illustrated encyclopedia* (Naval Institute Press, 1984)

Connecticut College. *Koiné 1962* (Connecticut College Yearbooks, 1962)

Ellsberg, Daniel. *The Doomsday Machine: Confessions of a Nuclear War Planner* (Bloomsbury, 2017)

Foster, Wynn. *Captain Hook: A Pilot's Triumph and Tragedy in the Vietnam War* (Naval Institute Press, 1992)

Foster, Wynn F. *Fire on the Hangar Deck: Ordeal of the Oriskany* (Naval Institute Press, 2001)

Francillon, René J. *Tonkin Gulf Yacht Club* (Conway Maritime Press, 1988)

Freeman, Gregory A. *Sailors to the End: The Deadly Fire on the USS Forrestal and the Heroes Who Fought It* (Perennial, 2004)

Freeman, Gregory A. *Troubled Water: Race, Mutiny, and Bravery on the USS Kitty Hawk* (Palgrave Macmillan, 2009)

Gillcrist, Paul. *Feet Wet: Reflections of a Carrier Pilot* (Presidio Press, 1990)

Gillcrist, Paul. *Vulture's Row: Thirty Years in Naval Aviation* (Schiffer, 1996)

Ginter, Steve. *Douglas A-4E/F Skyhawk in Navy Service* (S. Ginter, 2001)

Ginter, Steve. *Vought's F-8 Crusader Part four: Navy Fighter Squadrons* (S. Ginter, 1990)

Grant, Zalin. *Over the Beach: The Air War in Vietnam* (W.W. Norton, 1986)

Graubart, Julian I. *Golf's Greatest Championship: The 1960 U.S. Open* (Donald I Fine, 1997)

Gray, Stephen. *Rampant Raider: An A-4 Skyhawk Pilot in Vietnam* (Naval Institute Press, 2007)

Gregory, Shaun. *The Hidden Cost of Deterrence: Nuclear Weapons Accidents* (Brassey's, 1990)

Hansen, Chuck. *The Swords of Armageddon* (Chukelea, 2007)

Hansen, Chuck. *US Nuclear Weapons: The Secret History* (Aerofax, 1988)

Herzog, Rudolph. *A Short History of Nuclear Folly: Mad Scientists, Dithering Nazis, Lost Nukes and Catastrophic Cover-ups* (Melville House, 2013)

Hobson, Chris. *Vietnam Air Losses: United States Air Force, Navy and Marine Corps Fixed-Wing Aircraft Losses in Southeast Asia 1961–1973* (Midland Publishing, 2001)

Hope, Bob. *Five Women I Love; Bob Hope's Vietnam Story* (Doubleday, 1966)

Johnson, Leland. *Sandia National Laboratories: A History of Exceptional Service in the National Interest* (Sandia National Laboratories, 1997)

Keeney, Douglas L. *15 Minutes: General Curtis LeMay and the Countdown to Nuclear Annihilation* (St. Martin's Press, 2011)

LaPointe, Robert L. *PJs in Vietnam: The Story of Airrescue in Vietnam as Seen Through the Eyes of Pararescuemen* (Northern PJ Press, 2001)

Levinson, Jeffrey L. *Alpha Strike Vietnam: The Navy's Air War, 1964 to 1973* (Presidio, 1989)

Little, Jim. *Brotherhood of Doom: Memoirs of a Navy Nuclear Weaponsman* (Booklocker, 2007)

Maggalet, Michael H. and Oskins, James C. *Broken Arrow Vol 1: The Declassified History of American Nuclear Weapons Accidents* (Lulu, 2007)

May, John. *The Greenpeace Book of the Nuclear Age: the Hidden History, the Human Cost* (Pantheon Books, 1990)

Merideth, Lee W. *Grey Ghost: The Story of the Aircraft Carrier* Hornet (Rocklin Press, 2001)

Mersky, Peter. *US Navy and Marine Corps A-4 Skyhawk Units of the Vietnam War* (Osprey, 2007)

Mersky, Peter. *F-8 Crusader Units of the Vietnam War* (Osprey, 1998)

Mersky, Peter B. *RF-8 Crusader Units over Cuba and Vietnam* (Osprey, 1999)

Mersky, Peter B. and Polmar, Norman. *The Naval Air War in Vietnam* (Nautical and Aviation, 1981)

Miller, Jerry. *Nuclear Weapons and Aircraft Carriers: How the Bomb Saved Naval Aviation* (Smithsonian Institution Press, 2001)

Morgan, Rick. *A-3 Skywarrior Units of the Vietnam War: Osprey Combat Aircraft 108* (Osprey, 2015)

Nichols, John B. and Tillman, Barrett. *On Yankee Station: The Naval Air War Over Vietnam* (Naval Institute Press, 1987)

O'Connor, Mike. *MiG Killers of Yankee Station* (New Past Press, 2003)

Ohio State University. *The Makio. 1960–1962* (Ohio State University, 1960–1962)

Phelps, John B. *Accidental War, Some Dangers in the 1960s* (Ohio State University, 1960)

Powell, Robert "Boom". *Wave-Off!: A History of LSOs and Ship-Board Landing* (Specialty Press, 2017)

Rausa, Rosario. *Skyraider: the Douglas A-1 "Flying Dump Truck"* (Nautical & Aviation Pub. Co. of America, 1982)

Rhodes, Richard. *Dark Sun: The Making of the Hydrogen Bomb* (Simon & Schuster, 1996)

Rochester, Stuart I. *The Battle Behind Bars: Navy and Marine POWs in the Vietnam War* (Naval History and Heritage Command, 2010)

Rochester, Stuart I. and Kiley, Frederick. *Honor Bound: The History of American Prisoners in Southeast Asia 1961–1973* (Historical Office, Office of the Secretary of Defense, 1998)

Sagan, Scott D. *The Limits of Safety: Organizations, Accidents and Nuclear Weapons* (Princeton University Press, 1993)

Schlosser, Eric. *Command and Control: Nuclear Weapons, the Damascus Accident, and the Illusion of Safety* (The Penguin Press, 2013)

Sherman, Gabriel. *The Loudest Voice in the Room: How the Brilliant, Bombastic Roger Ailes Built Fox News-And Divided a Country* (Random House, 2014)

Sofko, James G. *USS* Ticonderoga *(CVA-14) Cruise Book 1965–66: The Year of Engagement* (1966)

Tanaka, M., Kawakita, R. and Kouzai, T. *The Sea of Ticonderonga* (Iwasaki Shoten, 1990)

Thomason, Tommy H. *Strike From the Sea: U.S. Navy Attack Aircraft From Skyraider to Super Hornet 1948–Present* (Specialty Press, 2009)

Thomason, Tommy H. *Scooter: the Douglas A-4 Skyhawk story* (Crécy, UK, 2011)

Toperczer, Istvan. *MiG-17 and MiG-19 Units of the Vietnam War* (Osprey, 2001)

U.S. Navy. *Wings of Gold* (U.S. Navy recruiting booklet, 1959)

Van Staaveren, Jacob. *Gradual Failure: The Air War Over North Vietnam, 1965–1966* (Air Force History and Museums Program, 2002)

Winchester, Jim. *A-4 Skyhawk: 'Heinemann's Hot Rod'* (Pen & Sword, 2005)

Wiper, Steve. *USS Ticonderoga CV/CVA/CVS-14: Warship Pictorial 22* (Classic Warships Publishing, 2004)

Logbooks and Cruise Reports

USS *Bon Homme Richard* and Carrier Air Wing Nineteen Cruise Report 21 April 1965–13 January 1966 (Naval History and Heritage Command)

USS *Gridley* (DLG-21) Deck Log (National Archives and Records Administration)

USS *Kitty Hawk* (CVA-63) Deck Log (National Archives and Records Administration)

USS *Ticonderoga* (CVA-14) Deck Logs 1964–66 (National Archives and Records Administration)

USS *Ticonderoga* Cruise Report 1965-66 (Naval History and Heritage Command)

USS *Ticonderoga* WestPac Intelligence Report 1965–1966. (Naval History and Heritage Command)

USS *Turner Joy* (DD-951) Deck Log (National Archives and Records Administration)

Reports

_____. Accident report F-8E BuNo. 149176 (Naval Aviation Safety Center, 1966)

_____. Accident report F-8E BuNo 150843 (Naval Aviation Safety Center, 1966)

_____. Air to Air Encounters in Southeast Asia. Vol 1 Account of F-4 and F-8 Events Prior to 1 March 1967 (Weapons Systems Evaluation Group, 1967)

_____. Commander in Chief Pacific Command History 1966, Volume 1 (Naval History and Heritage Command)

_____. Commander in Chief Pacific Command History 1965, Volume 1 (Naval History and Heritage Command)

_____. CINCPAC Operation Plan No.1-61: Pacific Command General War Plan (Commander in Chief Pacific Fleet, 1961)

_____. Formal Board of Investigation Report of Aircraft Accident 5 December 1965 Involving USS

_____. Ticonderoga CVA-14 Aircraft (Judge Advocate General's Office, released 2010)

_____. History of Accidents involving Nuclear Materials (Department of Energy, 1966 and 1971)

_____. History of the Mk 43 Bomb (Department of Energy)

_____. History of the Mk 57 Bomb (Department of Energy)

_____. Index to Nuclear Accidents (Unknown, declassified 1997)

_____. Naval Forces Vietnam Monthly Historical Summaries, April 1966, May 1966 (Naval History and Heritage Command)

_____. Narrative Summaries of Accidents Involving US Nuclear Weapons (Department of Defense, 1981)

_____. Nuclear Weapons: Actions Needed by NNSA to Clarify Dismantlement Performance Goal (U.S. Government Accountability Office, 2014)

_____. Nuclear Weapon Characteristics Handbook, September 1990 (Sandia National Laboratories, 1990)

_____. NWEF 1070-4 Summary of Navy Nuclear Weapons Accidents (1981, 1982, 1983 Supplement) (Naval Weapons Evaluation Facility, 1984)

_____. Summary of Air Force Nuclear Accidents (Sandia Corporation, 1968)

_____. US Navy in the Pacific Official Histories 1965, 1966 (Naval History and Heritage Command)

_____. Welcome Aboard Package USS *Ticonderoga* CVA-14. (Admiral Elmo R. Zumwalt, Jr. Collection, Texas Tech University, Vietnam Center and Archive)

Clifford, Lt Col C. C. Jr. and Kelso, Jack R. Preliminary Report Operation Blowdown (Defense Atomic Support Agency, 1964)

Dyson, F. G. *et al.* Tactical Nuclear Weapons in Southeast Asia (Study S-266) (Institute for Defense Analyses, Jason Division, 1967)

Handler, Joshua and Arkin, William M. Naval Safety 1989: The Year of the Accident. Neptune Papers No.4 (Greenpeace/Institute for Policy Studies, 1990)

Handler, Joshua and Arkin, William M. Naval Accidents 1945–1988. Neptune Papers No.3 (Greenpeace/Institute for Policy Studies, 1990)

Kristensen, Hans M. Japan Under the Nuclear Umbrella: U.S. Nuclear Weapons and Nuclear War Planning in Japan During the Cold War (Nautilus Institute, July 1999)

Melyan, Wesley R. C. and Bonetti, Lee. Rolling Thunder July 1965–December 1966: Project CHECO Report (HQ PACAF Directorate, Tactical Evaluation CHECO Division, 1967)

Peterson, Charles L. A Limited Evaluation of the Corrosion of Uranium and Weapon-Associated Metals in Substitute Ocean Water (Los Alamos Scientific Laboratory, 1966)

Porter, Capt, Melvin F. Tiger Hound (HQ PACAF Directorate, Tactical Evaluation CHECO Division, 1966)

Reese, H. L. AFRRI Special Report: DoD Nuclear Mishaps (Armed Forces Radiobiology Research Institute, 1986)

Russell, Admiral James S. Report of the Panel to Review Safety in Carrier Operations (Office of the Chief of Naval Operations, 1967)

Articles

Hanauer, Gary. "The Story Behind the Pentagon's Broken Arrows" in Mother Jones (April 1981)

Hansen, Chuck. "1,000 More Accidents Declassified" in The Bulletin of the Atomic Scientists (June 1990)

Hirose, Katsumi. "Plutonium in the Ocean Environment: Its Distributions and Behavior" in Journal of Nuclear and Radiological Sciences (Vol.10, No.1, 2009)

Norris, Robert S., Arkin, William M., and Burr, William. "Where They Were" in The Bulletin of the Atomic Scientists (November/December 1999)

Schneider, Barry. "Big Bangs From Little Bombs" in The Bulletin of the Atomic Scientists (May 1975)

"The H-Bomb Secret" in The Progressive (November 1979)

Vito, Capt A. H. Jr. "Carrier Air and Vietnam … an Assessment" in US Naval Institute Proceedings (October 1967)

"What the President Saw: A Nation Coming into Its Own" in Time (29 July, 1985)

Index